Successful Psychotherapy

Successful Psychotherapy

A Caring, Loving Relationship

C. H. PATTERSON, Ph.D.,
and
SUZANNE C. HIDORE, Ph.D.

JASON ARONSON INC.
Northvale, New Jersey
London

This book was set in 11 pt. Baskerville by TechType of Ramsey, New Jersey and printed and bound by Book-mart Press of North Bergen, New Jersey.

Copyright © 1997 by Jason Aronson Inc.

10 9 8 7 6 5 4 3 2 1

Library of Congress Cataloging-in-Publication Data

Patterson, C. H. (Cecil Holden), 1912-
    Successful psychotherapy : a caring, loving relationship / C. H. Patterson, Suzanne C. Hidore.
        p.   cm.
    Includes bibliographical references and index.
    ISBN 1-56821-795-1 (alk. paper)
    1. Psychotherapist and patient. 2. Psychotherapy—Philosophy.
    3. Therapeutic alliance. I. Hidore, Suzanne C.   II. Title.
    RC480.8.P367   1996
    616.89′14—dc20   95-52030

Printed in the United States of America on acid-free paper. Jason Aronson Inc. offers books and cassettes. For information and catalog write to Jason Aronson Inc., 230 Livingston Street, Northvale, New Jersey 07647 or visit our website: http://www.aronson.com

To Frances, Joseph, Penny, Jenifer,

Christopher, Tom, Vicki, and Chuck

To Anabel, in honor of her love;

To Sir John, the Knight in Shining *Amor*,

To Emily and Mike, who are the Light of Life.

Contents

Sometimes the Zeitgeist in a field so dominates scientific thinking that it precludes other viewpoints. When the characteristic line of thought is flawed or incomplete, it can obstruct progress in the field.

B. R. Crussan, 1991

Preface

In 1963, Carl Rogers wrote, "The field of psychotherapy is in a state of chaos" (p. 5). Although earlier he had felt that therapists were using different words and labels to describe the same experience, he had come to believe that therapists differed at the basic level of personal experiences. Rogers was hopeful that the chaos would encourage research that in turn would clear the confusion. At about the same time, Ungersma (1961) wrote:

> The present situation in psychotherapy is not unlike that of the man who mounted his horse and rode off in all directions. The theoretical orientation of therapists is based upon widely divergent hypotheses, theories and ideologies. . . . Individual practitioners of any art are expected to vary, but some well-organized schools of therapy also seem to be working at cross-purposes with other equally well-organized schools. Nevertheless, all schools, given favorable conditions, achieve favorable results: the patient or client gets relief and is often enough cured of his difficulties.
> [p. 5]

In 1974, Patterson wrote, "The days of schools in counseling and psychotherapy are drawing to a close" (p. ix). There was a recognition of common elements in the therapy relationship, and that commonality could have led to a convergence on a single basic theory. The research evidence supported these elements as the effective conditions in all the major theories. However, instead of a reduction in the number of theories or "schools," they have proliferated, along with the multiplying of methods, techniques, and strategies of intervention not warranting the designation of a school or theory. Although psychotherapy is now entering its second century, there appears to be little agreement as to its essential nature. Psychotherapy is *still* in a state of chaos.

Indeed, there is some question about whether there is any agreed-on definition of psychotherapy. The term covers a multitude of activities. Psychotherapy is viewed by some as a social influence process involving persuasion. Some, such as Ellis, carry it to a hard-sell extreme. Other cognitive therapists use reasoning, arguments, and disputation. Behaviorists utilize a variety of conditioning methods and techniques. Homework assignments are made. Psychotherapy thus extends to and is confused with tutoring and individual instruction. It includes a whole range of helping activities. All these, and more, are included by contributors to the *History of Psychotherapy* (Freedheim 1992), though none puts forward an explicit definition of psychotherapy. There is no index entry for *Psychotherapy, definitions of.*

At the 1949 conference on training in clinical psychology (The Boulder Conference), an unidentified participant proposed that "psychotherapy is an unidentified technique applied to unspecified problems with unpredictable outcomes. For this technique we recommend rigorous training" (Raimy 1950, p. 93). With a slight revision, this statement would appear to apply today. The updated version would be this: psychotherapy is innumerable techniques applied to unlimited problems with unpredictable outcomes. For these techniques we recommend rigorous and vastly inconsistent training programs.

Psychotherapy is psychological treatment for psychosocial problems, whether *sui generis* or as an aspect of physical or physiological conditions. It does not include treatment of educational problems, social skill deficiencies, career decisions or choices, and so forth—except as they are involved with or derive from psychosocial problems. Psychotherapy is defined here as a psychological relationship between a person or persons, designated as the clients, whose progress in self-actualization has been blocked or impeded by the absence of good interpersonal relationships; and a person, designated as the therapist, who provides such a relationship. The specific nature of this relationship is considered in the following chapters.

Rogers (1957a) published a classic article in which he defines three therapist and three client conditions that he hypothesizes as the necessary and sufficient conditions of therapeutic personality change. These conditions have long been identified with client-centered therapy. But Rogers does not so limit them. He writes:

> It is not stated that these six conditions are essential conditions for client-centered therapy, and that other conditions are essential for other types of psychotherapy. . . . [M]y aim in stating this theory is to state the conditions which apply to *any* situation in which constructive personality change occurs, whether we are thinking of classical psychoanalysis, or any of its modern offshoots, or Adlerian psychotherapy, or any other. [p. 101]

The present book could be considered an amplification or extension of Rogers's proposition. These conditions, it is contended, are the basic common elements of all the major theories.

These are all common elements in an effective therapeutic relationship between the therapist and the client. Thus, the system developed here could be called relationship therapy, a term used as the title of a book by the first author some twenty years ago (Patterson 1974). Before Rogers (1942) used the term *relationship therapy*, its use goes back to Jessie Taft (1933) and her associates who were influenced by Otto Rank.

This is a radical book. It presents an approach that is in sharp disagreement with most of the major approaches to psychotherapy. These approaches are characterized by the therapist as an expert who directs the therapy with active interventions and techniques. It is also in disagreement with the accepted conventional medical model in which the client must be first diagnosed before therapy can begin and in which treatment in psychotherapy is determined by the diagnosis.

An accumulation of research supports a set of common elements effective in psychotherapy (Bergin and Garfield 1994), but there has been little effort to base a single theory on them—something that would seem to be logical. Garfield (1982), noting that although such an attempt would not be popular, writes that it would be worth the effort.

One of the objections to this attempt will no doubt be that it is simplistic. Yet the objective of science is to discover, or develop, the universal laws that explain the domain. Physicists search for the unifying principles of the universe (Lederman and Teresi 1993, Weinberg 1993). Stephen Hawking (1993) is devoting his life to an attempt to reconcile two apparently contradictory theories: Einstein's unified field theory (the theory of relativity) and quantum mechanics, in a General Unified Theory.

Warren Weaver (1966), a biologist, states:

> As man's control of his environment has proceeded . . . he has progressively uncovered more and more complications, but, at the same time he has succeeded in discovering more and more unifying principles which accept the ever increasing variety, but recognize the underlying unity. He has, in short, discovered the many and the one. . . . [T]he diversity . . . is a surface phenomenon: When one looks underneath and within, the universal unity again becomes apparent. [p. 13]

And Subrahmanyan Chandrasekhar, an astrophysicist, in accepting the 1983 Nobel Prize, stated, "The simple is the seal of the true, and beauty is the splendor of truth."*

It would appear that this objective in the field of psychotherapy would be the development of a universal theory or system. Although there is an interest in integration, it is limited to methods or techniques (Patterson and Watkins 1996).

Some thirty-two years ago Schofield (1964) published a book

---

*Quoted in "In the Tradition," *University of Chicago Magazine,* 1991, 84(1):ii.

titled *The Purchase of Friendship*. The relationship denoted by Schofield
is not too far from the relationship described in this book as consti-
tuting psychotherapy. Love—brotherly love, or agape—would be a
good description of psychotherapy. Perhaps this book might have been
titled *Psychotherapy: The Purchase of Love*.

The universal system of psychotherapy presented here is based on
four propositions:

1. The first proposition states *a unitary theory of motivation.*
2. The second proposition states *a unitary theory of functional
   emotional or social-psychological disturbance.*
3. The third proposition states *a unitary theory of psychotherapy.*
4. The fourth proposition states *a unitary theory of primary prevention
   of social-psychological pathology.*

These propositions underlie the content of the ensuing chapters.
This book is the culmination of seventy years' experience (fifty by the
first author and twenty by the second author) in study, practice,
teaching, research, and writing in the field of psychotherapy.

1

The Chaos in Psychotherapy

Introduction

During the early years of this century—the first three or four decades—there was essentially one system of psychotherapy: psychoanalysis. Though there were a number of variants, such as those developed by Jung and Adler, orthodox Freudian psychoanalysis predominated. By the middle of the century, this situation had changed, and numerous other systems began proliferating.

Colby (1964) opens his review of the literature of the preceding three years with the words "Chaos prevails." As one immerses oneself in the study of the dozens of theories and approaches to psychotherapy, one indeed develops the feeling of chaos. Differences, inconsistencies, and contradictions appear at all levels, from philosophy to techniques. Concepts relating to the nature of human beings and the nature of emotional disturbance or abnormal behavior vary considerably, from a concept of the individual as determined by his or her environment to the concept of the person as capable of making choices and being free to do so. In 1969, Kanfer and Phillips wrote that not only do clinicians disagree in the theories they hold, but also "their practices and beliefs reflect even deeper inconsistencies and contradictions" (p. 276). The goals and methods of therapy related to these concepts differ — on the one hand, the control and change of specific behaviors by manipulating consequences in terms of rewards and punishments and, on the other hand, attempts to provide the conditions for the growth and development of the person's potential in the process of self-actualization.

The number of different theories or methods of psychotherapy is not known. The lead-in for an article by Parloff (1976) refers to 130 subschools of psychotherapy, but the author does not list them. The cover of the issue carries the words "The Psychotherapeutic Jungle." *The Psychotherapeutic Handbook* by Hebrink (1950) lists 255 methods of psychotherapy. Many in the list are simply techniques or are not actually psychotherapy. Karasu (1986) refers to 400 approaches. One writer (Singer 1974) discusses the training of psychotherapists as a "Tower of Babel." More recently, John Leo (1985), reporting for *Time* on the 1985 Phoenix Conference on the Evolution of Psychotherapy, quotes one participant as saying, "All the experts are here and none of them agree" (p. 59). Joseph Wolpe (1987) calls the conference "a babble of conflicting voices" (p. 133). Prochaska (1988) titles his review of the book containing the papers presented at the conference "The Devolution of Psychotherapy" and quotes from the introduction by Zeig (1987): "Here were reigning experts on psychotherapy and I could see no way they could agree on defining the territory! Can anyone dispute then, that the field is in disarray!" (pp. xviii–xix).

Further evidence of the diversity in psychotherapy could be documented. Included could be the flood of books on special methods and techniques, and the avalanche of announcements of workshops and institutes on specialized methods and techniques of treatment.

The diversity present in the field of psychotherapy extends from differences in philosophy and theories, basic concepts and goals, to methods and techniques. In the attempt to be unique, theorists as well as practitioners emphasize differences. Frank (1982) notes one factor:

Those features which distinguish them from each other . . . receive special emphasis in the pluralistic, competitive American society. Since the prestige and the financial security of psychotherapists depends to a considerable extent on their being able to show that their particular theory and method is more successful than that of any of their rivals, they inevitably emphasize their differences; and each therapist attributes his or her successes to those conceptual and procedural features that distinguish that theory and method from its competitors rather than to the features they all share. [p. 10]

This tremendous diversity in theory and practice constitutes a problem in the education of psychotherapists. What theories and practices should be taught in these curricula? It appears that this becomes a matter of the training and preferences of the faculty. It could be maintained that the curricula in this field are at the stage of the curricula in medical schools prior to the Flexner report (1960) originally published in 1910.

The Specific-Treatments Paradigm

In the 1960s the movement toward specific treatments for specific conditions was emphasized by a number of influential writers. Paul's (1967) statement is frequently cited: "The question towards which all outcome research should ultimately be directed is the following: *What* treatment, by *whom,* is most effective for *this* individual with *that* specific problem, and under *which* set of circumstances?" (p. 111). Krumboltz (1966) phrases it similarly: "What we need to know is which procedures and techniques, when used to accomplish which kinds of behavior change, are most effective with what kind of client when applied by what kind of counselor" (p. 22). Bergin and Strupp (1972) conclude that "the problem of psychotherapy research in its most general terms, should be formulated as a standard scientific question: What specific therapeutic intervention produces specific changes in specific conditions" (p. 8). Strupp and Bergin (1969) write:

We have become convinced that the therapy of the future will consist of a set of specific techniques that can be applied under

specifiable conditions to specific problems, symptoms or cases
. . . . It has become increasingly clear that psychotherapy as
currently practiced is not a unitary process and is not applied to
a unitary problem. [pp. 19–20, 68]

Urban and Ford (1971) advocate the same position. The task of
psychotherapy, they write, is "to articulate the conditions under which
specific tactics are appropriate for a particularized set of problems
. . . the discovery of which set of procedures is effective for what set
of purposes when applied to what kinds of patients with people"
(p. 20).

This paradigm has been the basis of behavioristic approaches to
psychotherapy. It has the appeal of scientific empiricism and of logic.
But it has yielded little in the way of matching specific techniques to
specific problems. A major problem is the requirements involved in its
premises. It would require (1) a taxonomy of client problems or of
psychological disorders (a reliable and valid diagnostic system); (2) a
taxonomy of therapeutic techniques or interventions; (3) a taxonomy
of therapist personalities; (4) a taxonomy of circumstances, conditions,
or situations or environments in which therapy is provided; and (5)
principles or empirical rules for matching all these variables. It is
apparent that a matrix including all these variables would require a
prohibitive number of cells. Parloff (1982) notes that "a systematic
approach to dealing with a matrix of 250 psychosocial therapies and
150 classes of disorders would require approximately 4.7 million
separate comparisons" (p. 723). Kisch and Kroll (1980) describe the
situation succinctly: "The compelling question of what aspects of
therapy work for what kinds of therapists for what kinds of patients is
probably empirically unanswerable because it is methodologically
unsolvable" (p. 406).

Stiles and co-authors (1986) note that such a design "renders the
specific schema unrealistic as a basis for progress. In principle, to
evaluate 10 types of client, therapist, technique, and setting a matrix
of 10,000 cells must be used" (p. 168). These authors conclude that

"after twenty years' work in the paradigm, researchers have yet to deliver many clear prescriptions" (p. 169).

Yet this is the model for the *Diagnostic and Statistical Manual of Mental Disorders (DSM-III)*, which in the 1980 third edition incidentally includes far more than 150 classes of disorders: over 260 diagnostic categories are listed (American Psychiatric Association 1980). Carson (1990), in a book review, makes some cogent criticisms of the *DSM-III-R* (American Psychiatric Association 1987). For example, "this diagnostic system, which essentially forces interdiagnostician agreement, and hence, ensures diagnostic reliability, has exposed in a much clearer light than heretofore the daunting problems of validity that attend the classic categories of psychiatric disorder" (p. 11). The manual has also been faulted because it deals with symptoms rather than with etiology (e.g., Persons 1991). These targeted symptoms have proliferated from slightly over 100 diagnostic categories in the first edition of the *Diagnostic and Statistical Manual of Mental Disorders* (American Psychiatric Association 1952) to over 260 in the third edition (American Psychiatric Association 1980) and 400 in the fourth edition (American Psychiatric Association 1994).

The most exhaustive attempt to match treatments to patients and problems is that of Beutler and Clarkin (1990) in their book *Systematic Treatment Selection*. Their attempt is not based on the *DSM-III-R* diagnostic system but on an elaborate system of patient variables, treatment settings or contexts, and relationship variables with strategies and techniques tailored to targets of change, levels of intervention, and mediating goals. The authors admit it is a complex process, perhaps too complex. Indeed, the complexity defies application. It is far from a usable prescriptive system (see also Seligman 1990).

The Movement Toward Integration

Recently, there has been an extensive effort toward integration. Goldfried (1982) and Goldfried and Newman (1986) provide historic surveys of the literature representing attempts to integrate varying approaches to psychotherapy over the past fifty years. The Society for the Exploration of Psychotherapy Integration was initiated in 1979 by Goldfried, Wachtel, and Strupp, and a newsletter began circulating in 1983. The *International Journal of Eclectic Psychotherapy*, which began publication in 1982, became the *Journal of Integrative and Eclectic Psychotherapy*. The *Journal of Psychotherapy Integration* began publication in 1991 as the journal for the Society. Norcross (1986a) refers to the psychotherapy Zeitgeist of the 1980s as "rapprochement, convergence, integration" (p. ix).

The movement toward integration in psychotherapy does not have the development of a single universal system of psychotherapy as its goal. It does not agree with the statement that "the objective of any movement toward eclecticism or integration in psychotherapy must be the development of a single comprehensive system of psychotherapy, including philosophical and theoretical foundations" (Patterson 1989c, p. 157). Although Norcross (1986b) earlier noted that "the promise of eclecticism is the development of a comprehensive psychotherapy based on a unified body of empirical work" (p. 11) he called Patterson's statement "patently false" (Norcross 1990, p. 297). Others are also in disagreement with this as an objective of integration. Arkowitz (1992), in his review and evaluation of integrative theories, expresses concern that "the integration of today may become the single-school approach of tomorrow. . . . Such a path takes us full circle back to where we started" (p. 273). Yet the development of numerous differing integrations or integrative therapies poses the same problem: "whether there will be competition among specific schools of integrative therapy" (Arnkoff and Glass 1992, p. 684). It does appear that the integration movement is not likely to move in the direction of a universal theory or system in the near future. Lazarus and Beutler (1993) disagree that integration is desirable: "We believe that integrationist views, as opposed to the technical eclectic approaches, may retard progress and lead in unproductive future directions" (p. 382). Goldfried and Castonguay (1992), in an article titled "The Future of Psychotherapy Integration," write:

It is doubtful that the integration movement will provide the field with one grand theoretical integration. Given the epistemological differences . . . it is hardly likely that this is possible. Moreover, we would maintain that as long as there exist theoreticians, it is likely that there will always be competing theories. [p. 8]

Norcross (1986b) writes, "The ideal of integrating *all* available psychotherapy systems is not likely to be met" (p. 6).

The Eclecticism Solution

Current attempts at integration focus on eclecticism in psychotherapy. Eclecticism is not a new development. Contemporary writers ignore the work of Williamson (see Patterson 1980) and Thorne (see Patterson 1986). Williamson wrote in the late 1930s, the '40s, and '50s, and Thorne in the '50s and '60s. Thorne, an M.D. as well as a Ph.D., used a medical model. Thus, eclecticism is not a new development, though it seemed to fall into disrepute from the 1950s through the 1970s. Most therapists were probably eclectic in the first half of the century, before the development of the current major theories. Psychoanalysis and its derivatives were the first theories to develop, and most of those therapists who were not eclectic adhered to some form of psychoanalysis or psychoanalytic (dynamic) therapy.

The number and percentage of psychologists (therapists) who considered themselves eclectic during the '40s and '50s are not known. Thorne (personal communication, June 2, 1967) gave a figure of zero for members of the American Psychological Association who identified themselves as eclectic, but the source of this figure is not known. Kelly (1961) reports a survey in which 40 percent of those responding in 1960 identified themselves as eclectic. Since then numerous surveys have found the percentage of psychologists (therapists) accepting the designation ranging from 30–65 percent, and fluctuating around 50 percent (Fee et al. 1982, Garfield and Kurtz 1974, 1976, Larson 1980, M. J. Mahoney et al. unpublished manuscript, Norcross and Prochaska

1982, Prochaska and Norcross 1983, Smith 1982, Swan and Mac-Donald 1978, Watkins et al. 1986).

Garfield and Bergin (1986) contend that "the new view is that the long-term dominance of the major theories is over and that an eclectic position has taken precedence" (p. 7). They came to this conclusion because no single theory has taken clear precedence over the others. Eclecticism, while the most frequently chosen label by therapists (clinical and counseling psychologists), still claims less than 50 percent of those responding to surveys. The *meaning* of eclecticism may be more the issue than the *numbers* that emerge in the surveys. The statement by Lambert and colleagues (1986) that "the *vast majority* of therapists have become eclectic in orientation" (p. 202, emphasis added) is an overstatement. Eclecticism has bred a variety of schools within the category. In addition, there are those practitioners who claim to be eclectic simply because they have no theoretical affiliation. Thus an important point not addressed adequately in surveys is just what eclecticism means.

What Is Eclectic Psychotherapy?   There is an increasing literature on eclecticism in psychotherapy. Various kinds of eclecticism have been proposed: theoretical eclecticism (Dimond et al. 1978), strategic eclecticism (Held 1984), radical eclecticism (Robertson 1979), technical eclecticism (Lazarus 1967), and perhaps others. Most discussions of eclectic therapy involve combining two theories or approaches, usually psychoanalysis and behavior therapy (e.g., Wachtel 1977). A number of books go beyond this, however: Beutler (1983), Hart (1983), Lazarus (1981), Norcross (1986a), Palmer (1979), and Prochaska and DiClementi (1984).

The general impression from all this literature is one of confusion. It is not clear just what eclectic therapy is. Those who call themselves eclectic appear to have little in common. They do not subscribe to any common set of principles. While they may not be antitheoretical or even atheoretical, there is nothing that could be called an eclectic theory. The most widely accepted form of eclecticism is technical eclecticism, which argues that techniques from various systems can be used without concern for the theoretical bases of the systems. Those who purport to be systematic have little credibility due to a lack of objective empirical research. Mahalik (1990) notes in a review of "systematic" eclectic models (Beutler's eclectic psychotherapy; Howard, Nance, and Myers's adaptive counseling and therapy; Lazarus's multimodal therapy; and Prochaska and DiClementi's transtheoretical approach): "None of the models have been well evaluated and none have received more than the beginnings of empirical support. Additionally, the great majority of research on the models has been conducted by the authors" (p. 675).

Garfield and Bergin (1986) note that "there is no single or precise definition of an eclectic orientation. . . . [I]t is exceedingly difficult to characterize an eclectic approach in terms of either theory or procedures" (p. 8). They further state that "because eclecticism does not represent any systematic view, no research on the nature of this 'approach' has been done, nor is it really possible" (p. 9). Garfield's (1982) earlier characterization still holds: "Eclecticism is perceived as the adherence to a nonsystematic and rather haphazard clinical approach" (p. 612). Strupp and Binder (1984) make a similar statement: "The term *eclectic*, which many therapists use to describe their orientation and practices, is so fuzzy it defies definition" (p. xii). In practice, eclectic psychotherapists appear to have little in common; they do not subscribe to any common principles or system. Lazarus and colleagues (1992) state that "the term frequently conveys nothing of substance—it simply implies that concepts from two or more of the more than 400 separate 'schools' of psychotherapy [Karasu 1986] have been blended, often in an arbitrary, subjective, if not capricious manner [Franks 1984, Lazarus 1988]" (p. 11).

Goldfried and Safran (1986) note that "there exists a real danger that . . . we may ultimately end up with as many eclectic models as we currently have schools of psychotherapy" (p. 464). Norcross's (1986a) edited book includes chapters by authors of the major eclectic positions, including Beutler (1983, 1986), Hart (1983, 1986), Lazarus (1981), and Prochaska and DiClementi (1984). Goldfried and Newman (1986), Goldfried and Safran (1986), Messer (1986), and Murray (1986) provide critical comments.

It causes one pause to consider that, in effect, there are as many eclectic approaches as there are eclectic therapists. Each operates out of his or her unique bag of techniques, on the basis of his or her particular training, experiences, and biases, on a case-by-case basis, with no general theory or set of principles as guides for practice. It is a method described most accurately as "flying by the seat of the pants." Although the expression may have a romantic flavor when applied to airplanes, should such free-wheeling, random practice be offered to human beings in distress? The practice of therapy must have an underlying rationale, which gives the therapist a guide to effective and consistent practice.

In addition to a lack of guidance in deciding under what circumstances a given therapeutic approach should be used, there is no way to test such undefined eclecticism. Thus there is no possibility of professional accountability.

The lack of theoretical foundation has been acknowledged. Prochaska and Norcross (1983) note:

The need for theoretical orientation has been frequently recognized, but few, if any, adequate models of systematic eclecticism have been created. . . . Beyond its conceptual relativity and personal appeal, eclecticism in its current state may not possess adequate clinical utility or validity for increasing numbers of therapists. [p. 171] . . . The real challenge for synthetic eclectic therapists and theorists alike is to construct models of systematic eclecticism that have both empirical validity and clinical utility. [p. 168]

The desirability of attention to theory is recognized by Arkowitz (1992) in his evaluation of the present state of technical eclecticism. With the limitless number of variables and their interactions, the task of research "seems overwhelming unless we have some coherent framework to guide the selection of relevant variables. It is here that theory is helpful, and perhaps even essential" (p. 289). Yet he does not see as desirable a single overarching system of therapy but refers to eclectic therapies. A true eclecticism is neither nonsystematic nor haphazard.

English and English (1958) define eclecticism as follows:

In theoretical system building, the selection and orderly combination of compatible features from diverse sources, sometimes
from incompatible theories and systems; the effort to find valid
elements in all doctrines or theories and to combine them into a
harmonious whole. . . . Eclecticism is to be distinguished from
unsystematic and uncritical combination, for which the name is
syncretism. [p. 168]

Eclecticism thus is, or should be, a systematic, integrative,
theoretical position. It appears that most of the approaches labeled
eclecticism are, in fact, syncretisms. Such approaches include those of
Palmer (1979), Garfield (1980), Beutler (1983), and Lazarus (1981).

Such eclecticism has been criticized. Rogers (1951) refers to the
attempt to reconcile various schools of thought as "a superficial
eclecticism which does not increase objectivity, and which leads
nowhere" (p. 8) and has also noted "a confused eclecticism, which has
been prevalent in psychotherapy, has blocked scientific progress in the
field" of psychotherapy (p. 24). Snygg and Combs (1949) write that "an
eclectic system leads directly to inconsistency and contradiction, for
techniques derived from conflicting frames of reference are bound to
be conflicting" (p. 282). From the point of view of research, eclecticism
has been considered undesirable, representing a confounding of the
treatment variable. Rogers (1956) notes that in research, to separate
truth from untruth, there must be an active consistency using specifically selected hypotheses. Such fluid definitions of eclecticism render
it impossible to study or practice systematically.

Since no body of theory or knowledge can be called eclectic
psychotherapy, it cannot be taught. It can only be developed on the
basis of experience. Thus the beginning therapist is in an unenviable,
and scientifically untenable, position. Such practice would seem to
border on the unethical. Garfield (1982) puts it simply: "Eclecticism is
perceived as the adherence to a nonsystematic and rather haphazard
clinical approach" (p. 612).

Paradoxically, eclecticism as an integrating force actually appears to be fostering divergence. But Norcross (1986b) writes that "a truly eclectic psychotherapy may begin with and be based on an operation-alization of common variables that play an important role in most therapies [Garfield 1973, 1980, Goldfried 1980, 1982, Prochaska and DiClementi 1984]" (p. 15).

The Common Elements Solution

It has been recognized for at least fifty years (Rosenzweig 1936) that there are basic common factors or elements in the diverse approaches to psychotherapy. Following Rosenzweig, other early writers recognizing common elements include Oberndorf (1946), Hathaway (1948), Wyatt (1948), Ziskind (1949), Collier (1950), Rioch (1951), and Black (1952). Frank has persisted in making this point since 1961 (Frank 1961, 1973, 1982).

Rosenzweig (1936) lists three factors: therapist personality, interpretations (whether right or wrong, they provide explanations of client behaviors), and theoretical orientations (though different, they have a synergistic effect on various areas of functioning). Others have listed other, usually more specific, factors, including advice, encouragement, explanations, therapist attention, warmth, persuasion, support, reassurance, suggestion, therapist expectation of improvement, and client expectation of improvement. Not all of these factors are common to all of the major theories or systems. Client-centered therapy, for example, rejects the use of advice, suggestion, persuasion, reassurance, and encouragement.

Frank's (1982) factors are more general. He has focused on a group of components centering on the concept of psychotherapy as a way of "directly or indirectly combating demoralization" (p. 19), which he sees as the core of client problems. The first of his four components is

an emotionally charged, confiding relationship with a helping person. . . . While the therapist's status or reputation in the patient's eyes may initially determine the therapist's ascendancy, success in therapy depends on the therapist's ability to convey to the patient that he cares about the patient, is competent to help, and has no ulterior motives. [Frank 1982, p. 19]

Without further analyzing the relationship, Frank (1982) lists as the second component a healing environment that first emphasizes the therapist's role as a healer through symbolically heightening the therapist's prestige and reinforcing the patient's expectation of receiving help, and second, is safe.

The third component is "a rational, conceptual scheme or myth that provides a plausible explanation for the patient's symptoms and prescribes a ritual or procedure for resolving them" (Frank 1982, p. 20). And the fourth is

a ritual that requires active participation of both patient and therapist and that is believed by both to be the means of restoring the patient's health. . . . The words myth and ritual are used advisedly to emphasize that, although expressed in scientific terms, therapeutic rationales and procedures cannot be disproved. [p. 20]

The functions of myth and ritual, according to Frank (1982), are as follows

1. "Strengthening the therapeutic relationship, thereby combating the patient's sense of alienation" (p. 21)
2. "Inspiring and maintaining the patient's expectation of help" (p. 21)
3. "Providing new learning experiences," which may occur in several ways—instruction, modeling, conditioning (p. 25)
4. "Arousing emotions," which provokes motive power for change (p. 25)
5. "Enhancing the patient's sense of mastery or self-efficacy, . . . (1) by providing the patient with a conceptual scheme that labels and explains symptoms and supplies the rationale for

the treatment program, and (2) by giving the individual experiences of success" (p. 27)

Frank's analysis is highlighted because it has been developed in some detail over a period of time and has received considerable attention, and perhaps acceptance. Two comments might be made here. First, Frank has developed his position on the basis of an analysis or study of healing in primitive societies, which involves myth and ritual. Second, the position emphasizes what are or may be regarded as the placebo aspects of psychotherapy (Fish 1973).

Implicit Commonalities.   A number of characteristics of psychotherapy appear to be present in all theories or approaches but are seldom explicitly noted.

First, all approaches and all therapists agree that human beings are capable of change or of being changed; disagreement is on how best to bring about change. Human beings are not predetermined; at any stage of development, they are still pliable. Learning theory approaches are based on this assumption. Skinner (1958) expresses it as follows:

It is dangerous to assert that an organism of a given species or age cannot solve a given problem. As a result of careful scheduling, pigeons, rats, and monkeys have done things in the last five years which members of their species have never done before. It is not that their forebears were incapable of such behavior; nature had simply never arranged effective sequences of schedules. [p. 96]

More dramatically, regarding the possibility of molding personality, he states, "Give me the specifications, and I'll give you the man" (Skinner 1948, p. 243).

Other approaches may not be so optimistic about the changeability of personality or behavior, but they clearly assume the possibility of change; otherwise there would be no point to engaging in psychotherapy.

Second, there is agreement that some kinds of behavior are

undesirable, inadequate, and harmful or result in dissatisfaction, unhappiness, or limitation of a person's potential and, therefore, warrant attempts at change. These behaviors may include cognitive or emotional disturbances or disorders, conflicts, unresolved problems, or those behaviors designated as neurotic or psychotic.

Third, all therapies and therapists expect their clients to change as a result of their particular techniques. This expectation may vary in its degree; in some instances, it approaches a highly optimistic or even enthusiastic expectation, while in others, it may be minimal, or minimal changes may be expected.

Every therapist believes in or has confidence in the theory and method that she or he uses. If the therapist did not believe that this approach was the best method, it would not be used; some other method would replace it. As in the case of belief in the ability of clients to change, therapists would not be engaged in the practice of therapy if they did not expect their clients to change and did not believe that their methods would lead to change. It might be hypothesized that success (or at least therapists' and perhaps clients' reports of success) bears a strong relationship to the degree of confidence that the therapist has in his or her approach. A common aspect of therapy thus appears to be the therapist's commitment to a particular theory or at least a particular method or set of techniques. The effect of this commitment, or the interaction of commitment and effectiveness of a method, is one of the problems in attempting to evaluate the effectiveness of a method apart from the therapist who uses it.

Fourth, individuals who enter and continue in therapy feel the need for help. They "hurt": they are suffering or are unhappy because of conflicts, symptoms, negative feelings or emotions, interpersonal problems or conflicts, inadequate or unsatisfying behaviors, and so on. They are, therefore, motivated to change. Therapists are not particularly interested in working with unmotivated or "involuntary" clients, even though such clients may obviously have problems. Persons who do not recognize their problems or do not feel any need for help do not often enter therapy, or, if they do, they usually do not continue.

Fifth, clients also believe that change is possible and expect to change. Frank (1959, 1961) has emphasized the universality of this factor in clients. Cartwright and Cartwright (1958) suggest that it is only this belief that leads to improvement in a positive linear manner. The other beliefs are probably present to some extent in all clients, however. If the client did not feel that she or he would improve and that the therapist and the therapist's methods could effect such improvement, the client would not enter or continue in therapy.

Finally, all therapists appear to expect and insist that the client be an active participant in the process. The client is not a passive recipient, as is the physically ill patient who is being treated by a physician, even in those approaches that are most directive and active. All learning (behavior change) appears to require some activity (whether motor, verbal, or intellectual) on the part of the learner.

The Relationship as a Common Element. Three general comments can be made about the common elements suggested in the literature reviewed so far. First, all of the variables, elements, or components involve or are aspects of an interpersonal relationship. Psychotherapy, it is generally agreed, is an interpersonal relationship, but not all interpersonal relationships are therapy or therapeutic. Psychotherapy must include, if it does not entirely consist of, an interpersonal relationship having certain characteristics or elements. This relationship is common to all methods or theories of psychotherapy.

Explicit Relationship Elements. The implicit commonalities underlie and/or enter into the relationship between the therapist and the client. More significant and more specific than the implicit elements, however, are a number of explicit elements that constitute the core of the therapeutic relationship. Therapy, by almost any definition, involves a personal contact between the therapist and the client. Many theories note the importance of the personal qualities that enter into the relationship without, however, specifying their nature. But some qualities have been identified, defined, and even measured. A classic article by Rogers (1957a) specifies (as assumptions) the necessary and sufficient conditions for therapeutic personality change. The three therapist contributions to the relationship and a corollary respecting the client are as follows:

1. All therapists manifest a real concern for their clients. They are interested in their clients, care for them, and want to help them. Rogers uses the term *unconditional positive regard*. Others have referred to warmth or nonpossessive warmth, respect, prizing, valuing, and accepting. While client-centered therapists would include a respect for the client's potential to take responsibility for her- or himself and to resolve her or his own problems, some therapists would not include this point. The client-centered nonevaluative, nonjudgmental attitudes also might not be shared by others, but a basic interest, concern, and desire to help another human being are common to all therapists and are a powerful aspect of the therapeutic relationship.

2. A second characteristic of all effective therapists is honesty, or a genuineness and openness. Rogers refers to it as *therapist congruence* — a consistency between the thoughts and feelings of the therapist and the therapist's expressions to the client. Therapists are sincere, authentic, transparent, and real persons. They are not engaged in trickery or deceit in their relations with their clients.

3. Empathic understanding is a third aspect of a therapeutic relationship. In some form or other, although it varies in terminology, all the major writers on psychotherapy refer to this characteristic of therapists as being important. Theorists vary in the degree of emphasis they place on empathic understanding, and therapists of different persuasions vary in the degree to which they provide it, but no one seems to deny its desirability, even its importance.

4. These attitudes or characteristics of the therapist lead to a therapeutic relationship only if they are recognized, perceived, or felt by the client. The therapist exists for the purpose of the relationship only as she or he is perceived by the client.

Agreement on the Relationship

The most widely known studies on the nature of the relationship as viewed by therapists are those of Fiedler (1950a,b, 1951), who found that therapists from different schools of psychotherapy agreed on the nature of the ideal therapeutic relationship. Factor analysis yielded one common factor of "goodness," whose items were concerned with empathy or understanding. Fiedler has also concluded that a good therapeutic relationship as viewed by these therapists is similar to a good interpersonal relationship. Other studies have found that the relationship is important in the effectiveness of behavior therapy (see Emmelkamp 1986). Emmelkamp (1986) believes that "it is becoming increasingly clear that the quality of the therapeutic relationship may be influential in determining success or failure of behavioral therapies" (p. 432).

There is currently widespread, if not universal, agreement among theorists and therapists on the influence of the relationship in therapy or behavior change (Bergin and Garfield 1994). Goldstein (1962), reviewing the literature on therapist and patient expectations in psychotherapy, concludes, "There can no longer be any doubt as to the primary status which must be accorded the therapeutic transaction" (p. 105).

Menninger and Holzman (1973), in the second edition of *Theory of Psychoanalytic Techniques,* view the relationship as the central focus of the therapeutic process. Goodstein (1977), reviewing a collection of papers published under the title *What Makes Behavior Change Possible?,* states that "among virtually all of the contributors there is an awareness of and attention to the therapeutic relationship as an essential ingredient of behavior change" (p. 579). The fourteen contributors include Frank, Strupp, Burton, Ellis, Raimy, the Polsters, Bandura, and Wolpe.

The behavior therapists, although admitting the presence of the relationship, have minimized its importance. Goldstein (1973), in discussing the relationship in behavior therapy, notes that "several writers in this area, especially Wolpe (1958, 1969), point out the need for establishing a good interpersonal relationship as an integral part of treatment process" (p. 281). He goes on to emphasize that the therapist establishes the relationship so that the therapist can be a reinforcing agent. The relationship is thus viewed as an objective tool carried on to manipulate the client rather than as a process of human interaction that is inherently healing. Goldfried and Davison (1970) suggest that "perhaps one of the reasons that behavior therapists have tended to deemphasize the importance of the relationship is the fact that their techniques have been shown to be effective in their own right" (p. 56). This is actually not a fact. The study that they and others cite as showing this effectiveness involved a laboratory study of fear modification that used an automated desensitization procedure (Lang et al. 1970). Instructions for the desensitization process were taped, and subjects listened to the tapes instead of being involved with a therapist. However, the tapes were of a human voice, and the experimental situation involved relationship elements (personal and interpersonal elements). Furthermore, the possibility of the subjects anthropomorphizing the machine was not considered (Schwitzgebel and Traugott 1968). Indeed, the experimenters themselves may have done so — the device was designated as "DAD" (device for automatic desensitization).

In addition, other research has shown that there is an influence of the relationship on conditioning. For example, Sapolsky (1960) has shown that the effectiveness of reinforcement depends on the relationship between the experimenter and the subject. Subjects who were given instructions that pictured the experimenter as attractive conditioned well, while those who were led to perceive the experimenter as unattractive did not condition during the experimental period (although there was evidence of delayed conditioning). Also, subjects who were matched with experimenters for similarity (compatibility) on the basis of a personality test conditioned better than did those who were incompatible. Similarly, "warm" experimenters were more effective than "cold" experimenters. Considerable evidence suggests that the rate and extent of conditioning are influenced by the personality and attitudes of the experimenter and the experimenter's relationship to the subject. As Ullmann and Krasner (1965) note, "Both the subject's and the examiner's expectancies, sets and so forth have a major effect on the individual's response to the situation" (p. 43). They go on to conclude that in therapy, "the best results are obtained when the patient and therapist form a good interpersonal relationship" (p. 43).

Observers of Wolpe and of Lazarus (when he was associated with Wolpe) note that relationship variables were present. Lazarus acknowledges this in his comment on the report: "Both Wolpe and I have explicitly stated that relationship variables are often extremely important in behavior therapy. Factors such as warmth, empathy and authenticity are considered necessary but often insufficient" (Klein et al. 1969, p. 262). Subsequently, Wolpe has stated, "The more the patient feels a responsive warmth towards the therapist, the more likely to be inhibited are those of his anxieties that are evident during the interview" (Burton 1976, p. 66).

Yet there are some who do not acknowledge the necessity or importance of the relationship. Gill (1976), a psychoanalytically oriented therapist, has reviewed a book in which therapists representing three approaches (behavior therapy, Gestalt therapy, and psychoanalysis) discuss the same three cases. He writes, "I confess that although I believe I understand why it is so, I remain astonished that so many therapists can remain blind to the fact that their allegedly specific methods of desensitization, rehearsing, and so on, owe their effects to unacknowledged interpersonal interaction" (p. 291). Bergin and Garfield (1994), in their summary of research, note that "there is massive evidence that psychotherapeutic techniques do not have specific effects; yet there is tremendous resistance to accepting this finding as a legitimate one" (p. 822).

That there is now general agreement on the importance of the relationship offered by the therapist, and in particular on the variables postulated by Rogers, is indicated by the statements of reviewers in the third edition of Garfield and Bergin's (1986) *Handbook of Psychotherapy and Behavior Change*. Beutler and colleagues (1986) write, "The importance of such qualities has subsequently been almost universally accepted by all psychotherapies, with varying levels of emphasis" (p. 276). Lambert and colleagues (1986) state:

> Virtually all schools of therapy accept the notion that these (accurate empathy, positive regard, nonpossessive warmth, and congruence or genuineness) or related therapist relationship variables are important for significant progress in psychotherapy and, in fact, fundamental in the formation of a working alliance. . . . These and related factors common across therapies

seem to make up a significant portion of the effective ingredients of psychotherapy. [p. 171]

Other relationship elements are or may be involved in psychotherapy. These variables are related to social, professional, and status differences between the therapist and the client—the concept of the therapist as an expert—and include professional authority, prestige, and status. "Bedside manner," the manifestation of self-confidence and self-assurance, and the charismatic manner of the therapist are other examples. Some approaches to psychotherapy emphasize this aspect, while others minimize it. To some extent, an element of authority is present in almost all therapeutic relationships. An authoritative role is usually assigned to the therapist by the client. Nevertheless, the degree of authority may vary tremendously, and it can be maximized or minimized in the relationship; it may be exploited or its explicit use may be avoided. That these variables contribute systematically to psychotherapy outcome has not been demonstrated. They are elements of the placebo (see Chapter 6).

This brief review of the relationship as the common element in psychotherapy is provided to serve as an introduction to the following chapters. The thesis of this book is that the relationship between the therapist and the client is the basis for a universal system of psychotherapy.

Conclusion

Although at first appearance the field of psychotherapy appears to be so diverse as to defy any attempt at integration, progress has been made. In their introductory overview chapter to their *Handbook of Psychotherapy and Behavior Change,* Garfield and Bergin (1986) write:

One might be inclined to say that more evidence is provided throughout these chapters to support Jerome Frank's long-held view that "common factors" are the main therapeutic ingredients of psychotherapy than for any other theory. . . . If this trend is further confirmed . . . then a major effort will have to be put into defining, measuring, and enhancing the therapeutically active factors that are common to the different approaches. [p. 18]

This book represents such an effort. The time is now ripe for the development of a universal system of psychotherapy. Such a system must be based on the common elements or factors of the major existing systems, if indeed it does not consist entirely of these elements. Later chapters will consider these elements, including therapist factors, considered here briefly, and client factors.

It has been argued that such a system is limited because its elements have been developed in a Western culture. However, the common elements involve the basic characteristics of human nature and are thus relevant to all times and cultures. A later chapter will deal with this issue.

Although the foundation for a new paradigm is in place, the currently accepted paradigm is strongly defended, so that a shift is unlikely to occur for some time. Mook (1988) quotes Max Planck, the physicist: "A new scientific truth does not triumph by convincing its opponents . . . but rather because its opponents eventually die and a new generation grows up that is familiar with it" (p. 5). But then he cautions, "Paradigms change by attrition as well as, or instead of, persuasion. But the process can also work the other way: a paradigm can be *locked in* by attrition as we lose, first those who hold alternative views, and later, those who even remember that there are any" (p. 5). This possibility is a danger that we currently face, as there are very few who accept the new paradigm, and thus few to whom these are passing it on. This book may serve to preserve the new paradigm, while those who cling to the old pass on.

2

Motivation as Self-Actualization

Introduction

The concept of motivation has been a central aspect of so-called dynamic systems of psychology, from Freudian psychoanalysis to neobehaviorism. However, there has been little agreement on identifying the motives underlying behavior, with the result that there are as many lists of motives as there are of instincts, the precursors of motives. As in the case of instincts, the question may be raised as to whether motives are necessary, and the question might well be answered in the same way—that is, in the negative. Postman (1956), reviewing one of the volumes of the Nebraska Symposium on Motivation, expresses the hope that at a future symposium someone will devote a paper to this question. His wish was in part granted by Kelly (1962), who states in opening his discussion, "I have no use for the concept of motivation. . . . Motivation is an invented construct" (pp. 83–84). In the introduction to this tenth symposium, Jones (1962) notes, "There seems to be increasing evidence over the years that the motivational concept as such has reached the end of its usefulness as a scientific concept" (p. viii).

English and English (1958) define *motivation* as follows:

1. the non-stimulus variables controlling behavior; the general name for the fact that an organism's acts are partly determined in direction and strength by its own nature (or enduring structure) and/or internal state. 2. a specific hypothesized process that energizes differentially certain responses, thus making them dominant over other possible responses to the same situation. [p. 330]

This is a rather vague and loose definition, but even so it is not generally accepted by psychologists. The lack of agreement as to what motivation is, and the inability to answer such questions as how many motives (or drives, impulses, desires, needs, etc.) there are, how they operate, how they are aroused, could well suggest that there may not be any validity or utility to the concept.

Littman (1958) attempts to find common elements among fifty-two motivational terms. Motivation as an energizing function or as an instigator of behavior is not present in all terms, nor is the concept of selection or direction of activity. Persistence in behavior, suggested by some as a characteristic of motivation, does not appear in most terms or definitions. Littman proposes, facetiously, a definition of motivation that would include all of the aspects proposed by various writers. This definition turns out to include all of behavior, and thus all of psychology.

Littman's definition may not be as facetious as he supposes. It points to something that has not been adequately recognized by many psychologists and that, when recognized, changes the whole problem of motivation. This is the fact that activity, or behavior, does not have to be energized, or stimulated, either from within or from without. This point disposes of the necessity for a concept of motivation to account for activity or to look for sources of energy that give strength to motives or drives.

The living organism is continuously active, continuously behaving. Life is activity, so that motivation, in its energizing aspect, is living activity. It is a given, and it does not have to be accounted for except as a property of living matter. As Littman (1958) expresses it, "It is not necessary that there be psychological activities (motives) to set behavioral systems into motion; systems may be so constructed that they already have the property of motion or activity" (p. 157).

Kelly (1962) suggests that we begin

> by assuming that the fundamental thing about life is that it goes on. It isn't that something *makes* it go on; the going on *is the thing itself*. It isn't that motives *make* man come alert to do things; his alertness is an aspect of his very being. Talking about activating motives is simply redundant talky-talk, for once you've got a human being on your hands, you already have alertness and movement, and sometimes a lot more of it than you know what to make of. [p. 85]

And Skinner (1948), a strict behaviorist, makes the same point. "No one," he says, "asks how to motivate a baby. A baby naturally explores everything it can get at, unless restraining forces have been at work. And this tendency doesn't die out, it's not wiped out. . . . We don't need to create motives" (pp. 101–102).

Is there no way of resolving this problem? Must we, with Littman (1958), accept the conclusion that "there are many different kinds of motivational phenomena" (p. 157), all separate, unique, specific, unintegrated? There have been, and are, many who feel that we do not. These are the psychologists, and others, who seek to understand the organism or the individual as an organized, integrated whole, who feel that there must be an organizing or unifying element or factor.

Early Unitary Concepts

There have been a number of unitary theories of motivation, and the first to propose such a theory probably lived before recorded history. Contemporary psychology includes many well-known figures who have arrived, more or less independently, at the conclusion that one single dominating need or motive lies behind all behavior.

The existence of aggression has been a stumbling block to many who have been concerned with human motivation. Its strength and practical universality have led to its being considered instinctive or innate. But many have suggested that this is not the case, that "it may be that what has often been considered instinctive or natural aggressiveness is always a reaction to threat, a reaction which is universal because threat, in some form or other is universal" (Patterson 1962, p. 115). Anthropologists have found societies with little trace or evidence of aggression (see Alland 1972). Ashley Montagu (1962) writes:

> My own interpretation of the evidence, strictly within the domain of science, leads me to the conclusion that man is born good and is organized in such a manner from birth as to need to grow and develop his potentialities for goodness. . . . [The view that aggressiveness is inherited] is not scientifically corroborated. In fact, all the available evidence gathered by competent investigators indicates that man is born without a trace of aggressiveness. [p. 11]

He refers to Lauretta Bender's finding that hostility in the child is a symptom complex resulting from deprivation in development. In her studies of infants, Charlotte Buhler (1961) also found that there is "evidence of a primary orientation toward 'reality' into which the baby moves with a positive anticipation of good things to be found. Only when this reality appears to be hurtful or overwhelming does the reaction become one of withdrawal or defense" (p. 71). Maslow also declares that impulses of hate, jealousy, hostility, and so on, are acquired. "More and more," he writes, "aggression is coming to be regarded as a technique or mode of compelling attention to the satisfaction of one's need" (Maslow 1949, p. 276). There is no instinct of aggression that seeks expression or discharge without provocation or without regard to circumstances.

In other words, aggression is not primary but is a reaction to deprivation, threat, or frustration. This is the frustration-aggression hypothesis put forward in 1939 by the Yale anthropologist Dollard and his psychologist associates. A more general term for the stimuli that provoke aggression is *threat*. Aggression is universal because threat, in some form or other, is universal. Analyst Bibring (1958), in criticizing Freud's theories, questions "whether there are any phenomena of aggression at all outside the field of the ego-preservative functions" (p. 483) and notes "the empirical fact that aggressiveness appears only or almost only when the life instincts or the ego instincts are exposed to harm" (p. 483). A popular novel purporting to demonstrate the innateness of aggressiveness in people inadvertently supports the view that aggression is the result of threat, since the development of aggression in the group of castaway boys occurs under conditions of fear and feelings of being threatened (Golding 1955).

The influence of the aggressive aspect of behavior has been so strong that in some cases it has been accepted as the basic and single motivation for behavior (Angyal 1941). Adler (Ansbacher and Ansbacher 1956), who was one of the first contemporary psychologists to propose a unitary concept of motivation, originally accepted aggression as the unifying principle. But he seems to have recognized that aggression occurs "when one of the primary drives is prevented from satisfaction" (p. 34) or as a result of neurotic feelings of inferiority, and he soon abandoned this principle.

Adler then sought the unifying concept elsewhere, and over a period of time he used varying terms to designate the basic striving and the "fictional" (because unattainable) goal of such striving. An early term was the striving "to be a real man" of the masculine protest. Other early terms were the striving for superiority, for power, for security, for self-esteem. Such striving was a compensatory process, developing out of a feeling of inferiority. As Adler turned from the neurotic to the normal or healthy individual, he turned from compensatory strivings to more positive concepts: completion and perfection. While the neurotic strives to overcome personal deficiencies, the normal individual is less self-centered and strives for a goal that includes the welfare of others. Adler saw no need for positing special forces as the source of energy for motivation: "The striving for superiority . . . is an intrinsic necessity of life itself" (Ansbacher and Ansbacher 1956, p. 103). "The striving for perfection is innate in the sense that it is a part of life, a striving, an urge, or something without which life would be unthinkable" (p. 104).

Many others have reached this solution to the problem of motivation, apparently independently and using somewhat differing terminology. Angyal (1941), defining life as "a process of self-expansion" (p. 29), makes the point that "we can say that the tendency of the organism is toward increased autonomy" (p. 47) or a tendency toward self-determination. He also refers to self-realization as being the intrinsic purpose of life (p. 354).

Lecky (1945), impressed by the integration and organization of the self, feels that a need for self-consistency and its preservation is the single basic need of the organism: "the goal for which the individual strives is the maintenance of a unified organization" (p. 45).

White's (1959) concept of competence, which he defines as "an organism's capacity to interact effectively with its environment," (p. 297) may appear to be a unitary approach to motivation. He refers to motivation as the urge toward competence. But White's concept is actually much narrower. Competence does not supplant or subsume the primary drives. It is an attempt to integrate many apparently spontaneous activities such as exploration, manipulation, sensing, mastery, and so forth. The feeling of efficacy as a goal seems limited and hardly acceptable as a basic, general goal of life.

Woodworth (1958) elevates a similar interaction with the environment to the status of a single motivating principle, however. He states that "the direction of receptive and motor activity toward the environment is the fundamental tendency of animal and human behavior" and "is the all-pervasive primary motivation of behavior" (pp. 124–125). Again, however, this would appear to be a limited and rather meager concept of life.

Thorne (1961) posits a drive for higher organization, which includes a person's need to maximize him- or herself, to achieve perfect functioning, and to organize his or her expanding experience into meaningful wholes. There is also a drive to achieve and maintain stability of organization, which includes self-preservation, homeostasis, habit systems, ideological controls, life goals and purposes, and lifestyle.

Even those who would repudiate the whole concept of motivation appear to be unable to avoid dealing with the problem of the direction or goal of behavior, and they develop concepts that are essentially motivational. Kelly (1958) declares that the concept of motivation is not needed to explain directionality of movement. Yet his theory of personal constructs assumes a motive or goal that is quite similar to those discussed earlier: "A person chooses for himself that alternative in a dichotomized construct through which he anticipates the greater possibility for extension and definition of his system" (p. 59).

Finally, Goldstein (1939), on the basis of extended experience with brain-injured veterans, concludes that self-actualization is the single basic motive of all behavior: "We can say, an organism is governed by a tendency to actualize, as much as possible, its individual capacities, its 'nature' in the world" (p. 196).

It appears, then, that a number of scholars has converged, more or less independently, to the position that the assumption of a single basic, dominant, integrating motive, or goal, is more useful in understanding behavior than an indefinite multiplicity of separate, independent, or even hierarchically arranged motives or needs. Whether this is an overemphasis on the law of parsimony or itself evidence of the need for integration, unity, perfection, or completeness is a matter for the future to decide. Suffice it to say that the concept seems to be increasingly accepted in psychology and may lead to the solution of the age-old problem of motivation and the understanding of behavior.

Maslow's Hierarchy of Needs

In the effort to understand the great variety of behavior manifested by the human organism, long lists of physiological, psychological, and social drives and needs have been proposed. A basic problem in motivation then becomes the organization of these needs into a system. The solution most frequently proposed is the ordering of needs in a hierarchy. Maslow's (1954) hierarchy is perhaps the most adequate attempt at such a solution. It starts with the basic physical needs, which are prepotent and take precedence, when they are unmet, over all other needs. When these basic needs are met, the safety needs emerge. Then come the belongingness need, the love need, the esteem need, and, finally, the need for self-actualization (Maslow 1970). The problem is that the order is not invariant, as Maslow himself recognizes. It is not always true that the lower, more basic physiological needs take precedence over the higher, less prepotent needs. A person may sacrifice life for honor. We need, therefore, some organizing principle to explain this apparent inconsistency. The resolution of this problem will be considered later.

Maslow (1943) includes as one of his needs the need for self-actualization, which he defines as a desire to fulfill one's potential, "to become more and more of what one is" (p. 270). It is not clear where he places self-actualization in his hierarchy. In one list (Maslow 1954, Chapter 5), it is the fifth of seven or eight needs. Maslow limits this need to self-fulfillment of potentiality and includes the esteem need as a separate category just above the self-actualization need. However, he also speaks of self-actualization as the "ultimate need" (Maslow 1954, p. 116).

Self-Actualization as the Single Basic Motivation

Much has been written about self-actualization in an attempt to develop and enhance the definition of the concept. Jahoda (1958) investigates concepts of positive mental health, synthesizing six approaches to the concept. Self-actualization is one of those approaches. She also lists autonomy and environmental mastery, linking them to the concept of self-actualization.

Jahoda's first criterion of mental health focuses on the "individual's style and degree of growth, development, or self-actualization" (p. 23). Jahoda concludes from the literature that "self" is defined as including self-esteem and a "self acceptance [which] implies that a person has learned to live with himself, accepting both the limitations and possibilities" (p. 24). She rejects words such as *egotism* and *self-centeredness* that indicate qualities of an exclusive attitude toward the self. This self-consciousness connotes an awareness of self and not an overemphasis of self. Jahoda states, "Implicit in Jung's general formulation, and explicit in those of the other authors, is the notion that the healthy individual demonstrates concern for others and does not center all his strivings on satisfying his own needs" (p. 35). Self-actualization does imply a clarity of self-image, an identity that with maturity becomes "more consistent and free from transient influence" (White 1952, p. 30).

Jahoda (1958) also discusses autonomy as a criterion of positive mental health. This concept further illuminates the concept of *self and other*. She cites Angyal (1952), who also addresses self and other balance in his discussion of autonomy. He conceptualizes a double orientation of self-determination and self-surrender:

> These two tendencies of the human being, the tendency to increase his self-determination in his expanding personal world, and the tendency to surrender himself willingly to a superordinate whole, can be summed up by saying that the human being comports himself as if he were a whole of an intermediate order. [Jahoda 1958, p. 133]

One thus actualizes oneself individually in a personally expansive sense and holistically as a subordinate part of the system with which one identifies.

Finally, Jahoda (1958) addresses environmental mastery as a criterion for positive mental health. One aspect of environmental mastery relates to self-actualization through the interaction of self with the interpersonal environment. The point is made by Foot and Cottrell (1955) that through effective interpersonal relationships, members of a group are able to realize both their individual and common goals. The opposite is illuminated by Rollo May (1954) in describing alienation, or ineffective interpersonal relationships, as a loss of the experience of community. Mastery here is not a domination but a concept of one becoming what one can be through effective interactions and promoting one's own goals as well as the goals of the group. The self and the community have the same goal: to fulfill potential. In the highest sense, these goals are exactly the same. Self-actualization is the process of an individual meeting her or his potential in concert with the group.

Rogers (1951) represents self-actualization as a part of a general actualizing tendency. The organism, or the individual, is inherently growing and forward moving. The individual has "an underlying flow of movement toward constructive fulfillment of its [the organism's] inherent possibilities" (Rogers 1980, p. 117). "The actualizing tendency is selective and directional — a constructive tendency, if you will" (p. 12). The basic tendency toward the maintenance and enhancement of the organism and of the self provides the motive force for therapy and personality change. "The organism has one basic tendency and striving — to actualize, maintain, and enhance the experiencing organism" (Rogers 1951, p. 487). Other terms that Rogers uses include *independence, self-determination, integration,* and *self-actualization.* In his presentation of his theoretical position, Rogers (1959) states that the self becomes differentiated as part of the actualizing tendency. As a result, a need may develop for positive regard from others and for positive self-regard. Rogers considers the need for positive regard from others and of oneself as secondary or learned needs. Since they may develop on the basis of and be shaped by experience, these needs may only be "potential" in the general actualizing tendency.

Combs and Snygg (1959) have perhaps developed this unitary theory of motivation most extensively: "From birth to death the maintenance of the phenomenal self is the most pressing, the most crucial, if not the only task of existence. . . . Man seeks not only the maintenance of *a* self. . . . Man seeks both to maintain and enhance his perceiving self" (p. 45).

The concept of self-actualization as the single basic need resolves the problem involved in Maslow's hierarchy. It provides the organizing principle for the separate, specific needs. It eliminates the confusion we face when we attempt to understand the order, or integrate, the multiplicity of often contradictory or opposing specific drives or motives that are attributed to human beings. There is no hierarchy in the sense that certain needs always take precedence over other needs. All the specific needs are subservient to the basic tendency for the preservation and enhancement of the self. The individual's specific needs are organized and assume temporary priority in terms of their relationship to the basic need for self-actualization. At any one time, the most relevant specific need assumes priority or prepotence or, to use Gestalt terminology, becomes the figure against the ground of other needs (Perls 1969a). When it is satisfied, the next most relevant need in terms of self-actualization assumes prepotence or becomes the figure, while the others recede into the background. All are organized by the basic need for self-actualization, and their significance or relevance is determined by this basic need.

Some Objections to Self-Actualization as a Unitary Motivation

Hilgard (1962), discussing the concept of a master motive and referring to some of the writers referred to earlier, concludes, "Because these theorists disagree among themselves as to the one master motive, we are on safer grounds to think of a group of ego-integrative motives, that is, motives with some sort of self-reference" (p. 144). It is, of course, true that many terms have been used by various writers — *self-enhancement, self-actualization, self-fulfillment, self-realization, self-esteem, completeness, perfection,* and so forth. But the diversity is more apparent than real. There appears to be a basic commonality that would require only agreement as to its designation.

A second objection may be formulated in the question whether the maintenance and the enhancement of the self are not a dualism. Are these not two independent motives, which may actually oppose one another at times, rather than a single motive? Preservation of the physical organism may mean the sacrifice of the psychological self or its actualization, fulfillment, or realization. Conversely, preservation of the psychological self may require the sacrifice of the physical organism. Maslow (1955) apparently was influenced by some such considerations in his concept of deficiency motivation and growth motivation.

But preservation or maintenance, and enhancement, may be seen as two aspects of the same motive, operating in different situations. Adler (Ansbacher and Ansbacher 1956) recognizes the different expression of the same basic motive in neurotics and normals. The neurotic, threatened and compensating for a deep feeling of inferiority, reacts to preserve or restore self-esteem, to overcome inferiority with superiority through the striving for power. The normal individual, on the other hand, free of threat, can strive for completeness or perfection. In the unhealthy individual, in the individual under stress who is threatened, enhancement or positive striving is impossible. The person must defend the self against attack or threat of attack and strive to safeguard, defend, or secure what he or she has. The energies of the individual are absorbed in preservation. Goldstein (1939) makes the same point. He considers the drive for self-preservation a pathological phenomenon. The drive for self-actualization, he suggests, undergoes a change in the sick (or threatened) individual in whom the scope of life is reduced, and she or he is driven to maintain (or defend) a limited state of existence. Preservation or maintenance of the self is thus a pathological form of self-actualization, the only form of self-actualization left to the threatened individual.

Another objection appears to be the belief that self-actualization is inimical to individuality. In this view, the self-actualizing person appears to be a collection of traits that are the same for all persons and manifest themselves in standard, identical behaviors. It is true that self-actualizing persons have many common characteristics or behaviors. But since what is actualized is the individual self, there is allowance for different interests and different potentials. Maslow (1956) makes the point that "self-actualization is actualization of a self, and no two selves are altogether alike" (p. 192).

A fourth, and opposite, widespread misconception is that a self-actualizing person is antisocial, or at least asocial. Salvatore Maddi (1973b), criticizing self-actualization as the good life, writes that this view holds that

actualization will tend to take place without the aid of socialization. Indeed, society is usually regarded, in this view, as an obstruction, because it forces individuals into molds, roles,

conventions that have little to do with their own unique potentialities. The best thing society can do is impinge upon the
individual as little as possible. [p. 20]

In another place, Maddi (1973a) writes:

According to Rogers, . . . what blocks individuals is society, in
the form of persons and institutions reacting with conditional
positive regard and therefore being too judgmental to be facilitative of self-actualization. . . . The definition of the good life
involves emphasizes spontaneity rather than planfulness, openness rather than critical judgment, continual change rather than
stability, and an unreflective sense of well-being. Enacting this,
one would more likely live in the woods than enter public life.
[p. 17]

This statement involves a subtle misrepresentation by quoting out of
context, using clever comparisons, and making unjustified inferences
and extrapolations from statements by Rogers.

The idea that the self-actualizing person is — or can be — antisocial
has also been expressed by Williamson (1965). He suggests that human
nature is potentially both good and evil and that "man seems to be
capable both of becoming his 'best' bestial and debasing self, as well as
those forms of 'the best' that are of high excellence" (p. 185). He also
contends that it cannot be accepted that "the nature or form of one's full
potential and self-actualization will thus be the 'best possible' or the
'good' form of human nature" (p. 185). While one could contend that
psychotherapy would provide the conditions for the actualizing of one's
"best" potential, Williamson (1963, p. 6) questions the "implicit
assumption that the 'best' potentiality will be actualized under optimum counseling relationships." He appears to believe that psychotherapy, by accepting self-actualization as its goal, is in danger of
encouraging "growth through demolishing all barriers restricting free
development in any and all directions, irresponsibly and without
regard for the development of others" (Williamson 1950, p. 183). He
questions the assumption that "any and all forms of growth contain

within themselves their own, and sufficient, justification" and asks, "Do we believe that the fullest growth of the individual inevitably enhances the fullest growth of all other individuals?" (Williamson 1958, p. 523). Again, note the use of extreme statements and the straw-man approach.

Smith (1973) also appears to accept this view of self-actualization as including undesirable, or antisocial, behaviors: "[T]he 'problem of evil' remains: people may realize their potentialities in ways that are humanly destructive, of others if not themselves" (p. 48). Indeed, some people *may* exercise their potentialities in antisocial ways, but (by definition) they are not self-actualizing people.

Even the eminent Harvard psychologist Robert White misinterprets self-actualization as self-centered or selfish. Recognizing that Maslow (1956) includes "focusing on problems outside oneself and being concerned with the common welfare" (p. 173), White (1973) questions its inclusion: "To call working for the common welfare 'self-actualization' instantly falsifies it into something done for one's own satisfaction" (p. 69). Thus, it is apparent that he views self-actualization as self, or selfish, satisfaction. "I ask readers," he continues, "to observe carefully whether or not self-actualization, in its current use by psychological counselors and others, is being made to imply anything more than adolescent preoccupation with oneself and one's impulses" (White 1973, p. 69). These remarks seem to reflect the equating of self-actualization with the ego-centered "culture of narcissism" of the "me decade" of the 1970s so widely popularized by writer Tom Wolfe (1976) and historian Christopher Lasch (1979).

Spence (1985), in her presidential address to the American Psychological Association, appears to accept this view. Referring to the rejection of materialism by the youth of the '60s and early '70s, she says:

> Although some were led to careers that were expressions of idealism, others turned their backs on the work ethic or substituted as a goal for material success, self-actualization and "doing their own thing." They and others who became swept up in this self-expressionist movement have in turn been denounced by

social commentators (e.g., Conger 1981) as the "me generation," representing what Christopher Lasch (1979) has called the culture of narcissism. Although the pursuit of self-actualization was stimulated by a rejection of materialistic goals, it represents another facet of unbridled materialism. [pp. 1289–1290]

These are serious misconceptions or misunderstandings, if not misrepresentations, of the concept of self-actualization as it is used by Maslow, Rogers, Patterson, and others. The implicit assumption in these criticisms is that there is an inevitable conflict between the individual and society and that the full development or self-actualization of individuals is inimical to the self-actualization of other individuals.

The formulation by Rogers of the self-actualizing person deals directly with this issue. Individuals live, and must live, in a society composed of other individuals. The person can actualize only in interaction with others. Selfish and self-centered behavior does not lead to experiences that are self-actualizing or satisfying in nature. The self-actualizing person "will live with others in the maximum possible harmony, because of the rewarding character of reciprocal *positive regard*" (Rogers 1959, p. 235, italics original). "We do not need to ask who will socialize him, for one of his own deepest needs is for affiliation and communication with others. As he becomes more fully himself, he will become more realistically socialized" (Rogers 1961, p. 194). The self-actualizing person is more mature, more socialized in terms of the goal of social evolution, though she or he may not be conventually or socially adjusted in a conforming sense.

We do not need to ask who will control his aggressive impulses, for when he is open to all his impulses, his need to be liked by others and his tendency to give affection are as strong as his impulses to strike out or to seize for himself. He will be aggressive in situations in which aggression is realistically appropriate, but there will be no runaway need for aggression. [Rogers 1961, p. 194]

Combs and Snygg (1959) also deal with this problem:

> We are so entirely dependent upon the goodwill and cooperation
> of others in our society that it would be impossible to achieve
> feelings of adequacy without some effective relationship with
> them. The adequate personality must be capable of living
> effectively and efficiently with his fellows. [p. 246]

White (1973) and the other critics doubt the existence of altruism, the respect for and devotion to others, which can and does enhance the existence of those who conduct their lives with that value as a guide. Ultimately altruism does create an opportunity to actualize one's own potential as one who lives in community with others and is responsible for providing whatever aid she or he can offer.

The self-actualizing person needs to live in harmony with others to meet his or her own needs to love and to be loved—in short, to be a self-actualizing person. In that way, the process of self-actualization guides one away from self-centeredness. Through the interdependency of needs of one person to another, the self-actualizing person provides the conditions for the self-actualization of others, rather than creating a self-centered way of being. In addition, the individual actualizes self within the external context. Such forces as culture, society, and family create a broader values context that influences the way each person actualizes her or his potentials.

The Conditions for Self-Actualization

Two kinds of conditions are necessary for the development of self-actualizing persons. First is the satisfaction of the biological needs required for the preservation and development of the physical organism: air, food, and usually clothing and shelter. Second, at the psychosocial level, caring, loving interpersonal relationships are necessary for the social-emotional development of the individual. It is true also that even biological survival requires a nurturing, caring, loving personal environment (Lynch 1977, Spitz 1945). Three necessary elements of the psychological environment are empathic understanding; respect and caring (unconditional positive regard, to use Rogers's term); and genuineness, honesty, sincerity. The nature of these conditions will be developed in later chapters.

3

The Common Etiology Is Lack of Good Interpersonal Relations

Introduction

The field of psychopathology has been dominated by attempts to develop a diagnostic system, represented by the development of the *Diagnostic and Statistical Manual of Mental Disorders,* now in its fourth edition (American Psychiatric Association 1994). The underlying assumption is that there are many, almost innumerable, kinds of mental illness. This is an assumption and not a fact. In addition, no one is really satisfied with the current taxonomy. Many practicing therapists, though dissatisfied with the diagnostic system, have simply accepted it as a necessary evil. By acquiescing to the underlying fallacy, they are failing to assert that psychological dysfunction and physical dysfunction are not specifically the same processes. The attempts to develop a diagnostic system go back to the beginning of psychiatry more than 100 years ago. The fact that such attempts have met with little success should suggest that no such differential conditions in fact exist.

The present chapter operates from an assumption that no differential conditions exist. This is for many a startling possibility requiring a reassessment of basic concepts. The problem involved with basing psychotherapy on a diagnostic system has been discussed elsewhere (Patterson 1948, 1959a Chapter 10). The medical model, followed by those who attempt to base psychotherapy on diagnosis, is not necessarily applicable to psychopathology. Freud himself rejected the medical model as a basis for psychology (Reik 1948) and set out to explore what was to him clearly a different field of study.

Before proceeding further, we should make clear that we are concerned with the so-called functional disorders in which psychotherapy is applicable. We recognize that there are mental disorders of definite organic origin, involving neurological disease, physiological disturbances, toxic conditions, and traumatic injury. There are also certain mental disorders that are possibly organic in nature, on a constitutional or endocrinological basis (e.g., the so-called endogenous depressions). Diagnosis of organic factors is an important medical function in these cases (assisted often by the use of psychological tests) and obviously influences therapy. Such diagnosis is, however, often difficult and sometimes inconclusive, and psychotherapy should not be denied pending decision as to the presence or absence of organic pathology. Moreover, although psychotherapy may not be indicated for a purely organic disorder, there are often mixtures of organic and psychological components in which psychotherapy is beneficial. In addition, the presence of a purely organic condition may, and often does, result in psychological reactions to which psychotherapy may be directed. However, the present discussion is primarily concerned with the recognized functional disorders, including psychosomatic dysfunctions of psychogenic origin, that are regarded as suitable for psychotherapy.

Diagnosis in Psychotherapy

There is a strong motivation toward classification. It appeals to the desire to simplify, to reduce data by categorizing. Classification is considered to be the basis of, the first step in, science. Strecker (1957) notes that " 'naming,' nosology, or classification, is the basis of all

science, indeed of all human knowledge" (p. 352). Zilboorg (1941), in
A History of Medical Psychology, states that

> to give a comprehensive nosology, to classify carefully, to
> produce a well ordered classification almost seems to have
> become the unspoken ambition of every psychiatrist of industry
> and promise, as it is the ambition of a good tenor to strike a high
> C. This classification ambition was so conspicuous that the
> composer Berlioz was prompted to remark that after their studies
> have been completed a rhetorician writes a tragedy and a
> psychiatrist a classification. [p. 451]

Two points are essential to address as one considers classification
of mental functions. First is the notion of classification in general, and
second, closely related, is the appropriateness of the physical context
for psychological dysfunction. A blind faith in the rightness of
classification generalizes the accepted principles of the physical and
biological sciences to psychology. Many dispute the equivalence of the
physical sciences, dealing with objects, with the science of psychology,
which deals with many concepts such as love and creativity that do not
exist in concrete, physical form. One can classify a leaf quite
exactingly. Attempts to classify emotions, with all of their individual
nuances, invariably diminish the subject. The approach is flawed.

It might seem that a logical analogy could be drawn between
internal medicine and psychiatry. Psychiatry, it might be maintained,
is a branch of medicine, and therefore the principles, methods, and
techniques that are applicable in internal medicine apply also, of
necessity, to mental disease and maladjustment.

If one looks a little more closely into the matter, however, a
question might be raised regarding the validity of the analogy between
physical disease and mental disease. The two are, as a matter of fact,
entirely different in many respects. In the first place, the nature of the
primary malignant process is entirely different. In one case it involves
primarily the physiological and chemical processes of bodily functioning; in mental disease of a functional type the disorder is primarily one
of psychological and social behavior. Two distinct levels of functioning

are represented that are different enough to raise considerable doubt as to the validity of any analogy between them. Again, physical disease is the result of specific, experimentally verifiable foreign agents, whether chemical, bacterial, or viral in nature. Such a statement cannot be made regarding functional mental disease, although some hope that eventually it will be possible to do so. Finally, in physical medicine there exists a wide variety of specific and experimentally or empirically verified remedies. Again, this is not the case in the field of mental dysfunction. In other words, while in physical medicine accurate differential etiological diagnosis is possible, leading to the selection of specific remedies, in the field of mental dysfunction no such specific etiological diagnosis is possible, nor are there specific, discrete psychotherapies that have differential effects on outcome.

As a matter of practice, psychiatric diagnosis has little rational connection with the choice of psychotherapy. Methods of therapy depend more on the specific training, experience, and preferences of the therapist than on the diagnosis. Those who feel that psychotherapy should be selective and specific, and thus "rational," chosen on the basis of diagnosis, have been unable to relate specific therapies to specific diagnoses, in terms of indications and contraindications, except possibly on the basis of the condition's severity. Attempts to list indications or contraindications are more often made in terms of symptomatic or basic treatment or the depth of therapy desired or possible, the time available, and so forth. In other words, the distinctions are based on the limits of the therapist and therapeutic situation rather than related to the diagnosis or etiology of the disorder.

Some confusion may arise because there is overlap between psychological and physical systems. With more information available, most notably in the areas of stress management, each system clearly influences the other. Some have assumed that the physical system dominates the psychological system. That view is not accurate in all cases. The stress management literature indicates that psychological responses create physical conditions. Thus, although the idea that physical disease creates psychological dysfunction is verifiable in some cases, the reverse is also true. The physical-to-psychological dysfunction scenario has been the justification for supposing that all psychological dysfunction requires treatment based on physical medicine. With increasing understanding of human psychological functioning, it has become apparent that the two systems are linked interactively, and it is not a case of physical prepotence. The model of treating psychological distress with physical procedures is rather like the problem of a square peg in a round hole. It is the conceptualization of the "whole" that we should revise.

Instead of creating new systems based on erroneous foundations, we must reconceptualize psychological dysfunction on its own terms. A rational therapy must direct attention to the basic element of maladjustment common to all mental disorders. If we found that there is a common basic etiology, then rather than being concerned about developing specific therapies, a rational psychotherapy would be concerned with principles and techniques that are most effective in reaching and remedying the underlying causes of maladjustment.

A few over the years have proposed a unitary theory of mental illness — or *emotional disturbance,* the term used here to distinguish functional from organic conditions. As early as the 1800s the topic was discussed in psychiatry. Zilboorg (1941) quotes Heinrich Neuman (1814–1884) as saying, "We shall never be able to believe that psychiatry will make a step forward until we decide to throw overboard the whole business of classifications. . . . There is but one type of mental disturbance and we call it insanity" (p. 438). Zilboorg further notes, "It would appear justifiable to state that with rare exception the tendency to develop classifications grew in inverse proportion to the psychiatrist's clinical interest in the patient as an individual" (p. 422). About the same time, Anton Messmer said, "There is only one illness, and one cure" (see Cushman 1992, p. 31). Stainbrook (1953, p. 12) cites Boyle as attempting in 1822 to reduce all psychopathology to the manifestation of one pathological process.

Maslow (1954) summarizes his discussion of psychopathogenesis under the heading of "Illness as Unitary" as follows:

What we have implied is that all or most illnesses come from this single source; i.e., psychopathogenesis seems to be unitary rather than multiple. . . . Perhaps what we now speak of as separate disease entities on the medical model are actually superficial and idiosyncratic reactions to a deeper general illness, as Horney claimed. [pp. 166–167]

Beginning in 1948, Patterson (1948, 1949, 1959a, 1974, 1985a) wrote of a unitary theory of emotional disturbance without, however, elaborating it in detail. And in 1958, and again in 1963, Menninger and his associates embraced a unitary theory. Their 1958 article is titled "The Unitary Concept of Mental Illness." In their 1963 book they note that many psychiatrists were coming to the conclusion that there is but one type of mental disturbance.

In 1959, Menninger reported that he began to question the existence of different mental illnesses at the beginning of his career but remarked, "I am somewhat ashamed to admit that it has taken me a quarter of a century to realize that this formula (treating the patient according to his/her diagnosis) rarely works out this way in actual practice" (cited in Hall 1959, p. 671). Menninger and his associates did not drop the use of the word *diagnosis*. They used it to distinguish varying degrees of disturbance, assuming a common underlying cause.

Ford and Urban (1967) note:

Most of the theories which have guided psychotherapy during the last half century have characterized all behavior disorders as resulting from a common nucleus, whether it was an Oedipus complex (Freud), a conflict between strivings for independence (Rank), a striving to overcome inferiority (Adler), or conflicts between learned and organismic evaluations (Rogers) to name only a few. [p. 336]

Thus many prominent practitioners and theorists have concluded that mental disturbance has some common underlying components.

The Nature of Emotional Disturbance

In addition to the single sources of emotional disturbance listed in the previous quotation, other sources have been proposed. Conflicting needs is noted by a number of writers, and the frustration of needs is specified by others. Alexander and French (1946), for example, write of "the failure of the ego in performing its function of securing adequate gratification for subjective needs under existing external conditions" (p. viii).

Threat to the self-concept has also been seen as the source of emotional disturbance. When the self-concept is disturbed, the personality reflects this disturbance. The self-concept *is* central in the personality; thus it is only natural that when the self-concept is disturbed, the personality reflects this disturbance. The self-concept becomes disturbed when the maintenance or enhancement of the self is frustrated or threatened. Frustration of or threat to the satisfaction of the basic need of the individual results in a lowered evaluation of oneself, a loss of self-esteem, a reduced self-regard. In general, some positive rather than negative evaluation of the self is one of the conditions necessary for normal psychological adjustment.

An organism or individual under threat becomes defensive, withdraws, and restricts or narrows its range of activity. "Threat is the individual's awareness of menace to his phenomenal self" (Snygg and Combs 1949, p. 118). "Under threat the impulse of the organism is to protect its organization and its concepts become more strongly defended than ever" (p. 91). "A self under threat has no choice but to defend itself in one form or another" (p. 135). It may attempt to overcome the threat, avoid the threat, or, if neither one of these methods is successful, it may distort or deny the threatening situation. Snygg and Combs (1949) and Hilgard (1949) point out that the common defense mechanisms described by psychoanalysis are means of dealing with threats. "All the mechanisms imply a self-reference, and . . . are not understandable unless we adopt a concept of the self" (Hilgard 1949, p. 375). Mechanisms may also be seen as bolstering self-esteem through self-deception. "The need for self-deception arises because of a more fundamental need to maintain or restore self-esteem" (Hilgard 1949, p. 377). When the individual is in an environment that is perceived as threatening, the individual will behave in ways intended to protect the self. Some of those behaviors may be poor adaptations interpersonally and may ultimately result in further deterioration.

Deprivation and conflict have long been associated with personality disturbance, but deprivation and conflict do not result in disturbance unless the self-concept is involved. Maslow (1954) makes this point clearly:

> [There is a] distinction between a deprivation that is unimportant to the organism (easily substituted for, with few serious after effects) and, on the other hand, a deprivation that is at the same time a threat to the personality, that is, to the life goals of the individual, to his defensive system, to his self-esteem, to his self-actualization, i.e., to his basic needs. . . . Only a *threatening* deprivation has the multitude of effects (usually undesirable) that are commonly attributed to frustration in general. [p. 156]

The frustration or deprivation of biological needs is not necessarily, or even usually, a source of psychological threat or personality disturbance. "Deprivation is not psychopathogenic; threat is" (Maslow 1954, p. 158). Conflict, also, is pathogenic only when it involves a threat to the self, as when a choice involves the giving up of a necessary goal or satisfaction related to the esteem needs. "It is possible to subsume most individual instances of threat under the rubric 'inhibiting or threatening-to-inhibit development toward ultimate self-actualization' as Goldstein has done" (Maslow 1954, p. 166). A threat to or frustration of the satisfaction of the basic need of the individual results in a lowered evaluation of oneself. The outcome is a loss of self-esteem, a loss of self-worth.

Emotional or personality disturbances have, then, a common characteristic—a loss of self-esteem. This is a conclusion that has been reached by a number of psychologists, apparently independently. White (1964) throughout his book stresses the significance of self-esteem for an ordered or normal personality. Another expression of this point of view is that of Stanton (1956). In a discussion of the influence of the therapeutic environment in mental illness, he writes:

> The non-specific therapeutic measures rest upon the assumption that there are common factors in all serious functional illness.

This assumption seems well founded at least from the point of view of modern psychoanalytic formulations. All patients are believed to retain throughout their illness an area of intact functioning which was ignored only a few years ago. At the same time, all patients are thought to suffer from low self-esteem. [p. 38]

A loss in self-esteem is a consequence of frustration of the drive toward actualizing one's potential; anxiety, guilt, and aggression are also results of failures in achieving one's goals, or self-actualization. The discrepancy between what one is and what one is capable of produces the symptoms of anxiety and guilt.

People who have lost self-esteem must focus their energy on defending their failing selves rather than growing. Such persons feel "stalled out" and unable to go forward in life, which increases their feelings of being incapable and worthless. Because they continue to feel threatened, they must maintain the status quo, hold onto what they have to prevent further dissolution of self. Fear is the primary energizing force. The focus of energy is in a defensive process rather than in a growth process.

Focusing on defensive maneuvers diverts attention or focus from growth and from the characteristics of the self-actualizing person. Such defensiveness does not allow people to be open to their environment and the full experiencing of their organism and their senses; thus their relationship with reality is disturbed. Not being able to accept or respect themselves, they are not able to accept or respect others, resulting directly in disturbed interpersonal relationships. They are self-centered, focusing on defense, rather than problem centered, that is, able to devote themselves to a problem or cause outside themselves. They are inordinately dependent, lacking independence or responsibility for self; they are inhibited, lacking in any spontaneity; and they wear a mask or facade rather than being genuine. Their creativity is suppressed by rigid control, so that they are handicapped in utilizing and developing their potentials.

These, and other symptoms, have been recognized as characteristics of emotionally disturbed persons. But they are symptoms—

symptoms of the frustration of the actualizing drive. The kinds and nature of symptoms are wide and varied. Attempts to classify and treat symptoms, or syndromes of symptoms, do not, or are unlikely to, remedy the root cause. The symptoms and clusters vary among individuals as a result of many differences among individuals, re- sulting from their genetic, neurological, and physiological makeup and their differing life experiences. These factors include sex, race, color, culture, age, and so forth, those factors that create experiences unique to each individual. To some extent, then, symptoms may be consid- ered incidental and/or accidental — individually evolved expressions of a single source. Though differently expressed, symptoms all derive from one basic, single origin: the frustration of the drive toward self-actualization.

The Primary Source of Emotional Disturbance

When one reviews the literature on the nature and source of sociopsy- chological disorders, it becomes evident that such conditions develop where there has been, and generally still is, a lack of good interpersonal relationships. *Estrangement from community* is a term that has often been used. But that is an abstraction. The community consists of individuals living in relationship to each other — what sociologists call the *primary group,* consisting of the family and a few others. There is an interde- pendence of needs between the individual and the primary group.

The psychological origins of emotional disturbance derive from the lack of or inadequate interpersonal relationships, particularly in the early period of infancy and childhood. The evidence that emotional disturbance arises from a lack of good human relationships is pervasive and generally acknowledged. Ford and Urban (1963), in their evalu- ation of systems of psychotherapy, state, "All of these theorists seem to agree that the situational conditions necessary for the development of behavior disorder are the ways other people behave toward the growing person" (p. 649).

An individual's self-esteem fails to develop and wanes when

others do not respect that person, when one is not valued or accepted and understood by others, when one does not receive love and its resulting attention and compassion from others. The presence of such relationships is necessary for the development of an adequate self and for the actualization of that self. The absence of good relationships leads to psychosocial or emotional disturbance.

Walsh (1991) documents the lack of love in the lives of the emotionally disturbed. "Many of those involved in the treatment of schizophrenia view love deprivation as the major predisposing environmental variable" (p. 12). He refers to Buss's (1966) contention that persons who do not receive parental love but experience coldness and rejection are predisposed toward passivity, isolation, and suspicion. These characteristics may develop to schizophrenic levels. Walsh provides evidence for the operation of this effect through the brain system. He quotes Restak's statement based on Heath's studies of Harlow's love-deprived monkeys: "The infant who is deprived of movement and physical closeness will fail to develop the brain pathways that mediate pleasure. In essence, such people may be suffering at the neuronal level from stunted growth of their pleasure system" (Walsh 1991, p. 123).

Thus considerable evidence indicates that the absence of loving relationships in infancy and childhood leads to the kinds of feelings, attitudes, and behaviors characteristic of those who are labeled as depressed, neurotic, schizophrenic, suicidal, psychopathic (personality disorder), and criminal or lawless (Walsh 1991, pp. 117–152). Freud is right in saying that psychopathology originates in childhood, but not in the specific traumatic experiences he claims. It appears that the unifying or common element in functional emotional disturbances is the absence of a loving, caring relationship with a committed caregiver during infancy and childhood.

The lack of loving relationships causes disturbance in the development of the self; abuse of the relationship (physical, sexual, emotional) is devastating to the self, literally shattering the self in some cases. Psychotherapy is the providing of a good human relationship for those who have been abused in relationships or have lacked such a relationship. The next chapters will develop this thesis.

Conclusion

The notion that there is a common or single basic etiology for all functional emotional disturbance is not a new idea. It is actually implicit in all the major methods of psychotherapy. Perhaps instead of continuing to act on the assumption that there are different kinds of emotional disorders, with differing sources or origins, we should operate on the assumption that there is no basic essential difference and attempt to discover and understand the common etiology. The theory presented in this chapter is such an attempt.

We are aware that this approach requires a paradigm shift, a basic realignment of beliefs, values, and perspectives in psychology. This will be and has been resisted by anyone who, although sensing the current system is inherently mistaken, prefers the familiar and its stake in being right to the challenge of learning to work in alignment with the true nature of the psychological dysfunction.

Simply stated, all psychosocial disorders develop when there is — or has been — a lack of good interpersonal relationships in the person's life. The assumption that there is a common etiology for all emotional disturbances has implications for a theory and system of psychotherapy. It suggests that if there is a common etiology, then there should be a single, common treatment. The following chapters consider this proposition.

4

The Goal: Self-Actualizing Persons

Introduction

In Chapter 2 we proposed the drive toward self-actualization as the basic psychological motive of the person and gave a general definition of self-actualization. Drives are directed toward goals; goals are the obverse of drives or motives. In this chapter we propose self-actualization—or the self-actualizing person—as the goal of the therapy process, and we describe the nature of the self-actualizing person.

Proposed Goals of Psychotherapy

Historically, the literature on psychotherapy has contained very little regarding its goals. One would think that the goals, objectives, or purpose of such an important process would be of great concern. In 1967, Mahrer wrote, "The literature of psychotherapy has relatively little to offer on the goals of psychotherapy—their identification significance, and organization. On this point, clinicians, researchers, and theoreticians have been seriously inarticulate" (p. 1). In contrast, the goals and objectives of the educational process have been targeted and clarified. It is difficult to understand how so much could be written about the process of psychotherapy with so little consideration of its goals, since ends influence means. In therapy, goals give guidance to the process. When there are no stated goals toward which to work, one wonders how therapists can consistently guide their work.

Within the last twenty years increased attention has been given to goals of psychotherapy. Two influences have perhaps contributed to this greater concern. One has been the greatly increased research on the effectiveness of psychotherapy, with the focus on outcomes of the process. The second has been the influence of behaviorism, with its focus on specifying objectives, even though concern has been with relatively immediate, concrete, easily measured outcomes. The emphasis of the behaviorists on stating and defining the objectives of treatment is an example for those who advocate other methods or approaches, even though there might be disagreement with the highly specific and limited objectives of behavior therapy.

Yet even now, the matter of goals in psychotherapy is neglected in the literature. Theories of psychotherapy include some consideration of goals (Patterson and Watkins 1996). On the other hand, the clinical literature seldom gives much attention to the matter of goals. Individual therapists do, of course, have goals. Their goals are limited and specific (as in the case of behavior therapists and cognitive behavior therapists) or often implicit.

The continued neglect of goals in psychotherapy is evident in two recent publications. A special issue of *Psychotherapy* edited by Norcross (1992), with forty-one contributors, gave no direct attention to goals. The 900-page *History of Psychotherapy*, edited by Freedheim (1992), indexes one reference to goals under "Psychotherapy, common goals in" and the discussion is not related to goals of the psychotherapy process. Mahrer (1967) suggests that a list of goals would be valuable for research purposes as a basis for deriving outcome criteria for psychotherapy. Outcome research, however, is almost entirely limited to criteria represented by existing instruments unrelated to theory.

There appear to be as many goals of psychotherapy as there are writers. The number and variety of goals are almost endless; a complete listing would be unwieldy and confusing. Even a listing of the goals proposed by the chapter authors in Mahrer's book (including Ellis, Dreikurs, Fine, Gendlin, Greenblatt and Levinson, Kelly, Raimy, Rosen, Saul, van Kaam, Whitehorn, and Wolpe, among a total of sixteen) would be a long one. Included are such specific goals as the removal or elimination of symptoms, the reduction or elimination of test anxiety, phobias, fear of speaking in public, frigidity, impotence, enuresis, alcoholism, and so on. Chapter authors speak of unlearning nonadaptive habits and learning adaptive habits; reduction of anxiety; relief from suffering; curing of a mental disease or illness; personality reorganization; effective biological and social functioning; and adjustment to the environment, society, or culture. Still other authors express even broader and more general goals: insight, self-understanding, optimal functioning, maturity, the facilitation of growth, the development of a philosophy of life, and the achievement of meaning in life (see Frankl 1965). Burton (1972), after a survey of the literature, lists forty different aims of psychotherapy, most of them general rather than specific.

At one end of an organized list are highly specific goals, including the reduction or elimination of discrete symptoms and other specific behaviors targeted by the behaviorists. At the other end are highly general goals. Freud includes the enhancement of pleasure and satisfaction in love and work as goals. It would appear to be almost impossible to combine or integrate these and other goals into a generally acceptable goal.

The concept of mental health might seem to be an organizing focus. But concepts of mental health vary, being defined in almost as many ways as the goals of psychotherapy. Jahoda (1958), recognizing the lack of a psychologically meaningful description of mental health, examines five criteria: (1) absence of mental disorder or symptoms, (2) normality of behavior, (3) adjustment to the environment, (4) unity of the personality, and (5) correct perception of the environment (see Chapter 2 for a further consideration of Jahoda's concepts). Jahoda discards the first two, since symptoms are normal or abnormal depending on the cultural context, so that it is difficult to define what

is normal in any absolute sense. Adjustment may be "passive acceptance of social conditions to the detriment of . . . mental health" (p.
23) and thus represent conformity. Psychotherapy has been accused of
being an instrument of social control and for maintaining the status
quo (Halleck 1971). Jahoda (1950) proposes a criterion of active
adjustment, or "active mastery of [the] environment" (p. 217), involving a choice of what one adjusts to and a deliberate modification
of environmental conditions. This mastery does not connote dominance but "aims at creating an environment with which one can feel at
home" (p. 217). Integration, unity of the personality, or self-
consistency, she feels, is useful as a criterion. However, it is not
acceptable alone since it does not imply freedom from conflicts with
the environment. Correct perception of reality, both of the world and
of oneself, while difficult to establish, since the majority judgment is
not necessarily correct, is still useful as a criterion. One is reminded of
the remark of Nathaniel Lee, the English dramatist, on being confined
to the Bedlam insane asylum: "The world and I differed as to my being
mad, and I was outvoted" (De Grazia 1952, p. 146). Thus, Jahoda
proposes a triple criterion, including mastery, integration, and accurate perception of reality, in which Smith (1950) concurs.

Jahoda's proposal or solution to the problem of the nature of
mental health and of the goal of psychotherapy does not seem to have
been adopted or to have influenced the field, though a considerable
period of time has elapsed during which it has received attention. We
have noted that Jahoda's concept of positive mental health does not
appear to be adequate. Two other suggested ideas are psychological
effectiveness and White's (1959) concept of competence. Both Bonner
(1965) and Maslow (1962) point out that competence conceptualizes
behavior in the adjustment framework. One must ask, Competence for
what? Effectiveness for what? These questions indicate the need for a
criterion of competence and effectiveness, so that these cannot themselves be the criterion. An ultimate goal must itself be the criterion.

Thus, we still need an integrating or ordering concept that can
encompass the suggested goals, which are of varied degrees of
specificity as well as nature. A resolution of this problem is offered
here, with a division into immediate goals and long-term goals.

A Levels Concept of Goals

One of the difficulties of specifying or agreeing on the goals of psychotherapy is the fact that the goals stated by different writers vary in specificity or, to use another term, level. If goals could be organized in terms of levels, perhaps we would find, or gain, greater agreement. Parloff (1967) proposes two levels of goals: mediating and ultimate. Mediating goals, according to his classification, are those that are aspects of the psychotherapy process — for example, recovery of repressed memories. He notes that while there may be great differences in mediating goals, "differences in the stated ultimate goals will in all likelihood be small" (Parloff 1967, p. 9). Halleck (1971), discussing the need for study of the optimum human condition, suggests that although psychiatrists may not agree on specific treatment for a given patient, they might agree that some general principles could be used as guidelines for treatment. It is to this problem that the search for, and agreement on, ultimate goals are directed.

The Ultimate Goal

Ultimate goals are broad and general in nature. They are concerned with long-term outcomes and relate to the following questions: What do we want to be? What should people strive to be? What should people be like? What kind of persons do we want and need? These questions have been the concern of philosophers since before Aristotle. It is also recognized that the ultimate goal should transcend culture so that it is inclusive of our expanding world community.

Self-Actualization as the Ultimate Goal. A number of terms or concepts appear to transcend these limitations and to constitute an ultimate goal, including *self-realization, self-enhancement, full functioning,* and *self-actualization.* Perhaps the most commonly used term is the last. We propose that self-actualization is the ultimate goal of psychotherapy.

This is not a new proposal. Many writers have referred to it in one form or another. Hahn and MacLean (1955) write that "most leaders in the field agree that the desired outcome of counseling is self-realization and self-direction on the part of the client" (p. 24). May (1967) believes and quite clearly states that the goal of therapy is to assist clients in actualizing their potentials. Rogers (Whiteley 1987) states that the goal of a growth model of therapy is to remove blocks to growth so that the person can continue in a functional role.

The Self-Actualizing Person.   A number of writers have contributed to the description and definition of the self-actualizing person, sometimes using other designations for such a person. Combs and Snygg (1959) discuss the characteristics of the "adequate" person, the person who has developed an adequate self. Adequate persons perceive themselves in positive ways: they have positive self-concepts; they accept themselves. The adequate person also accepts others:

> We are so entirely dependent upon the goodwill and cooperation of others in our society that it would be impossible to achieve feelings of adequacy without some effective relationship with them. The adequate personality must be capable of living effectively and efficiently with his fellows. [Combs and Snygg 1959, p. 246]

In addition, adequate persons are aware of and able to accept all their perceptions without distortion. From a behavioral point of view, adequate persons are characterized by efficient behavior, since they are not handicapped by defensiveness and are more open to experience. They are spontaneous and creative because, being secure, they can take chances, experiment, and explore. Being secure and accepting themselves, they are capable of functioning independently; they find their own feelings, beliefs, and attitudes adequate guides to behavior. Finally, adequate persons are compassionate. They can relate to others with concern rather than with the hostility and fear of defensiveness.

In discussing the actualizing tendency, Rogers (1969) notes that it leads to or is manifested by growth and motivation, differentiation, independence and autonomy, and self-responsibility. Rogers's concept of the fully functioning person is similar to the adequate-person concept of Combs and Snygg. Rogers (1963b) describes three major characteristics of fully functioning persons. First, they are open to experience, to all external and internal stimuli. They have no need to be defensive. They are keenly aware of themselves and the environment. They experience both positive and negative feelings without repressing the latter. Second, fully functioning persons live existentially. Each moment is new. Life is fluid, not fixed. They are changing, in process, flexible, and adaptive. Third, fully functioning persons find their organism "a trustworthy means of arriving at the most satisfying behavior in each existential situation" (Rogers 1963b, p. 20; see also Rogers 1961, Chapter 9). Their behavior is determined from within; the locus of control is internal. Since they are open to all experience, they have available the relevant data on which to base behavior. Behavior is not always perfect, since some relevant data may be missing. But the resulting unsatisfying behavior is corrected on the basis of feedback. Such a person is a creative and self-actualizing person.

Kelley (1962) describes the fully functioning person in similar terms. Such persons think well of themselves and feel able or competent while being aware of limitations. They also think well of others, recognizing their importance as opportunities for self-development. Fully functioning persons develop and live by human values rather than by external demands. They are creative. A characteristic not mentioned by Rogers or Combs and Snygg is the ability of the fully functioning person to recognize the value of all experience, including mistakes, as a source of learning and to profit from them.

These descriptions of the self-actualizing person have been developed through observation, experience, and, in Rogers's case, research in education and psychotherapy. Maslow (1943) defines self-actualization as a desire to fulfill one's potential, "to become more and more of what one is" (p. 382). He formulates a general definition of self-actualizing people as being characterized by "the full use and exploitation of talents, capacities, potentialities, etc. Such people seem to be fulfilling themselves and to be doing the best that they are capable of doing. They are people who have developed or are developing the full stature of which they are capable" (pp. 161–162).

Selecting a group of people, living and dead, who seem to be self-actualizing, he attempts to find what they have in common and what differentiates them from ordinary people. Fourteen characteristics emerge:

1. More efficient perception of reality and more comfortable relations with it
2. Acceptance of self, others, and nature
3. Spontaneity; lack of rigid conformity
4. Problem-centeredness: sense of duty, responsibility
5. Detachment; need for privacy
6. Autonomy, independence of culture and environment
7. Continued freshness of appreciation
8. Mystic experiences; oceanic feelings
9. Gemeinshaftsgefühl; empathy, sympathy, compassion for all human beings
10. Deep interpersonal relations with others
11. Democratic character structure; respect for others
12. Discernment of means and ends
13. Philosophical, unhostile sense of humor
14. Creativeness (For more detail, see Maslow 1956 and Patterson 1985.)

The self that is to be actualized is in fact the concept of the self developed by the individual through transactions with the physical and, especially, the social environment. The self-concept is the organization of the perceptions of the self, and it is the self-concept, rather than any "real" self, that is of significance in personality and behavior. As Combs and Snygg (1959) note, the existence of a real "Self" is a philosophical question, since it cannot be observed directly. The self-concept becomes the significant determinant of response to the environment. It governs the perceptions or meanings attributed to the environment.

Criticism of Self-Actualization as a Goal of Psychotherapy.
Criticism of self-actualization as a goal of psychotherapy centers around three points: generality, positive assumptions of the nature of

human beings, and reliance on the concept of self. The first two are interrelated.

The first criticism is that a goal so unspecified and general as self-actualization does not give direction to the therapist. This ultimate goal is global, since it is intended to be relevant to psychotherapy in general. Even though it is global in its definition, it is not without direction. Its underlying assumption is a positive, forward-moving nature of humankind; that is, people are motivated to grow and develop their full potential if provided with an environment that allows that natural course to unfold.

Rogers (Whiteley 1987) points out that human nature is like the other organisms in our environment. No one asks if a plant will grow to be a good plant or a bad plant. We know that given the proper environment, a plant will grow to its potential. It is only about human beings that we seem to want to ask the good or bad nature question.

A reliance on self-actualization assumes a forward-moving nature of humankind given the proper environment in which to grow. That is the environment given by the therapist. A human being is not an unruly beast to be controlled by the therapist lest it run amok due to its own evil nature. A human being is to be provided an environment in which the person can continue to grow and to develop her or his potential.

The direction given to the therapist is that this forward-moving energy can be relied on to motivate clients toward solutions to life problems. This means that the therapist is a facilitator and not a controller. The client is the primary healer, relying on his or her own motivation toward growth. The therapist facilitates growth by creating an environment optimal for personal growth.

Admittedly, there can be exceptions to the basic nature assumption. Some individuals may have aberrant conditions such as brain malfunction or a chemical imbalance that interrupt the normal functioning of their potential. Some human beings have been so abused that they seem to have lost any positive potential, yet in these cases one can argue that the potential for growth still exists, and it may be more a matter of our ability to offer conditions that are more powerful than the force of abuse.

The third criticism is that self-actualization is a term that focuses on the individual, and thus it may be limited in its transcultural application. This point is basically a culture-centric perspective, since "self" as an individual entity is only one definition. All cultures recognize the existence of a self, though its relational definition and focus of energy may vary. The outcome of self-actualization is inevitably influenced by cultural factors. Self-actualization will vary in differing cultural contexts. This point is developed fully in Chapter 8 on cultural issues in therapy.

Characteristics of Self-Actualization as the Ultimate Goal.

Self-actualization as the goal of psychotherapy has a number of significant characteristics.

First, it constitutes a criterion in the sense that it is not vulnerable to the question, For what? Self-actualization is a given, inherent in the biology of living organisms.

Second, self-actualization as a goal avoids the problems of the medical model and its illness–health dilemma. The goal is more than the elimination of pathology and the achievement of some undefined (and undefinable) level of "normality." It is not a negative concept, such as the absence of disturbance, disorder, or "mental illness." It is a positive goal.

Third, it avoids the problems of an adjustment model, with its question of adjustment to what, and the accompanying questions of conformity and (political) control (see Halleck 1971).

Fourth, self-actualization as a goal eliminates the conflict or dichotomy between intrapersonal and interpersonal goals. It encompasses both aspects of the person.

Fifth, self-actualization as a goal encompasses all persons. Self-actualizing persons share characteristics and behaviors. Yet it allows for individual differences—each person has somewhat different potentialities that can be actualized.

Sixth, the goal is a process, not a static condition to be achieved once and for all. It is not an end, which once achieved is no longer a goal, but a continuing process of becoming. A goal should be an ideal that is continuously striven for though never completely reached. The goal is thus better stated as being the ongoing development of self-actualizing persons.

Seventh, self-actualization as a goal is not derived from religion, philosophy, ethics, or even psychology. It is biologically and organismically based, built into the organism. It is a given.

Eighth, self-actualization is not the isolated goal of psychotherapy, limited to the treatment of disturbed or abnormal individuals. As noted earlier, it goes beyond the absence of disturbance or abnormality. It is the goal for all persons, the "normal" as well as the abnormal, all of whom, though not suffering from psychopathology, are dissatisfied, unhappy, unfulfilled, and not fully utilizing one's potentialities, not being the person one is capable of being. Thus, self-actualization is the goal of life, and, as such, it should be the goal of society and of all its institutions — religion, education, marriage and the family, political and economic-occupational systems. Psychotherapy is of a piece with the rest of life, not something apart from it. Its purpose is to contribute, with other social institutions, to the personal development and fulfillment of individuals (see Chapter 8 for a discussion of individuation and community). In fact, psychotherapy has come into existence as a means by which society provides special assistance to those whose progress toward self-actualization has been blocked, interrupted, or impeded in a particular way, specifically by the lack of good human relationships.

Ninth, another aspect of self-actualization is particularly significant. Goals are related to drives or motives — in fact, they are the other side of motivation. Thus, when we talk about the goal of life, we become involved in purpose, needs, drives, or motives, since goals are influenced by — indeed, determined by — needs. The ultimate goal of psychotherapy, and of life itself, should directly relate to the basic needs of human beings.

Finally, if the single basic motivation of all persons is the drive toward self-actualization, then it logically follows that the goal of psychotherapy is to facilitate progress toward self-actualization in those persons in whom it is frustrated by psychological factors or an adverse psychological environment.

Mediate Goals

Mediate goals are the usual goals considered by psychotherapists. They include the specific and concrete goals of behavior therapists. Contributors to Mahrer's (1967) book focus on this level of goals, such things as reduction of symptoms; reduction of anxiety, psychological pain and suffering, and hostility; elimination of unadaptive habits; acquisition of adaptive habits.

Other mediate goals include good marital and family relationships; vocational and career success and satisfaction; educational achievement, including study skills and good study habits; development of potentials in art, music, athletics, and so forth.

The ultimate goal is a common goal, applicable to all individuals. Mediate goals provide or allow for individual differences. People have differing and multiple potentials; they actualize themselves in varying ways.

A number of implications of the separation of goals into ultimate and mediate become apparent. First, while the ultimate goal is universal, applying across time and cultures, mediate goals vary with individuals, time, and cultures. It is here that client choices and decisions operate in a most practical sense.

Second, mediate goals may be considered as mediating goals, between the immediate goal and the ultimate goal. That is, they are steps toward the ultimate goal. In some instances they may overlap with aspects of the ultimate goal—the development of self-understanding, self-esteem, or self-acceptance, for example.

Third, the ultimate goal provides a criterion for the acceptability of mediate goals, something that is either lacking or implicit in behavior therapy.

Fourth, while mediate goals may be considered as subgoals or steps toward the ultimate goal, they may also be seen as by-products of the ultimate goal. Self-actualizing persons normally and naturally seek to achieve the mediate goals on their own, or they seek and obtain the necessary assistance, such as tutoring, instruction, information, education and training, or reeducation, to achieve them. As by-products, they are not necessarily goals to be directly achieved or specifically sought. Thus, in psychotherapy, they need not be determined or defined in advance but are developed by the client during, or even following, the therapy process. It appears that it may be sufficient, in some cases, to provide the conditions leading to the development of self-actualizing persons; thus, as individuals become more self-actualizing, they develop an increasingly realistic awareness that helps them identify, pursue, and achieve their own specific goals.

Finally, it is apparent that many of the mediate goals are the objectives of other elements of the helping process, of education, reeducation, and skill training.

The Immediate Goal

The immediate goal of psychotherapy is to initiate and continue the process that will enable the client to progress to the ultimate goal. This process will be considered in the next three chapters.

Goals as Values

Goals are values, and, conversely, values are goals. Therapists who value educational achievement, economic or occupational success, or social success will see these as desirable goals for their clients, while therapists who value independence and responsibility will see these as goals for their clients. Whether the client or the therapist should determine goals has been a troublesome question, with the behaviorists insisting that clients should determine their own goals. Yet, therapists have *their* own goals. Many feel, however, that therapists should not impose their own goals on the client.

Should therapists abandon their own goals and accept those of the client? The model presented here provides a solution to this dilemma. The problem of the therapist imposing goals on the client arises when therapists have a variety of relatively specific goals, which may not be relevant to all clients. The acceptance of a single, broad, ultimate goal applicable to all clients would change this situation. The reluctance of therapists to adopt such a goal is based on the difficulties of defining a goal that appears to be applicable or best for all clients. Halleck (1971) points out that "philosophers, theologians, political scientists, and psychologists have struggled with this problem for centuries, searching for value systems founded upon religious beliefs, social utility, ethical relativism, or human biology" (p. 196). Self-actualization is a goal that more and more psychologists and psycho-therapists appear to be adopting. This acceptance comes, in part, because of the increasing awareness of diversity issues, including cultural encapsulation (see Wrenn 1962, 1985).

Self-actualization is seen not only as a goal but as the basic, dominant motive of life. Its acceptance as a goal in therapy prevents the therapist from imposing an external, arbitrary goal on the client. Thus, therapists are recognizing and accepting a goal that is *inherent* in all clients. The ultimate goal is not determined explicitly by either the therapist or the client but by the motive of life itself.

Within the context of the ultimate goal, the client has the freedom to determine subgoals. Therapists who disclaim any ultimate goal or who are unaware of their implicit (and more specific) goals may impose their own goals on the client without being aware of it. This may be encouraged by the fact that many clients, when they enter therapy, have no clear or explicit goals. On the other hand, therapists sometimes disagree with or refuse to accept the stated goals of the client. The behaviorists often appear to direct or force the client into defining a problem or goal that their techniques can deal with, ignoring or rejecting other problems or goals as being too vague, general, or not susceptible to operational definition.

The specific goals of therapy are thus selected by the client, in terms of their contribution toward his or her becoming a more self-actualizing person, or, from another point of view, they are by-products of increasing self-actualization. As a more fully self-actualizing person, the client is then more capable of achieving these specific goals. If clients require assistance from others—information, education, or training—they may seek and obtain it, or they may be referred by the therapist to sources of such specific help.

Self-actualization is the goal not only of psychotherapy, but since it is the basic motivation of the human being, it is, or should be, the goal of society and all its institutions—the family, the school, the church, as noted earlier. It is the goal of all helping relationships. Psychotherapy is only one way of facilitating self-actualization. It is appropriate for those individuals whose self-actualization is prevented or inhibited by the lack or inadequacy of good human relationships.

5

The Therapist I: Necessary Conditions

Introduction

"If the cause of all disorder is basically the same, it follows that one psychotherapeutic approach will suffice for all" (Ford and Urban 1967, p. 336). Ford and Urban do *not* accept the premise of this statement. This is, however, the implicit premise of most of the major approaches to psychotherapy (behavior therapy being the major exception) and the premise on which most practicing therapists operate.

If the origin of psychologically based emotional disturbances is the lack or inadequacy of good interpersonal relationships in the past (and often the current) lives of clients, then the provision of a good interpersonal relationship is the specific treatment for such clients. The lack of good interpersonal relationships constitutes a major impediment to the process of self-actualization. Psychotherapy, then, by providing a good interpersonal relationship, is the specific treatment for the frustration of the drive toward self-actualization.

The Therapy Relationship

Concern with the nature of the therapeutic relationship has been evident in every theory and approach to psychotherapy, including behavior therapy. Nearly everyone accepts the assumption that the relationship between the therapist and the client (or the therapeutic alliance) is the major factor in psychotherapy. And as noted in Chapter 1, the common elements in a good therapeutic relationship have been sought. Here we are concerned with the therapist conditions. The client conditions will be considered in Chapter 7.

After reviewing the major theoretical approaches to psycho-therapy in a chapter titled "Central Therapeutic Ingredients: Theoret-ical Convergence," Truax and Carkhuff (1967) found three sets of characteristics: (1) "the therapist's ability to be integrated, mature, genuine, or congruent"; (2) "the therapist's ability to provide a non-threatening, trusting, safe or secure atmosphere by his accep-tance, nonpossessive warmth, unconditional positive regard, or love"; and (3) "the therapist's ability to be accurately empathic, be with the client, be understanding, or grasp the patient's meaning" (p. 25). Accurate empathy, respect, or nonpossessive warmth and genuineness are "aspects of the therapist's behavior that cut across virtually all theories of psychotherapy and appear to be common elements in a wide variety of approaches to psychotherapy and counseling" (p. 25). Truax and Carkhuff note that these are the therapist conditions for client therapeutic personality change posited by Rogers (1957a).

These conditions are stated clearly by Rogers (1957a) in his classic article "The Necessary and Sufficient Conditions for Thera-peutic Personality Change":

> For constructive personality change to occur, it is necessary that these conditions exist and continue over a period of time: . . .
>
> • The second person, whom we shall term the therapist, is congruent and integrated in the relationship.
>
> • The therapist experiences unconditional positive regard for the client.
>
> • The therapist experiences an empathic understanding of the client's internal frame of reference and endeavors to commu-nicate this experience to the client. [p. 96]

These therapist conditions have usually been considered as characterizing client-centered therapy. But Rogers (1957a) clearly states that they are not restricted to client-centered therapy:

> It is *not* stated that these . . . conditions are essential for client-centered therapy, and that other conditions are essential for other types of psychotherapy. . . . [M]y aim in stating this theory is to state the conditions which apply to *any* situation in which constructive personality change occurs, whether we are thinking of classical psychoanalysis, or any of its modern offshoots, or Adlerian psychotherapy, or any other. [p. 101]

A universal system of psychotherapy, then, consists of those elements or conditions that are shared by all the different systems of psychotherapy.

Empathic Understanding

In English, the word *understanding* has come to mean knowledge *of* or comprehension *about* something. One of the goals of science is understanding — understanding of objects and the results of their manipulation. It is an understanding that derives from an external frame of reference. This is not the kind of understanding we refer to when we use the word in psychotherapy. Here we are concerned not with knowing *about* clients but knowing how they feel and think and perceive things — themselves and the world about them. It is an understanding from an internal frame of reference rather than from the external, so-called objective, frame of reference. Some languages, such as French and German, have two verbs for *to know*, one meaning to know from the external frame of reference and the other simply to know, subjectively. Because English does not make this distinction, we need a modifier for the word *understanding; empathic* is used for this purpose.

Empathic understanding has long been recognized as an important element in psychotherapy. In this section we discuss its nature, how it can be measured, and what it looks like in action.

The Nature of Empathy

Empathy should not be confused with sympathy. It does not involve identification with the client. This is clear in Rogers's (1961) definition: "[Empathy is] an accurate . . . understanding of the client's world as seen from the inside. To sense the client's private world as if it were your own, but without losing the 'as if' quality—this is empathy" (p. 284). It is an understanding from within the perspective of another person. In contrast to most other methods of psychotherapy, which "seek to indoctrinate the listener into their own assumptive worlds" (Frank and Frank 1991, p. 70), the therapist enters the assumptive world of the client and accompanies the client in the exploration—and change—of that world.

A phrase in the language of the Native Americans expresses it: "to walk in his moccasins." Great novelists are experts in empathic understanding, leading their readers to empathize with their characters. The theme of one novel, *To Kill a Mockingbird* (Lee 1960), is dependent on the concept of empathy. At one point in the story Atticus Finch, the lawyer, trying to help his two young children understand people's behavior toward him, says, "If . . . you can learn a simple trick . . . you'll get along a lot better with all kinds of folks. You never really understand a person until you consider things from his point of view—until you climb into his skin and walk around in it" (p. 34).

Empathy, of course, is not a trick, nor is it simple. Our society tends to be externally oriented, or we become preoccupied with our own frame of reference. We do not normally or easily see things from another person's point of view. The external frame of reference is encouraged by an educational system that values the scientific method and trains students to work from the external, "objective" mind-set. On the other hand, most of us can relatively easily assume another's point of view. Trainees in counseling or psychotherapy generally have the capacity to understand the nature of empathy and can put themselves in the place of another person—at least momentarily.

The challenge is to persist in this frame of reference, since it is not our usual behavior in everyday human relationships. Although many students can achieve some level of empathic contact with clients, they are generally unable to maintain it without training. They "pop out" of the client's internal frame of reference due to a failure of concentration or a major distraction from their own frame of reference, which is external to the client's. Maintaining consistent contact with the client's internal frame of reference requires discipline.

The discipline of empathic listening is challenging to therapists in two ways. First, maintaining another's (the client's) frame of reference is not our habitual focus of attention. Therapists most easily remain in their own frame of reference. The problem is that, when a therapist is listening from her or his perspective to a client who is speaking from a unique internal perspective, the therapist may perceive a message different from the one the client has sent. Even highly competent professionals occasionally are unable to maintain empathic contact, which results in misunderstanding. This is clearly the point made in the case of Helen R. (Strupp 1990). When the female client voices her anger at men for her feeling of oppression, the therapist shifts to his own frame of reference and responds as a male. He responds defensively to the client's feeling about men rather than to her more central fear of oppression. By shifting out to his own frame of reference, he became defensive and misunderstood his client's point. The challenge here is to maintain empathy, especially when pulled to defend one's own issues.

The second challenge is the risk of the therapist by fully understanding the client in being confronted by dissonance in his or her own worldview. When the therapist's worldview conflicts with the client's, sometimes it is clearly the therapist's worldview that becomes untenable. Such a confrontation can motivate the therapist to alter her or his perceptions. The therapist may, by entering the understanding of the client's perceptions, find it impossible to hold previously unrecognized prejudicial perceptions. In a comment on the published case of Helen R., Snyder (1992) points out:

In order to respond with full empathy, a therapist needs to take a risk. This is particularly critical when the therapist is a member of a "dominant" group and the client of a "subordinate" one

(Miller 1976). It may feel awkward under these circumstances because we often don't understand and even resist understanding the lifeworlds of people who are in a group subordinate to our own. It is easier to take a risk of analysis or interpretation than to take a risk of empathically resonating with what has been heard. [p. 319]

To "empathically resonate," a therapist risks personal understanding of the client's perceptions, sometimes coming face to face with experience that challenges his or her own worldview.

Students are sometimes bothered by the apparent subjectivity of empathic understanding. They are trained to seek or obtain "objective facts." But the so-called facts are nothing more than the subjective perceptions and impressions of other observers, usually with added evaluative or judgmental aspects.

Gathering the facts has been stressed in training because of the medical model emphasis on diagnosis and the scientific research emphasis on objectivity. A wise student is encouraged to ask, "For what am I gathering facts?" (The use of diagnosis is discussed in Chapter 3.) In most systems of psychotherapy, diagnosis is not a direct guide to psychotherapy treatment. If the therapist does not require diagnosis as a specific guide for treatment, as is concluded in Chapter 3, then for what reason must a therapist gather "facts"? Researchers are suspicious of subjective experiences because they are difficult to quantify and verify. Objectification may be appropriate when dealing with the data of many cases but inappropriate for a therapist when dealing with a real person or a small group of persons in therapy. The therapeutic process usually involves expression of emotion — a subjective experience. The outcome of experienced emotion can be objectified, but there is no naturally occurring object called "emotion." It occurs and is experienced subjectively.

If one is seeking "facts" to understand the client, then the relevant facts are the client's feelings, ideas, beliefs, and perceptions. Those facts are gathered through empathic listening to what the client offers. The therapist will not find those facts existing in their fullest potential from any source external to the client. Those facts exist meaningfully, immediately, and most distinctly in the client.

Perhaps one of the resistances to this concept of the client knowing the relevant facts is that the therapist has to acknowledge "not knowing" something. Casement (1991) offers this explanation:

It is all too easy to equate not-knowing with ignorance. This can lead therapists to seek refuge in an illusion that they understand. But if they can bear the strain of not-knowing, they can learn that their competence as therapists includes a capacity to tolerate feeling ignorant or incompetent, and a willingness to wait (and to carry on waiting). [p. 9]

Letting oneself be guided by the client creates an opportunity for the client to form a basic trust in the therapist (Casement 1991). Clients are aware on some level that they are the ones who know most deeply their own experiences. A therapist who assumes or accepts the stance of omniscience will inevitably make an error known to the client. Such errors in the context of omniscience will create a loss of trust and potentially motivate resistance. A therapist who is able to admit not-knowing and who communicates to the client that an attempt is being made to understand creates an atmosphere of learning. The client comes to trust the therapist through realizing that the therapist is willing to learn from her or him. It is of note that the client also learns to trust her- or himself in that context as well, as is revealed in this client statement.

Client: You seemed confident that I could lead the way. That gave me confidence that I could take charge of my illness.

The following question is sometimes raised regarding discrepancies between the client's perceptions and those of others: Should the therapist check the client's perceptions against those of her or his associates, family, or teachers? If the client's perceptions are greatly out of line with others', this will usually be apparent; often it will be brought to the therapist's attention by those in the client's environment. An exception is in the case of addiction in which chemical dependency, as a biophysical process, masks the discrepancy between the addict's perception of the situation and reality. Therapy should not begin until after the client has entered treatment for the chemical dependency. In cases in which the discrepancies are less evident, the therapist will usually become aware of them as therapy continues. The client will speak of them through issues of confusion or conflict.

The central question is what therapists should or can do about such discrepancies. Usually they should do nothing about them immediately, since there is nothing effective they can do until a relationship is established. When this is achieved, the client likely will recognize and become aware of them, and then in therapy can deal with them. Or, if they are apparent, and the client does not seem to be progressing toward awareness of them, the counselor may respond to them through confrontation.

Empathy involves at least three aspects. First, assuming that the client is willing to allow the therapist to enter her or his private world and attempts to communicate perceptions and feelings, the therapist must be *receptive* to the communication of the client. Second, the therapist must *understand* the communication of the client. To do this the therapist must be able to put her- or himself in the client's place, to take the client's role. Third, the therapist must be able to *communicate* her or his understanding to the client.

Since we cannot actually *be* another person, we are inevitably outside, in an "as if" situation. This separateness is necessary. It is a protection against too close an identification and against empathy becoming sympathy. The client's feelings are *not* those of the therapist. The therapist only enters the perceptual world of the client as a way of helping the client clarify and understand experience. Attempting to become totally one with the client would emotionally exhaust the therapist who works with many clients.

Differences between therapists and their clients are barriers to empathy. (This issue is discussed in Chapter 8.) We can empathize to some extent at least, and sometimes to a great extent, with any other person on the basis of our commonalities as human beings. As Sullivan (1947) puts it, "We are all much more simply human than otherwise" (p. 7).

Fortunately, therapists do not need to understand or empathize completely with clients to be able to help them through therapy. This point is especially true in client-centered therapy because the therapist does not take responsibility for leading or curing the client. In the role of facilitator, the therapist is trying to understand and clarify the client's perceptions of the problems. If this understanding occurs with at least some success in the beginning of therapy, the relationship has a chance of continuing and of being successful. Indeed, clients who perceive that the therapist is trying to understand them will show remarkable persistence at making themselves clearly understood.

Measuring Empathic Understanding

Truax developed a Tentative Scale for the Measurement of Accurate Empathy (Truax and Carkhuff 1967), a nine-point scale with definitions of each point and examples. Carkhuff (1969) revised the scale and converted it into a five-level system for measuring empathic understanding in interpersonal processes (see Patterson 1985a). Carkhuff and Berenson (1967) describe the movement from low to high empathy:

> The emphasis, then, is upon movement to levels of feeling and experience deeper than those communicated by the client, yet within the range of expression which the client can constructively employ for his own purposes. The therapist's ability to communicate at high levels of empathic understanding appears to involve the therapist's ability to allow himself to experience or merge in the experience of the client, reflect upon this experience while suspending his own judgments, tolerating his own anxiety, and communicating this understanding to the client. [p. 27]

At low levels of empathy therapists are less sensitive to the client's expressions and are responding to or with their own feelings and perceptions. They are not in the client's frame of reference but may be evaluating and judging the client and his or her behavior, reacting with suggestions, advice, moralizations, and so on. Their responses are irrelevant to the feelings and perceptions of the client.

Examples of Empathy

Client: Sometimes I get so depressed I don't know where I'm going.

Counselor: Well, you know, it's around exam time and lots of kids get to feeling a little down at this time of year.

Client: Yes, but this has nothing to do with exams. That's not even bothering me.

Counselor: You mean none of the exams is bothering you? Surely one of them must be bothering you! [Carkhuff and Berenson 1967, p. 32]

In the first response, the therapist is so focused on his or her own assumption that he or she rushes ahead of the client. The therapist, perhaps being uncomfortable with the feeling expressed by the client, is making excuses rather than responding to what the client said. In the second response, after the client directly states that exams are not the problem, the therapist reasserts his or her focus and denies again the client's knowledge of the source of the problem.

At a minimally facilitative level, the therapist is with the client and the client feels this.

Client: Sometimes I get so depressed I just don't know what to do.

Counselor: Sometimes you feel like you're never going to get up again.

Client: Right, I just don't know what to do with myself. What am I going to do? [Carkhuff and Berenson 1967, p. 31]

At a highly facilitative level, therapists go beyond the words or even expressed feelings of the client to the implications of her or his statements. The therapist is still responding to the client and not intruding feelings or perceptions. The client's feelings may be blurred and confused so that she or he does not recognize all their meanings or implications, which may be clarified by the therapist.

Client: Gee, those people! Who do they think they are? I just can't stand interacting with them any more. Just a bunch of phonies.

They leave me so frustrated. They make me so anxious. I get angry at myself. I don't even want to be bothered with them anymore. I just wish I could be honest with them and tell them all to go to hell! But I just can't do it.

Therapist: Damn, they make you furious! But it's not just them. It's with yourself too, because you don't act on how you feel. [Carkhuff 1969, vol. I, pp. 117–118]

It is impossible for a therapist to maintain the highest level of empathy continuously. And it is unnecessary. In fact, it is probably undesirable. At the beginning of therapy an extremely high level of empathy can be threatening and inhibit the communications of clients. Clients may well feel that the counselor understands them better than they do themselves, which can serve to shift the locus of responsibility away from the client. Carkhuff (1969) suggests that in the early stage the therapist is most effective if she or he focuses on a minimal level of facilitative conditions. Since empathic responses must become more accurate as the therapist listens to and gains an understanding of the client, it is reasonable to predict that even with experienced therapists, initial responses are less empathic than later responses.

Carkhuff makes an important distinction between the ability to discriminate an accurate empathic response and the ability to communicate empathically. If one is presented with a number of responses at various levels of empathy, one is able relatively easily, or with relatively little training, to recognize or identify the better or best responses. It is much more difficult to construct or compose a good response. Discrimination is a necessary but not sufficient condition for communicating empathy. Individuals who are able to make accurate discriminations are not necessarily able to communicate accurately. Those who can communicate accurately can also discriminate accurately, however.

Respect

Rogers (1957a) includes unconditional positive regard as one of the therapist conditions for constructive personality change. He credits

Standal (1954) with originating this term. Positive regard is unconditional when it does not depend on the client's behavior. The attitude of
respect creates a specific environment within the relationship. "It is an
atmosphere which simply demonstrates 'I care'; not 'I care for you *if*
you behave thus and so' " (Rogers 1961, p. 283). Rogers uses other
terms to describe this condition, including acceptance of the client as
a person, with negative as well as positive aspects. Here we call it
respect. In this section we look at the nature of respect as well as how it
is measured and manifested.

   Caring about, prizing, valuing, and *liking* are other terms for the
respect condition. It is a nonpossessive caring. The client is regarded
as a person of worth just as he or she is, simply for being. There are
no conditions for acceptance. Clients need not change or be different
in order to be accepted. "It involves an acceptance of and a caring for
the client as a 'separate' person" (Rogers 1961, p. 283), allowing the
person to have her or his own feelings and experiences and having the
ability to give those feelings and experiences their own meanings
according to the client's understanding.

   This does not mean that the therapist accepts as right, desirable,
or likable all aspects of the client's behavior or that he or she agrees
with or condones all of the client's behavior. Therapists maintain their
own values and ethics. Judgments are simply not applied to the
original being of the client. At all times in the relationship the therapist
exists in an attitude of acceptance of the being of the client.

   One outcome of an attitude of respect is that the respected
individual learns that, ultimately, responsibility for evaluating self lies
within the self. Healthy existence requires that, although others may
be sought for advice or input, the person must judge for her- or
himself. Otherwise, the person will have to rely on others for all value
judgments. The values of the self vary with different cultures, and the
individual must determine within her- or himself how her or his values
direct choices. There are as many external opinions as there are blades
of grass. To rely exclusively on external sources for ultimate decisions
in one's life is a confusing and anchorless experience. Rogers (1957a)
states that the locus of control for judgment should remain with the
client and that judgment on the part of the therapist shifts that
responsibility.

Respect is expressed in the therapist's listening to the client and in the effort to understand the client, as well as in her or his communication of that understanding. Respect increases with understanding. The basic respect for the client as a human being increases perceptibly with understanding of her or his perceived meaning in life and uniqueness of self.

The therapist initiates a valuing process that begins with the therapist's manifested respect for the client and ends in the client respecting and valuing self. The client perceives that someone is listening and valuing and begins to listen to and value him- or herself. This is not a selfishness. This is a core feeling of being worthy of existence, a survival need. Without this core feeling of worth, beings become hopeless and may attempt to destroy their physical existence.

Nonpossessive warmth is another term that has been applied to the respect condition. There is a real interest in the client, a sincere concern for her or him, a trust, a love. It "does not imply passivity or unresponsivity; nonpossessive warmth is an outgoing positive action involving active, personal participation" (Truax and Mitchell 1971, p. 317). Although initially respect is expressed by communicating with some warmth of tone, respect can be communicated in many different ways. These include inviting the client to initiate ideas, following the lead of the client, accurately reflecting the statements being made by the client, being open and honest, and communicating the attitude that the client knows what he or she is experiencing and is capable of accurately expressing that experience.

> We must emphasize that it is not always communicated in warm, modulated tones of voice; it may be communicated, for example, in anger. In the final analysis, it is the client's experiences of the expression that counts, and the client may experience the therapist's attempt to share his own experience fully as an indication of the therapist's respect for the client's level of development. [Carkhuff and Berenson 1967, p. 28]

Carkhuff and Berenson believe that "unconditional positive regard" is a misnomer. They consider the attitude an initial suspension of negative judgments. However, the focus of the unconditional acceptance is on the being of the client, not on behaviors. The client is accepted, without conditions, as a worthy and valuable human being. This is unconditional positive regard.

Measuring Respect

Truax (Truax and Carkhuff 1967) developed a five-point Tentative Scale for the Measurement of Nonpossessive Warmth, which was revised in 1969 (Carkhuff 1969; see also Patterson 1985a). The variable of unconditionality is defined as an acceptance of the experience of the client without imposing conditions. Warmth involves a nonpossessive caring for the client as a separate person and, thus, a willingness to share equally his or her joys and aspirations as well as depressions and failures. It involves valuing the client as a person, separate from any evaluation of her or his behavior or thoughts (Truax and Carkhuff 1967).

Examples of Respect

In the first example, it is obvious that the therapist shows complete lack of respect or warmth for the client and is evaluative:

Client: I just can't wait to get out of school—I'm so excited. I just want to get out and get started on my career. I know I'm going places.
Counselor: What's the matter with you, don't you like school? [Carkhuff and Berenson 1967, p. 34]

The next example also involves disapproval of the client's behavior as well as evaluation and lack of warmth:

Therapist: . . . another part here too, that is, if they haven't got a lot of schooling, there may be a good argument, that, that they—are better judges, you know.
Client: Yeah . . .
Therapist: And you're in a *position* that you can't argue with them. Why is it that these people burn you up so much?

Client: They *get by with* too many things. . . .

Therapist: Why should that bother you?

Client: 'Cause I never got by with anything.

Therapist: They're papa figures, aren't they? [Truax and Carkhuff 1967, p. 61]

Another example:

Client: I want to meet people but I am afraid to join clubs and stuff because I might get in with kinds I don't really fit in with. I don't know any of the kids here.

Therapist: You shouldn't be so scared. They won't bite, you know. Just jump right in and be friendly. Everyone feels that way. You're going to be just fine.

Now contrast these with the following dialogue, in which the words can only give an indication of the warmth present:

Client: . . . ever recovering to the extent where I could become self-supporting and live alone. I thought that I was doomed to hospitalization for the rest of my life and seeing some of the people over in the main building, some of those old people who are, who need a lot of attention and all that sort of thing, is the only picture I could see of my own future. Just one of (*Therapist*: Mhm) complete hopelessness, that there was any . . .

Therapist: (Interrupting) You didn't see any hope at all, did you?

Client: Not in the least. I thought no one really cared and I didn't see any way that I could end it all completely and not become a burden or an extra care, I would have committed suicide, I was that low. I didn't want to live. In fact, I hoped that I—I would go to sleep at night and not wake up, because I, I really felt there was nothing to live for. (*Therapist*: [very softly] Uh huh.) Now I, I truly believe that this drug they are giving me helps me a lot, I think it is one drug that really does me good. (*Therapist*: Uh huh.)

Therapist: But you say that, that during that time you, you felt as though no one cared, as to what (*Client*: That's right) what happened to you.

Client: And, not only that, but I hated *myself* so that I didn't *deserve* to have anyone care for me. I hated myself so that I, I, I not only felt that no one did, but I didn't see any reason why they *should*.

Therapist: I guess that makes some sense to me now. I was wondering why it was that you were shutting other people off. You weren't *letting* anyone else care.

Client: I didn't think I was *worth* caring for.

Therapist: So you didn't ev — maybe you not only thought you were — hopeless, but you wouldn't allow people . . . (therapist's statement drowned out by client). [Truax and Carkhuff 1967, p. 67]

Therapeutic Genuineness

Therapists who are genuine are "for real," open, honest, sincere. They are involved in the relationship and are not simply mirrors, sounding boards, or blank screens. The sessions are real encounters. And that is the reason why the *exact* nature of the relationship cannot be predicted or controlled in advance. Therapists are freely and deeply themselves, without facades, not phony. They are not feeling and thinking one thing and saying something different. They are, as the existentialist would say, authentic or, to use Jourard's (1964) term, transparent.

Berne (1961) writes, "If the therapist plays the role of a therapist, he will not get very far with perceptive patients" (p. 233). *All* clients are perceptive and respond to pretense in some way, at some level. A therapist who pretends to be understanding when she or he is not will be perceived as pretending and lacking in genuineness. Or a therapist who, for example, starts out by being accepting of the client and then shifts to making judgments will be perceived as incongruent and lacking in honesty. Clients will decide how relevant that pretense is and how they will deal with the lack of faith engendered in that guise. It should be noted that a therapist who intends to be genuine may not always be genuine. This lack of perfection is human and acceptable. It is the therapist who frequently "plays a role" who may be perceived as lacking genuineness.

Genuineness appears to have become the major emphasis of many approaches to psychotherapy. The major theories have given it a more important place. Even psychoanalysis, in which the therapist is a rather ambiguous figure, a blank screen, has moved from this position to the acceptance of the therapist as a real person. If there is one thing that unites many of the apparently extremely diverse innovations in psychotherapy, it is the concept of genuineness.

The characteristics of a self-actualizing person (see Chapter 2) are relevant here in considering the genuineness of the therapist's personal attitudes — attitudes that go deeper than a learned professional role. Therapists must be self-actualizing persons if they are to provide the conditions that facilitate the self-actualization of their clients. The nature of the therapist's presence in the relationship is a reflection of the philosophy, attitudes, and beliefs that underlie his or her practice. Rogers (1986) makes this point when he writes, "It [therapy] is a basic philosophy rather than simply a technique or a method. When this philosophy is lived, it helps the person expand the development of his or her own capacities. When it is lived, it also stimulates constructive change in others" (p. 138). Thus, there must be present in the therapist the characteristics of the self-actualizing person that are genuinely reflected in the therapist's work. Behaviors that on the surface are respectful to the client but are supported by a personal attitude of disdain are incongruent.

There is a real danger involving a misinterpretation of genuineness as supporting an "anything goes" policy. All genuineness is not therapeutic. Carkhuff and Berenson (1967) comment on this problem:

However, a construct of genuineness must be differentiated from the construct of facilitative genuineness. Obviously, the degree to which an individual is aware of his own experience will be related to the degree to which he can enable another person to become aware of his experience. However, many destructive persons are in full contact with their experience; that is, they are destructive when they are genuine. The potentially deleterious effects of genuineness have been established in some research inquiries. Hence the emphasis upon the therapist's being freely and deeply himself in a nonexploitative relationship incorporates one critical qualification. When his only genuine responses are negative in regard to the second person, the therapist makes an effort to employ his responses constructively as a basis for further inquiry for the therapist, the client and their relationship. In addition, there is evidence to suggest that whereas low levels of genuineness are clearly impediments to client progress in therapy, above a certain minimum level, very high levels of genuineness are not related to additional increases in client functioning. Therefore, while it appears of critical importance to avoid the conscious or unconscious facade of "playing the therapeutic role," the necessity for the therapist's expressing himself fully at all times is not supported. Again, genuineness must not be confused, as is so often done, with free license for the therapist to do what he will in therapy, especially to express hostility. Therapy is not for the therapist. . . . Under some circumstances, the honesty of com-munication may actually constitute a limitation for the progress of therapy. Thus, with patient's functioning at significantly lower levels than the therapist, the therapist may attend cautiously to the client's condition. He will not share with the client that which would make the client's condition the more desperate. [pp. 29, 81]

Therapeutic genuineness does not require that therapists always express all of their feelings; it only requires that whatever they do express is real and genuine and not incongruent in the context of the therapy environment. And at a minimal level, genuineness is not being insincere, dishonest, phoney, or incongruent. Genuineness is not impulsive, though the two erroneously appear to be equal in the minds of many, instructors as well as students.

Truax and Mitchell (1971) make an important point (and Carkhuff and Berenson would appear to agree in their comment just quoted):

From the research evidence and an examination of the raw data itself relating genuineness to outcome, as well as collateral evidence, it is clear that what is effective is an absence of defensiveness and phoniness—a lack of evidence the therapist is not genuine. In other words, it is not the positive end of the genuineness scale that contributes to therapeutic outcome. Instead it is a lack of genuineness which militates against positive client change. The highest levels of the genuineness scale do not discriminate between differential outcomes. The scale itself and the evidence concerning genuineness would be more precise if we dropped the term genuineness and call[ed] it instead by some negative term that would include both defensiveness and being phony. [p. 316]

It sounds almost like a riddle that with an emphasis on the importance of being genuine, one cannot not "force" being genuine. It is a way of being that one allows rather than creates.

Patterson (1974) proposes the term *therapeutic genuineness*. Therapists must consider the *consequences* of expressing themselves and *how* they go about it, asking, "Is it therapeutic for the client?" The therapist needs to take time to consider the origin of the feeling about to be expressed. The therapist does not unthinkingly blurt out such things as "You bore me." Rather, if therapists feel bored, they look at themselves and the relationship to see if they are contributing to the feeling. A therapist might say, "To be honest, I am feeling you are giving me a long lecture, and in the face of your saying you feel at times this is not moving fast enough, I am wondering if we are both letting you lecture on rather than address your more pressing concerns."

Measuring Therapeutic Genuineness

Truax (Truax and Carkhuff 1967) constructed a five-point Tentative Scale for the Measurement of Therapist Genuineness or Self-Congruence. He states that this was the most difficult scale to develop. Examination of the scale suggests that a high rating would not necessarily represent therapeutic genuineness. It was this scale that Garfield and Bergin (1971) used in their study that found that genuineness correlated negatively with empathy (– .66) and warmth (– .75). Carkhuff's (1969) revision of the scale to measure facilitative genuineness in interpersonal processes appears to correct this deficiency (see also Patterson 1985a).

Examples of Genuineness

In the first example, the therapist is evasive rather than open and honest:

Client: Do you think I'm crazy?

Therapist: Well, that all depends on what you call crazy. What do you think?

Client: I think I want to know if you think I'm crazy.

Therapist: You don't know?

Client: I just want to know what you think.

Therapist: You're afraid I think you are crazy.

The therapist is avoiding a content response and not responding to (but interpreting) the feelings expressed by the client. Essentially the responses are evasive. Contrast this with the following:

Client: Do you think I'm crazy?

Therapist: No. I think you're working on some really confusing experiences . . .

Client: (interrupts) Yeah, and sometimes I feel crazy or like I don't know what to do.

Carl Rogers makes a statement in one of his films that if he is thinking about something or feeling something, he should express it because it will come out in one way or another. This is more than a fleeting thought. It is a persistent feeling or sense. The withholding of a persistent feeling can be a form of dishonesty in a relationship. Again, as Patterson (1974) warns, the mediating variable is that the honesty must be therapeutic in its impact.

Implications

Trust in the Client

Implicit in respect for the client is trust in the client. The therapist must trust the client to the extent that the client is given control of the nature and rate of development of the therapeutic process. The therapist's trust in the client is not limited or restricted. It is complete. The client is the expert on the client. The client knows, implicitly, how fast he or she can proceed in therapy. The client is responsible for decisions about what is important to discuss, definition of problems, and solutions to problems. The client must be allowed to "do it for him- or herself." Anything that deprives the client of this experience fosters dependency, potentially creates resistance, and ultimately detracts from the self-actualizing process. Decisions and solutions that do not originate in the client are not as likely to be implemented or followed through successfully.

Thus the therapist does not engage in questioning, guiding, leading, probing, directing, suggesting solutions, advising, admonishing, pushing, pulling, explaining or interpreting, or imposing her or his insights on the client. Reassurance, praise, or encouragement are not offered. The client maintains—or in some cases, reclaims—responsibility for him- or herself in the therapy, as he or she must do in life.

A continuing question the therapist poses to her- or himself is "How much do I trust my client?" The presence of the actualizing tendency in the client makes it possible for the client to control and direct the therapy process. Each client has multiple potentials and the ways or manner of their actualization. The therapist has faith in the client, trusting that the actualizing tendency will manifest itself under the therapist-offered conditions. The actualizing tendency means that it is not necessary for the therapist to engage in active interventions. The therapist is not a director — the specific path to self-actualization is not known to the therapist. The therapist trusts the actualizing tendency in the client and has faith that the tendency will manifest itself under the therapist-offered conditions. The client is thus encouraged to take responsibility for directing and controlling his or her own progress. This is accomplished specifically by the therapist being consistently responsive to the client in the process.

Moore (1992) calls this way of being "action-through-nonaction." According to Moore:

> The basic intention in any caring, physical or psychological, is to alleviate suffering. But in relation to the symptom itself, observance means first of all listening and looking carefully at what is being revealed in the suffering. An intent to heal can get in the way of seeing. By doing less, more is accomplished. [p. 10]

Moore cautions therapists not to confuse care with heroics. Well-intentioned heroism is an active force. Action-through-nonaction is simple, flexible, and receptive, requiring patience and responsiveness on the part of the therapist.

Therapist Patience

A basic requirement of the therapist is patience. The process cannot be speeded up by the therapist. The providing of the basic therapist conditions allows for the optimum rate of progress by the client. Therapeutic progress, like learning, does not follow a straight line. There are plateaus — perhaps even temporary regressions — where the client rests, absorbs what has preceded. Some have suggested that an optimum level of pressure or stimulation should be provided by the therapist. What is optimum is never defined. For example, Strupp and Binder (1984) write about the therapist as "someone who evokes anxiety. . . . As always in therapy, the trick is to steer a course which on the one hand maintains sufficient tension, thereby keeping the patient motivated, and on the other, prevents the experience of too much anxiety" (pp. 191–192). Rogers (1961), however, states, "If I can free him [the client] as completely as possible from external threat, then he can begin to experience and to deal with the internal feelings and conflicts which he finds within himself" (p. 54). Active interventions by the therapist can be, and usually are, threatening. The client is subject to internally aroused anxiety as he or she engages in therapy. The therapist avoids creating external anxiety or threat, since the internally produced anxiety will provide the optimum level for the client's progress. Patience is a natural outcome of respect for the client.

Therapist Responsiveness

The therapist conditions are designed as responsive, as compared with the therapist as the initiator in the process. The therapist remains consistently in the responsive mode, following the client, who leads in the process. Thus the therapist does not engage in questioning to guide the client in his or her self-exploration. The therapist does not engage in leading, probing, directing, suggesting alternatives or solutions, advising, admonishing, pushing, pulling, explaining, interpreting, or imposing her or his insights onto the client. Reassurance, praise, or encouragement are not offered because these are judgments. For the therapist to be nonjudgmental out of a motive of keeping responsibility for judgment with the client, the therapist cannot judge positively or negatively as this would create a shift of judgment from the client to therapist.

The Essence of the Conditions

When one brings together the various aspects of the facilitative conditions — empathy, warmth, respect, concern, valuing and prizing, openness, honesty, genuineness, transparency, intimacy — it becomes apparent that they constitute love in the highest sense, or agape, to use the Greek term.

Thomas Moore (1992), a psychotherapist and theologian, points out that love is the essence of psychotherapy. Logic or mere understanding is not enough. Love, with its patient and careful attention, creates the environment of healing. Moore concludes, "It has often been noted that most, if not all, problems brought to therapists are issues of love. It makes sense then that the cure is also love" (p. 15).

A loving relationship is the therapy for all disorders of the human spirit and of disturbed interpersonal relationships. It is not necessary to wait for a "breakthrough" or a discovery of new methods or techniques in psychotherapy or human relations. We already have, in essence, the answer — the answer that has been reached through thousands of years of human experience and recognized by the great philosophers of various times and cultures.

The therapist is not a technician, operating objectively on the client. He or she cannot be detached or disengaged but must be involved in a personal, human encounter. If the therapist is to help clients, she or he must feel for them, love them in the sense of agape. It is perhaps a basic fact of human relationships that you cannot really help people without becoming involved with them, without caring for them. Burton (1967) has noted that "after all research on psychotherapy is accounted for, psychotherapy still resolves itself into a relationship best subsumed by the word 'love' " (pp. 102–103).

Psychotherapy is a human relationship involving two unique individuals. Thus, each relationship is unique. Since this is so, the nature or outcome of the relationship cannot be predicted in detail. But it is not necessary to predict the specifics of the relationship. The therapist need only begin, enter the encounter, without concern about its exact nature or outcome. The therapist must commit to the client and to the relationship without knowing just what will develop or just what it will mean.

If the therapist must have assurance about what will happen and how the relationship will go, he or she will be unable to commit to it. If a therapist cannot trust her- or himself in the relationship, that therapist cannot help the client. The relationship must be free to develop spontaneously. If the therapist has preconceived notions about its nature, he or she will control and restrict the relationship. The need for control, for predictability of the specifics, represents a lack of tolerance for ambiguity and indicates that the individual is unsuitable for the practice of psychotherapy. The therapist must have confidence in her- or himself as a person. Too many students and therapists are seeking something to *do to* their client rather than being concerned about how to *be with* them.

The therapy process is predictable in its general nature and ultimate outcome. *If* the conditions for therapeutic personality change are present in the therapist as a person, *then* a relationship will develop that will lead to the client becoming a more self-actualizing person and, in the process and/or as a result, changing in specific ways or achieving those particular goals that the client desires and that are aspects of or by-products of a self-actualizing process.

Is Love Conditional?

There has been considerable discussion about the conditionality of the therapeutic conditions. An analysis of a therapy interview conducted by Rogers indicates that his responses are not noncontingent but vary with the client's statements (Truax 1966). Thus, the level of the conditions varies during therapy and in relationship to the behavior of the client. Yet love, in its purest form, is unconditional. It is given without demanding something in return. It is bestowed on a person not for what one is but for the being of that person, for his or her very existence.

The solution to the problem would appear to relate to distinguishing between the client as a person — the being — and the client's behavior. The client is unconditionally accepted and respected as a being who exists. The therapist manifests a fundamental respect, concern, and warmth regardless of what the client is or of the client's behavior in or out of the therapy relationship. This basic, minimum level of love, of respect and warmth, is unconditional — it does not depend on any action or attribute of the client. It simply exists as a foundation for all relationships.

When there is a fundamental acceptance of the person, there is no need for that person to be anything more than who he or she is in order to be accepted. As one client expressed the recognition of that basic unconditionality, "You're there with me, but not making me *be* anything or say anything that I'm not." This approach frees the client from needing to defend the self through pretense. Clients, in the presence of the therapist, can deal with themselves directly.

Another positive outcome of a fundamental attitude of respect for the person is that the client comes to feel that he or she is, at a very core level, an acceptable person. Here is an example of a client statement of this recognition:

> *Client*: I've told you things I've never shared with anyone, and you still . . . I don't know . . . you haven't changed your attitude toward me. It sort of changes how I feel. I mean, if you don't think it's so bad with all you know about me, well, maybe I'm not so bad. It sounds silly . . . now that I wasted all that time and energy hiding and being ashamed to tell anyone . . . and angry.
> *Therapist*: You now feel angry . . .
> *Client*: Yeah, for a minute there I felt angry. You know, why me, why did it happen that way, why did they let things go on, why, why, why? And then really just relieved that I don't have to feel it anymore . . . against myself. Like, just go on now, let it go and move on.

This client moved from feeling the therapist's attitude of acceptance to rediscovering her own acceptance of herself. Self-acceptance facilitates the actualizing tendency. We all want to accept ourselves, and that is the antecedent of the reawakening of our potential.

But one who loves and respects another is, of course, affected on some level by the other's behavior. Therapists who care deeply about their clients are affected by a client's behavior, both in and out of therapy. They are pleased or disappointed, happy or sad, approving or disapproving, depending on how the client behaves. The therapist's responses are to some extent contingent on the client's behavior.

But throughout all this differential responsiveness, there is a basic respect, concern, caring, or love for the client as a person. Without respect the therapist could not help the client. The client would not continue the relationship. Without respect the therapist would not be a significant person to the client, and if the therapist were not a significant person, her or his responses would not be meaningful or important to the client and would have no effect on the client.

When one really cares about another, one wants to help the other be a better person and prevent him or her from making mistakes. Thus, there is the temptation to intervene actively in the life of the other. If one loves another, one cannot allow the other to make a mistake, to fail, to do something that clearly seems to be bad or wrong. Or can one? Does a real love, a greater love, respect the right of the other to make her or his own decisions, even to make mistakes or to fail? And how is one to know what is a mistake or what actions will lead to failure, what is good or bad, right or wrong, for another? And even where certain actions are clearly wrong or bad, can or should one, even on the basis of love, intervene, thus indicating a lack of faith in the other? Possibly so, in extreme instances where irreparable damage seems sure to be done. But it might be maintained that under the conditions of real love, which include faith and confidence in the other person, the other will not choose to act in a way that is clearly bad, wrong, or harmful to self or others. The question perhaps revolves around the extent of the love or caring one has for the other, the respect one has for his or her integrity, the faith one has in the other, and the relationship she or he is providing for the other.

Kitchner (1984) discusses the difficulty of pondering ethical questions that are beyond strictly dichotomous right and wrong answers. Each therapist must come to her or his own understanding of the extent of the application of respect for client choice in a therapy relationship. Professional ethics provide therapists with guidelines in cases of intended harmful behavior (American Psychological Association 1992). A therapist is ethically bound to intervene when the client clearly communicates an intent to harm self or others. If a client knows this and communicates directly or indirectly to the therapist of such intent, a case can be made that the client wants and invites intervention. Therapists can recognize the complicated nuances of choice behavior.

Patterson (1985a) explicates the perspective of total respect for freedom of choice:

> Love must allow the loved one to make his or her own choices
> and, in the extreme case, must leave open the possibility that

death rather than life may be chosen, because it has such
confidence that the power of love will lead to the choice of life.
But the risk that death might be chosen must be taken because
love requires that the loved one have the freedom of choice.
[p. 94].

Is Love Controlling?

A final aspect of the conditions — or of love — is significant for the
problem of control. In reinforcement terms, the most potent reinforcer
of human behavior is a good human relationship. The conditions are
not effective, in the long run, unless they are real or genuine. When it
is real and genuine, love prevents one from using or exploiting another
for one's own purposes. It would thus appear that there is a built-in
protection in the conditions against excessive control or manipulation.

Yet this does not appear to eliminate the possibility of control by
misguided persons of good intentions. Possessive love, as is well
known, can be harmful. Is there then no protection against influence
by those who can offer love and understanding? It appears that
brainwashing is most effective where there is real belief in what is
being imposed and where there is real concern for the person being
influenced — a desire to "save his soul," so to speak. In Orwell's (1949)
novel *1984,* Winston, even though tortured by his inquisitor, O'Brien,
felt love for him because O'Brien understood him.

It has been pointed out that we should take comfort "in the
knowledge that the behavior of those who exercise control is generally
governed more by the behavior of those controlled than by anything
else" (Day 1972). But is it? History, and *Walden Two* (Skinner 1948),
do not demonstrate this. It is only true on the assumption that behavior
is mainly controlled by automatic reinforcement.

Perhaps here is the key, as Skinner himself has suggested. When
there is awareness that one is being controlled — even by the loving and
understanding of another — then one is not in the position of responding automatically to reinforcement. Looking at it in another

way, if respect is not a part of love, it is not real love. Or, if respect as well as empathic understanding and genuineness are not present, the individual responds differently. But if respect is present, there is no attempt to control in a manipulative sense or in terms of what the controller thinks is best. It is our ability to be aware of being controlled that is our protection. Respect for another prevents the controller from manipulating another, and the awareness of lack of respect prevents the other from being manipulated by a possessive love and understanding.

How the Conditions Relate

The three conditions of empathy, respect, and genuineness interrelate both in terms of contributing to each other in the therapy process and being statistically correlated (in most studies). Rogers (1975) and Truax (Truax and Carkhuff 1967) suggest that genuineness is basic, since warmth and empathy can be threatening or meaningless without it. In turn, empathy must be based on warmth and respect. However, warmth and respect are known to increase with the depth of understanding of another, and the attentiveness and listening characterizing the attempt to understand another is evidence of respect for the client. Truax and Carkhuff (1967) write, "We begin to perceive the events and experiences of his life 'as if' they were parts of our own life. It is through this process that we come to feel warmth, respect and liking for a person who in everyday life is unlikable, weak, cowardly, treacherous, vile, or despicable" (p. 42).

Rogers (1975) suggests that each of the conditions may be the primary or most important element in different situations or kinds of relationships. In everyday relationships in the home, school, and at work, genuineness is probably most important as "a basis for living together in a climate of realness" (p. 9). In special situations of nonverbal relationships — parent and infant, therapist and mute psychotic, doctor and seriously ill patient — warmth or caring may be most important. But when the other person is troubled, hurt, anxious, confused — the situation in which clients find themselves — then empathy "has the highest priority" (p. 9).

The Research Evidence

Research on the therapist conditions posited by Rogers (1957a) has been voluminous. In 1954, Rogers and Dymond edited a volume reporting a series of studies done at the University of Chicago. In 1967, Rogers and his colleagues edited a volume reporting on an extensive research project involving hospitalized schizophrenics. The 1967 review by Truax and Carkhuff lists 439 references. The 1971 review of Truax and Mitchell includes ninety-two references. They conclude in their review:

> Therapists or counselors who are accurately empathic, nonpossessively warm in attitude and genuine are indeed effective. Also these findings seem to hold with a wide variety of therapists and counselors, regardless of their training or theoretic orientation, and with a wide variety of clients or patients, including college underachievers, juvenile delinquents, hospitalized schizophrenics, college counselees, mild to severe outpatient neurotics, and a mixed variety of hospitalized patients. Further, the evidence suggests that these findings hold in a variety of contexts and in both individual and group therapy. [p. 310]

Gurman (1977) agrees, concluding in a review that there is "substantial if not overwhelming evidence in support of the hypothesized relationship between patient-perceived conditions and outcome in individual psychotherapy" (p. 523).

Early research, as with any fledgling project, tended to have methodological and statistical problems. Thus, for some time in the late 1970s many reviews of research focusing on methodology were negative (Bergin and Lambert 1978, Bergin and Suinn 1975, Gurman 1977, Lambert et al. 1978, Mitchell et al. 1977, Orlinsky and Howard 1978, Parloff et al. 1978). However, the early research set the stage for more sophisticated methods and more specific research questions that confirmed positive results.

Updated reviews of research on the therapeutic relationship in the late 1980s once again reported positive outcomes. Orlinsky and Howard (1986) state that "50 to 80 percent of the substantial number of studies in this area were significantly positive, indicating that these dimensions were very consistently related to patient outcome" (p. 311). Lambert and colleagues (1986) joined the growing support by observing, "[That] these personal qualities bear a striking resemblance to each other, across studies and methodologies, is evidence that they are important in psychotherapy outcome and are prominent ingredients of change in most, if not all, therapies" (p. 159). They conclude that the common factors "seem to make up a significant portion of effective ingredients of psychotherapy" (p. 202).

In the recent review of research accumulated since 1985, Beutler and colleagues (1994) introduce their review in part with the following statement:

> Rogers's (1957) conceptualizations of the "necessary and sufficient" conditions for effective psychotherapy formed the foundation for the preponderance of research on the psychotherapy relationship over three decades. Most contemporary investigators would probably agree that these facilitative qualities play a central role in therapeutic change. In clinical practice, they are equally well accepted and have been assimilated into much of contemporary theory. These variables are the ones most often considered when the topic of "common" or "shared" psychotherapy characteristics come up. These are the qualities of the therapy relationship to which much of the therapeutic change is attributed. [p. 243]

In the mid-1980s, the "therapeutic alliance" was proposed as a component of the relationship (Gelso and Carter 1985). It seems that "the alliance" was intended to be a step forward in clarifying the facilitative conditions as qualities of the client and the relationship itself, as well as the therapist. Rogers (1957a) much earlier stated the essential importance of the client perceiving the conditions. It was, in fact, the fourth condition. Thus, the clarity is more a matter of semantics than substance. This alliance has been recognized as very similar to Rogers's conceptualization of the therapeutic relationship (Beutler et al. 1994). Whatever its intention, the outcome of the introduction of the term *therapeutic alliance* was an explosion of research that has reconfirmed the importance of Rogers's facilitative conditions as basic to an effective psychotherapy relationship.

In a review of nine major review articles on relationship variables, Patterson (1984) concludes that few things are as certain in the field of psychology as is the consistently strong evidence supporting the "necessity if not sufficiency of the therapist conditions of accurate empathy, respect, or warmth, and therapeutic genuineness" (p. 437). That conclusion is echoed in numerous reviews of the literature (Beutler et al. 1986, Lambert and Bergin 1983, Orlinsky and Howard 1986).

In a twenty-four-study meta-analysis using the therapeutic alliance as a relationship measure, the results were in favor of the therapeutic relationship as a predictor of outcome. The largest effect size was observed when clients evaluated both the outcome and the quality of the relationship. In addition to supporting the effect of the quality of the relationship on outcome, this result supports Rogers's (1957a) fourth condition that the client must perceive that the conditions are being offered by the therapist. Piper and co-authors (1991), in evaluating relationship quality and outcomes in short-term psychodynamic therapy, demonstrate a significant relationship does exist. Rounsaville and colleagues (1985) found similar positive results for interpersonal psychotherapy. Luborsky and colleagues (1985) studied the quality of the relationship among nine counselors and 110 drug therapy clients. They found that the quality of the relationship after the fifth treatment sessions was strongly predictive of outcome. Other studies report similar results using relationship quality as a predictor of success for nonpsychodynamic therapies (Safran and Wallner 1991, Williams and Chambless 1990). Studies in Germany (Rudolf 1991) and the Netherlands (Dormaar et al. 1989) confirm the importance of the relationship to outcome in different cultural contexts (Beutler et al. 1994).

Interestingly, studies of various therapy orientations have noted few differences in effect sizes associated with different theoretical orientations. Even reviews limited to one disorder (Nietzel et al. 1987) have not found differences in outcomes attributed to therapist orientations. It is certainly possible that this result reflects the strong underlying universal qualities of the therapeutic relationship that contribute to outcome in all psychotherapy.

Beutler and colleagues (1994) conclude their review of literature on the therapeutic relationship with this comment: "Collectively, the quality of the therapeutic relationship, by its various terms, has consistently been found to be a central contributor to therapeutic progress. Its significance traverses theoretical schools, theory-specific concepts, and diversity of measurement procedures" (p. 244).

6

The Therapist II: Other Conditions

Introduction

Rogers (1957a) hypothesizes that the three therapist conditions considered in the last chapter are not only the necessary but also the sufficient conditions for therapeutic outcomes. But the question can be raised as to whether other conditions are necessary, or useful or effective, or contribute to the efficacy and efficiency of psychotherapy.

The therapist variables that have been suggested are innumerable. Many, if not most, of them are techniques or methods rather than basic conditions. It is the latter with which we are concerned here. We shall consider two groups that have been proposed — social influence variables and the action variables proposed by Truax and Carkhuff (1967) and Carkhuff and Berenson (1967) — and another variable, concreteness, proposed by Truax and Carkhuff (1967) and Berenson (1967).

Social Influence Variables

In 1961, Frank suggested that psychotherapy is a process of persuasion. In 1966, Goldstein proposed that research in psychotherapy should be directed toward studying variables derived from research in social psychology, particularly the psychology of interpersonal attraction, and he, with Heller and Sechrest (Goldstein et al. 1966), provided an analysis of relevant research in social psychology. A considerable literature on the process of persuasion in social psychology was drawn upon (e.g., Hovland et al. 1953).

In 1968, Strong (see also Strong 1978, Strong and Claiborn 1982, Strong and Matross 1973) proposed applying the social-psychological concept of cognitive dissonance to the interpersonal influence process in psychotherapy. He suggested that the greater the extent to which therapists are perceived as expert, attractive, and trustworthy, the greater would be their credibility and thus their power to influence clients.

There are three main therapist variables in the concept of psychotherapy as a social influence process. The first is actually a loose cluster of variables designated as *perceived expertness,* or credibility. It also appears to include respect and perceived competence. Contributing to this client perception of expertness are indications of status (degrees, diplomas, office decor, and furnishings), prestige (reputation), and power and authority. While trustworthiness is often considered a separate variable, it is also included with expertness in the concept of credibility.

The second variable is *perceived attractiveness.* Included in this are therapist–client similarities in opinions, attitudes, beliefs, values, and background; therapist liking for the client; therapist likability, friendliness, and warmth; and therapist self-disclosure.

The third variable is *therapist expectancy.* Therapist confidence in him- or herself and/or in the methods and techniques used leads to the client expecting change or improvement. This expectancy is communicated to the client through various subtle, unintentional ways as well as through direct expressions of optimism, suggestions, and reassurance.

It is interesting to consider social influence variables in relation to the nature of the placebo. In their review of the placebo effect, Shapiro and Morris (1978) discuss these variables, including expectancy, as ways in which the placebo operates.

Related to or an element in therapists' expectations of positive results are their belief and faith in themselves and in their methods or techniques, factors that Shapiro (1971) emphasizes as important elements in the placebo effect. These factors appear to be the same factors that Orne (1962) calls the "demand characteristics" in psychological experiments both in and outside the laboratory. Rosenthal (1966), among others, demonstrates the influence of the experimenter's beliefs, expectations, and desires on the outcome of psychological experiments both in and outside the laboratory. In psychological research these are unwanted, or placebo, effects. They should be regarded as such in psychotherapy, as indeed they are by Shapiro and Morris.

These variables appear to constitute the "good guy" factor in psychotherapy (Muehlberg et al. 1969). LaCrosse and Barak (1976) suggest that the common factor in expertness, attractiveness, and trustworthiness is what Strong calls the "influence" or the "persuasiveness" of Frank and of LaCrosse or the "power" of Strong and Matross and of Dell (Corrigan et al. 1980). They then note that "these terms are also related to what might be described as 'charisma' or 'impressiveness'" (LaCrosse and Barak 1976, p. 172). All of this suggests an image of the therapist as a person exuding or projecting self-confidence, self-assurance, competence, power, and persuasiveness — a charismatic snake-oil salesperson. The placebo in psychotherapy will be considered in more detail in Chapter 9.

Research on Social Influence Variables

Some reviewers support these variables in spite of the mixed results and the fact that the studies reviewed are only analogue studies and do not include outcome studies. Strong (1978) states that "as a whole, these studies show that therapist credibility is an important variable in psychotherapy" (p. 108). This would seem to be an unjustifiable conclusion. In regard to perceived therapist attractiveness, he concludes that "studies of the effect of client attraction to the therapist on the ability of the therapist to influence the client have obtained mixed and generally pessimistic results" (p. 108).

Corrigan and colleagues (1980) conclude that "the effects of expertness and attractiveness on counselors' ability to influence clients are, at best, unclear. . . . Those studies that successfully manipulated attractiveness failed to find differential effects on client change" (p. 425). Yet these authors recommend further research on these social influence variables in counseling as "interesting and reasonable," though they admit that "the question of the utility of considering counseling as a social influence process remains" (p. 437).

Beutler and colleagues (1986), in their review of research on social influence variables, found some evidence from nonanalogue studies that therapist credibility, expertness, and trustworthiness are related to therapy outcome. However, these findings, based on only two studies, must "be tempered with the observation that self-reports and therapist reports of internal change may be more susceptible to the influence of these influence attributes than are more objectively measured behavioral changes" (p. 281). One of the studies (LaCrosse 1980) was of atypical clients—those in an outpatient drug treatment program, only two of the thirty-six being voluntary clients. There is also a question about the validity and probable bias of ratings by the clients of both their therapists and outcome with the possibility of a spurious element in the correlations of the two sets of ratings.

In addition to the fact that, other than analogue studies, less than a handful of studies of actual clients exist, three observations may be made. First, the analogue research suggests that social influence factors may affect client perceptions of the therapist early in the relationship, but they probably are not lasting and are superseded by less superficial variables as therapy progresses. Second, these variables are probably not independent of the therapist empathy, respect, and genuineness. LaCrosse (1980) found significant correlations between social influence variables and the Barrett-Leonard Relationship Inventory, which measures client perceptions of therapist empathic understanding, congruence, level of regard, and unconditional positive regard. Thus, such effect as social influence variables could be due to their association with or participation in the core therapist conditions. Finally, the social influence variables appear to partake of the well-known placebo effect.

Carkhuff's Action Conditions

Carkhuff and Berenson (1967) propose three other conditions that they call action conditions, in distinction to the responsive conditions of empathy, respect, and genuineness. These are confrontation, therapist self-disclosure, and the immediacy of the relationship.

Confrontation

There appears to be some confusion regarding the nature of confrontation in psychotherapy. The primary dictionary definition includes an element of hostility. Moreover, it implies a confrontation between two persons. This is not the kind of confrontation of concern here. It is not a personal confrontation of the client by the therapist. The kind of confrontation we are considering is that indicated by a secondary aspect of the dictionary definition: to set side by side for comparison or to place before.

Confrontation is an expression by the therapist of his or her experience of discrepancies in the client's behavior or verbalization. Carkhuff distinguishes three broad categories of discrepancy: (1) discrepancy between clients' expressions of what they are and what they want to be (real self, or self-concept, versus ideal self); (2) discrepancy between clients' verbal expressions about themselves (awareness or insight) and their behavior as it is either observed by the therapist or reported by the clients; and (3) discrepancy between clients' expressed experience of themselves and the therapist's experience of them (Carkhuff 1969). A fourth category should be added to cover discrepancies between clients' experience of themselves and others as reported at different times, either in the same session or in different sessions.

Confrontation is the attempt to bring to awareness the presence of cognitive dissonance or incongruence in the client's feelings, attitudes, beliefs, perceptions, or behaviors. It consists of reflecting discrepancies or inconsistencies between or among client statements relating to these areas. Confrontation does not create these discrepancies — it simply sets out or places before the client discrepant statements the client has made. The confrontation is between inconsistent communications of the client, not between the therapist and the client. Often these communications relate to ambivalent feelings and attitudes toward persons in the client's life. But always the sources for the confrontation come from the client; they are not interpretations deriving from the therapist. The therapist remains in the client's frame of reference and does not take the initiative from the client.

In the early stages of therapy, the therapist is tentative in her or his confrontations, usually formulating them as questions since the therapist is not too confident about them. "Premature direct confrontations may have a demoralizing and demobilizing effect upon an inadequately prepared helpee" (Carkhuff 1969, Vol. II, p. 93). The therapist may say something like, "You seem to be saying two different things" or "Now you say this, but earlier you seemed to be saying that."

Later in the therapy, more direct confrontations may focus specifically on discrepancies. "The increasing specificity will lead to the development of an understanding of the distortions in the helpee's assumptive world and, hopefully, to reconstruction of that world" (Carkhuff 1969, Vol. I, p. 211). Direct confrontations precipitate an awareness of a crisis in the client that, when faced, leads to movement to higher levels of functioning. The goal is to enable clients to confront themselves and, when desirable, others. "Confrontation of self and others is prerequisite to the healthy individual's encounter with life" (Carkhuff 1969, Vol. II, p. 93).

An important use of confrontation is to indicate to clients that insight is not enough and that, although they have insight, their behavior has not changed. Confrontation enables clients to go beyond insight and to recognize the need to change their behaviors. Confrontation is not limited to negative aspects of clients or to facing them with their limitations. It also includes pointing out discrepancies involving resources and assets that are unrecognized or unused (see Patterson 1985a for Carkhuff's Scale for Measurement of Confrontation in Interpersonal Process).

Examples of Confrontation

Therapist: Although you said your behavior has gotten you in trouble, you have also said you really do enjoy yourself . . . it's

not all negative. There is some very good feeling about yourself
there.

Client: Yes, you're right. I do, yeah, I do feel that (smiling). It isn't
bad. What I am isn't bad; it's just that I have used it in the wrong
ways. I don't have to change me so much as learn to manage what
I do in better ways.

The therapist is confronting two conflicting statements made by the
client. This points out to the client a conflict experienced within herself
and that she now has made clear to herself. She sees that her behavior
is negative and is the focus of change in this instance.

All confrontation runs some risk of threatening the client. The
association of confrontation with high levels of the core conditions
suggests that confrontation may be useful or effective only in the
context of *high* levels of empathy and respect. This point further
suggests that since high levels of these conditions may not be present
or perceived by the client in the first interview or early interviews,
confrontation should not be employed until the relationship has been
well established. The option to confront is earned by the therapist by
building a nonthreatening relationship. Once the relationship is
established, the therapist can respond to incongruencies. When ap-
proached in this way, confrontation becomes a process of clarification
rather than a threat to the self.

It is possible that confrontation should not be considered as a
separate condition or dimension of psychotherapy. Perhaps it could be
included in empathic understanding. The recognition and communication of discrepancies in the client's verbalizations and behaviors do
seem to be aspects of empathy. Within a relationship characterized by
the core conditions, confrontation is a matter of clarifying or bringing
the client's feelings and thoughts to greater awareness instead of an act
of conflict. When the therapist clarifies or reflects the incongruence
(confrontation), the client often responds with statements like the
following:

Therapist: You said you always act like your mother, and then you
said you always act like your father. That's confusing.
Client: Yes, that's exactly the problem. I'm feeling both of those ways
at once, and I have to come to some kind of understanding of that

very conflict. I'm not her and I'm not him. I have to find who I am. The difficulty, of course, is not being what he *expects* me to be and not being what she *expects* me to be, and just be who I am and not worry about what they'll think of me.

Therapist: You act like that person to please that person . . . for their approval.

Client: If I stop pleasing other people all the time, I just might find me. (pause) That's a scary thought! I'm not sure I want to be me.

When the therapist is following empathically what the client is saying, she or he will sense the conflict in the statements. When the therapist reflects the feeling of confusion (assuming it is accurate), the client will recognize it as his or her feeling and begin to explore it. The client in this case revealed a concise picture of the problem in the conflicting statements. The therapist did not confront the content of the statement but reflected the confusion that the therapist empathically understood from the client's statements.

Therapists of most of the major approaches have avoided confrontation. Direct confrontation has been limited to clients who are aggressive, manipulative, or confronting themselves; thus the therapist reacts to, rather than initiates, confrontation. This type of confrontation is not what we are addressing here. In addition to the possible dangers when it is not associated with empathy and warmth or concern, confrontation, like genuineness, can be used to vent the therapist's aggressiveness and internal anger, frustration, and other negative feelings. The word itself is perhaps not a felicitous one, with its connotations of aggressiveness and face-to-face conflict. It would be helpful if a more appropriate word could be found.

The reasons for avoidance of confrontation are not the issue so much as the consequences of the action in the relationship and the process, namely distrust and resistance. First, when the client is representing her or his confusion in the form of conflicting statements and the therapist does not seem to notice, the client can assume the therapist is not listening. Second, if a therapist avoids confrontation, there is the issue of lack of genuineness or honesty and an apparent double standard, as in the following example:

Therapist: I think it's very important to be completely open and honest with each other.

Client: Well, how do I seem to you, how do I come across when you listen to me?

Therapist: Well, er, umm . . . I like you. You're a nice woman.

Client: Don't equivocate!

Therapist: Maybe we need to get to know each other better.

Client: Maybe. [Carkhuff and Berenson 1967, pp. 176–177]

In summary, confrontation is a clarification of conflicting client statements rather than a conflict between the therapist and the client. It is responsive, not directive. Effective confrontation emerges from the therapist's sense of empathic understanding of the client's confusion or internal conflict, not an attack on the client. Confrontation should be employed only after the relationship is established. In addition to working on negative aspects presented by the client, confrontation is effective in raising awareness of positive aspects.

Therapist Self-Disclosure

What the effects of self-disclosure are is not clear from the research available. Yet there are those who advocate therapist self-disclosure. Beutler (1978) states that "the degree either of experimenter or therapist self-disclosure precipitates a similar disclosure level in subjects and patients" (pp. 134–135). But Strong and Claiborn (1982) write that "therapist disclosure to encourage patient disclosure does not seem like a good use of the therapist's power unless some specific disclosure is needed" (p. 157).

Self-disclosure early in therapy as a model for client self-disclosure is unnecessary if the client understands the nature of therapy. Most clients expect to talk about themselves; indeed, they usually come to therapy for that purpose. If clients do not understand this, then simply structuring the client's role is more efficient and effective than modeling, since the client can misunderstand or fail to understand the modeling. Clients do not expect therapists to talk about themselves and may be embarrassed, puzzled, or mystified when they do. Clients are more involved in the problems that brought them to therapy than interested in the therapist's personal life.

Therapist disclosure of similarities with the client in the effort to increase his or her attractiveness may reduce the client's perception of the therapist's competence and expertise or may be perceived as reassurance that the client's problems are not as serious as she or he had thought, possibly resulting in less motivation for therapy or less desire for change. On the other hand, therapist disclosure of differences may create a distance that would not have been perceived by the client without that emphasis. Strong (1978) suggests that therapist self-disclosures provide social comparison data and thus increases or decreases patients' evaluations of themselves, the severity of their problems, the validity of their ideas, and even their self-esteem.

Therapists disclose themselves in everything they say and do, and clients form a picture or perception of the therapist from these disclosures. The question is, in how much disclosure should the therapist engage, particularly verbal disclosure of specific personal information and experiences, especially those not related to the therapy or the therapy relationship? The therapist should be very cautious about such disclosures. Disclosure of the therapist's present feelings or thoughts during therapy is essentially a matter of genuineness.

Therapist self-disclosure must be for the client's benefit. It is the client who must engage in self-disclosure for therapy to occur, not the therapist. Therapists should not engage in self-disclosure for their own benefit or therapy. Therapy is for the client, not the therapist.

As therapy nears ending, however, clients become less focused on themselves. Resolution of their own problems no longer requires all their attention. They become more aware of the therapist as a person and more interested in the therapist as an individual, and they may express this interest by asking questions about the therapist as a person. The occurrence of this behavior in therapy may be an indication that therapy is nearing or is at its end.

Just as there is some question about whether confrontation is not a part of empathy (with perhaps an aspect of genuineness), so there is some question as to whether therapist self-disclosure is a part of honesty and genuineness (with perhaps an aspect of empathy). Carkhuff (1969) notes that "the dimension of self-disclosure is one facet of genuineness. . . . Spontaneous sharing on the part of both parties is the essence of a genuine relationship" (pp. 208–209; see Patterson 1985 for Carkhuff's Scale to Measure Facilitative Self-Disclosure).

Example of Therapist Self-Disclosure

Client: I'm afraid of those kind of spooky movies, so I just don't watch them. I wonder if that's crazy—you know, I shouldn't be so afraid.

Therapist: I don't watch those kind of movies either. They scare me.

Client: Yes? I'm glad to hear that. There are so many bad things that go on anyway in the world. I don't have to see more of that.

Therapist: There are a lot of *real* things that frighten you.

The therapist chose to respond to the portion of the initial statement based on the emphasis the client gave it. The disclosure allowed the therapist to share personal experience with the client without judging the behavior.

Immediacy of the Relationship

Immediacy refers to the current interaction of the therapist and the client in the relationship. Concern with immediacy is significant because the client's behavior and functioning in the therapy relationship are indicative of his or her functioning in other interpersonal relationships. Gestalt therapy recognizes this in a concern with the here and now (Perls 1969a,b). The Adlerians also focus on immediate behavior in the counseling situation. Kell and Mueller (1966) emphasize what they call the *eliciting behaviors* of clients in the therapy relationship, particularly self-defeating behaviors. If the essence of psychotherapy is a relationship, and we are concerned about the functioning of the client in interpersonal relationships (indeed, it is because of inadequate functioning in interpersonal relationships that most clients come to a therapist), then the client's functioning in the therapy relationship should be important.

> The way he [the client] relates to the counselor is a snapshot of the way he relates to others. . . . Clients come to counseling manipulating, hostile, rejecting, testing. They invest or do not invest; they are afraid; they present weakness; they attempt to seduce; they stay in a shell; they hide; they try to force the counselor to be responsible; they try to force punishment from the counselor; they apologize for being human. If the counselor does not focus on trying to understand these things, growth possibilities for clients can be missed. [Cudney 1968, pp. 135–136]

The therapist has the opportunity to deal directly with the client's problem behavior, and the client has the opportunity to learn and to change his or her behavior.

Carkhuff (1969) has suggested that immediacy bridges the gap between empathy and confrontation, making possible

> a translation in the immediate present of the helper's insights into the helpee's expressions. The helper in responding immediately to his experience of the relationship with the helpee not only allows the helpee to have the intense experience of two persons in interaction but also provides a model of a person who understands and acts upon his experience of both his impact upon the other and the other's impact upon him. [vol I, p. 192]

There are many complexities in considering how to respond to the immediacy of the relationship. The therapist must be sensitive toward the client's feelings about her or him and deal with them rather than ignore them. It is particularly difficult for the therapist to recognize negative feelings as related to him- or herself or, if the therapist does recognize those feelings, to respond to them. The difficulty is increased by the fact that the client's message may be, and often is, indirect; that is, it is concealed in references to other persons than the therapist. Carkhuff (1969, p. 194) gives as an example the statement by a client that she has difficulty relating to her physician, which is a way of stating that she has difficulty relating to the therapist. It is obvious that this is an inference, or even an interpretation, that is based on the therapist's feeling or intuition or, if the inference is accurate, on her or his sensitivity. There is the danger that the therapist may be mistaken, that she or he is imposing her or his own interpretation or projecting rather than being sensitive to the client. In addition to depending on her or his own experiencing of the client, the therapist is going beyond or ignoring the content of the client's communication to respond to the unspoken message. "Usually when the helpee cannot express himself it is not so much a function of his inability to express himself as it is of the attitudes he holds about the helper in relation to himself" (Carkhuff 1969, vol I, p. 212). While an accurate response by the therapist can facilitate progress, an inaccurate response can be threatening and damaging. It is wise to avoid harmful responses in cases in which the potentially harmful response is at best a guess. If the client is trying to communicate a negative feeling, the client will likely repeat it until it is understood.

While the relationship at every moment could be examined in terms of its immediacy, responding to this is not always appropriate. It is most appropriate to focus on immediacy when the client refers to it or when therapy seems to be stalled. A way to address this, of course, is for the therapist to offer her or his experiencing of the process. If therapy is stalled, then in some cases focusing on the immediacy of the relationship may reveal issues in the relationship that need to be addressed. Possibly the impasse involves feelings, attitudes, or behavior of the therapist of which the therapist is unaware. In addition, it is also useful to look specifically at the relationship in terms of immediacy when the process seems to be going well — that is, to look at its positive aspects.

Immediacy, while involving the relationship of the client to the therapist, is not dealt with as a psychoanalytic transference relationship. The immediate intent of the relationship is to create an environment in which the client can be safe and secure enough to initiate change. A secondary intent, which follows personal change, is that the client can transfer to other relationships the learning about how to *be* in a healthy relationship. Obviously, the client's relationship with the therapist is initially related to and influenced by his or her habits or methods of relating to others. It is emphasized that the working implication of this therapeutic relationship is initially and continually as an example of a healthy interactional way of being between two people.

As in the case of the other action dimensions, therapist responses of immediacy at a high level are not suddenly presented to the client. Before the therapist knows and understands the client, there is necessarily some uncertainty about his or her experience of the client. And before the client has developed a good relationship with the therapist, he or she is not prepared for the disclosure. Therefore, the therapist's expression of immediacy is tentative: "Are you trying to tell me how you feel about me and our relationship?" As the relationship develops, the therapist becomes more sure of his or her communications, and interpretations of immediacy are then unnecessary.

One may ask whether immediacy is independent of or qualitatively different from the responsive dimensions. To be sensitive to clients' perceptions, feelings, and attitudes toward the therapist or to how they are relating to the therapist would appear to be a part of empathy. Carkhuff (1969) refers to immediacy as "one of the most critical variables in terms of communicating a depth of understanding" (p. 192). The expression of the therapist's experiences of the client appears to be an aspect of genuineness. The pointing out of the meaning of the client's words or behavior in terms of his or her relationship with the therapist appears to be similar to confrontation. Thus immediacy may be empathy and/or genuineness and/or confrontation that involves a particular content — the relationship between the therapist and the client (see Patterson 1985 for Carkhuff's Scale for Measuring Immediacy of the Relationship in Interpersonal Process).

Examples of Immediacy.   In the following example, the therapist ignores the client's feelings about him, focusing instead on the client's general reaction of discouragement:

> *Client*: I'm not sure I should continue these sessions. I don't feel I'm getting anywhere. You — they don't seem to be helping me. I don't get the feeling you are very concerned.

Therapist: You're pretty discouraged and feel like quitting and giving up.

Client: Yeah . . . it doesn't seem worthwhile to continue.

Contrast this with the following dialogue, in which the therapist responds with a high level of immediacy (as well as confrontation) to the client's (implicit or explicit) feelings of aggression toward the therapist:

Therapist: John, you really want to destroy our relationship here.

Client: It's more than that.

Therapist: You want to kill me.

Client: No, not really, I . . . .

Therapist: John, you want to kill me.

Client: Yes, I want to kill you. I know you haven't earned it, but I want to kill you, maybe for everyone I hate.

Therapist: That's too easy.

Client: All I know is I want to kill you.

Therapist: You can't.

Client: I can! I can! One way or another I will. So I can't take you this way but I'll find another way. I'll fail you. I'll lead you astray. You'll think I'm improving but I'll fail. I'll be your failure case. You'll be responsible.

Therapist: You'll do anything you have to, to undermine me, to destroy me, even something that hurts you.

Client: Yes, yes.

Therapist: If you can in some way defeat me, you won't have to change your way of living. You do stupid things to protect a stupid way of life, and that's stupid.

Client: Oh, I want to change. I do, I can't help it. I can't help it. God, I've been wrong to hurt you.

Therapist: You had to find out whether you could take me. If you could, I couldn't help you, and I can. [Carkhuff and Berenson 1967, p. 149]

The following dialogue illustrates the therapist's inference that the client's statement about others also applies to the therapist:

Client: I'm never sure where I stand with anyone.

Therapist: That applies here as well, right, Jim?

Client: Yeah, I guess it does. I've been thinking of bringing it up — guess I was afraid to learn that you, too, would give some meaningless bunch of words.

Therapist: You're telling me you're not sure you trust me enough to go further — even though we have shared a great deal.

Client: Guess I was sure you'd think I was crazy — earlier I felt I might shock you.

Therapist: Look — at this moment I experience this: Whatever Jim fears most does not cause me *any* anxiety — I'm not sure I can get it all into words — but your impulses don't scare me — and I trust that. I feel drained of energy. Damn it, you have your own strength — have it, for crying out loud — then you will know. [Carkhuff and Berenson 1967, p. 189]

Integration of the Responsive and Action Dimensions

The separation of the therapeutic conditions into two groupings — the understanding or responsive conditions and the initiating or action conditions — is not a hard-and-fast separation. To some extent all the conditions are or can be present throughout the therapy process. Understanding or empathy is essential for confrontation and immediacy. Warmth or respect also is essential as a base for the action conditions. The action conditions must have a context of warmth and understanding. This is important, particularly for the beginning therapist, who may be tempted (or encouraged by a misunderstanding of the place of the action conditions) to move quickly into high levels of action conditions without adequate understanding or the basis of empathy and warmth or respect.

The division of therapy into dimensions or conditions that lead to insight and dimensions or conditions that lead to action is probably not warranted (Carkhuff and Berenson 1967). The understanding conditions, in addition to providing the basis for insight, also contribute directly to action or make action possible for the client whose therapeutic relationship lacks high levels of the action conditions. On the other hand, the action conditions can stimulate and contribute to client insight. It is possible, as has been indicated earlier, to consider the action conditions not as new or different conditions but as extensions of the understanding conditions to new areas. Thus therapist self-disclosure is genuineness or openness applied to the therapist's personal life. Immediacy is empathy applied to the therapist–client relationship of the moment. In addition, the action conditions may be to some extent, if not entirely, essentially high levels of the understanding conditions. That this is the case seems to be recognized implicitly by Carkhuff (1969).

The deliberate use of the action dimensions — particularly by the beginning therapist, who is apt not to be particularly high in the responsive dimensions — should be cautious. Confrontation inherently has the possibility of being threatening to the client, and therapist self-disclosure and immediacy can also be threatening, in which case they can hold up or slow down rather than facilitate client progress. In fact, we believe that all therapists should focus on providing the highest levels of the responsive dimensions, and appropriate expression of the action dimensions will follow as the therapy relationship develops. This view is supported by the fact that there is an almost total absence of research to support the effectiveness of the action dimensions in therapy, while there is some indication that these dimensions can lead to client deterioration rather than improvement. These three action conditions are thus not necessary independent conditions.

Concreteness

There is one other aspect of therapy that the writers consider very important, though it is almost entirely neglected. That is concreteness, or specificity, first suggested by Truax and Carkhuff (1967). Concreteness, or specificity, involves the use of specific and concrete terminology rather than general or abstract terminology, in the discussion of feelings, experiences, and behavior. Being concrete avoids vagueness and ambiguity. It leads to differentiation of feelings and experiences rather than generalization. Concreteness or specificity is not necessarily the same as practicality, nor is it objectivity. It does not apply to impersonal material — it is *personally relevant* concreteness. It is "the fluent, direct and complete expression of specific feelings and experiences, regardless of their emotional content" (Carkhuff and Berenson 1967, p. 29).

Specificity is the opposite of much of the verbalization of many therapists who attempt to generalize, categorize, and classify with broad labels the feelings and experiences of the client. Many interpretations are generalizations, abstractions, or higher-level labeling (or the inclusion of a specific experience under a higher-level category). Concreteness is the opposite of such labeling. It suggests that such interpretation is not useful but harmful. In addition to being threatening, abstract interpretations cut off client exploration. Rather than permitting an analysis of a problem into its specific aspects, labeling leads to the feeling that the problem is solved and the issue closed. A simple, though perhaps extreme, example would be applying the label "Oedipus complex" to a male client's description of his feelings and attitudes regarding his father and mother. The client might well feel that this solves his problem, that he has insight, and that nothing further need or can be done.

The level of concreteness may vary during different phases of the therapy process. It should be high in the early stages, but later, when the client moves into deeper and more complex material, a high level may be undesirable or even impossible until confused and mixed feelings and emotions are expressed and become clearer. Later, in the ending phases when the client is planning and engaging in action, high levels would again be desirable. In the early stages, concreteness can contribute to empathic understanding because clients are encouraged to be more specific in their communication. (See Patterson 1985 for the Carkhuff Scale for Measuring Concreteness or Specificity.)

Examples of Concreteness

The first example is of a general, abstract response that clearly will not help the client focus on the specifics of the problem:

Client: I don't know just what the problem is. I don't get along with my parents. It's not that I don't like them or that they don't like me. But we seem to disagree on so many things. Maybe they're small and unimportant, but . . . I don't know, we never have been close. . . . There has never, as far as I can remember, been a time when they gave me any spontaneous affection. . . . I just don't know what's wrong.

Therapist: It seems that your present situation is really of long standing and goes back to a long series of difficulties in your development.

Compare this with the following concrete response to the same client statement:

Therapist: Although you feel confused, you do feel your parents haven't shown you direct love or affection. You're not sure they love you. Is that it?

A second therapy excerpt exemplifies a therapist encouraging the client to specify the client's own statement. The therapist is responding to the lack of clarity in the client's thoughts. By focusing on being specific, the therapist helps the client define the problem:

Client: I need to do it so my mom will change how she sees me.
Therapist: Wait, I'm not clear on what is "it."
Client: Well, I guess, let her know I have an opinion.
Therapist: Sounds like, with "I guess," you're not sure.
Client: Oh, I'm sure I should say I do have an opinion. I guess . . . well, I *know*, uh, I don't believe I can do that.
Therapist: So you know what you want to do but are in conflict about actually doing it.
Client: Right. Facing her . . . that's the challenge.

As the client became more specific, he realized that the problem was in asserting himself with a controlling person. Specificity helps the client focus.

Concreteness serves three important functions. First, it keeps the therapist's response close to the client's feelings and experiences. Second, it fosters accurateness of understanding in the therapist, allowing for early client corrections of misunderstanding. Third, concreteness encourages the client to attend to specific problem areas (Carkhuff and Berenson 1967).

By responding in specific and concrete terms to long, general, vague ramblings of the client, the therapist helps the client sift out the personally significant aspects from the irrelevant aspects. Although it might appear that questions of the who, what, when, where, and how type would be useful, this is not the case in a therapeutic relationship. Questions and probing should not dominate the therapy process because they create a context in which the therapist is in control and omniscient, and, simultaneously, the client is unknowing and dependent. The client is thus responding to the therapist rather than the other way around, completely undermining the therapeutic process, which is intended to keep responsibility with the client. Questions should be limited to situations in which the therapist does not understand or cannot follow the client and must ask for clarification.

The Research Evidence

Confrontation

Research on confrontation suggests that high-facilitative therapists, during the first therapy session and even during the first fifteen minutes of the session, use more confrontations focused on the therapy relationship and, within the first thirty minutes, use more confrontations focused on resources rather than pathology and on client actions rather than personality, than do low-facilitative therapists. Low-facilitative therapists focus on client limitations. Beutler et al. (1986), in their review of research on confrontation, refer to a study in which clients reacted to "directive confrontation negatively, with noncompliant responses" (p. 288). Other research reports inconsistent results, with some finding low levels of confrontation being positively related to outcome and others finding positive results with high levels.

One of the problems involved in the study of confrontation involves the definition of the variable. Most studies do not define confrontation as we do in this chapter.

Therapist Self-Disclosure

An early study by Dickenson (1969) found no relationship between therapist self-disclosure and client improvement in individual therapy. Hayward (1974) also found no relationship. A study by Derlega and colleagues (1976) found that therapist self-disclosure increased client self-disclosure only when the client was informed that therapist self-disclosure was appropriate.

Most of the research on therapist self-disclosure consists of analogue studies. In a review of research since 1970, Watkins (1990) reports on thirty-five studies, all of them analogue studies. Generalization from analogue studies to actual therapy situations is impossible. Beutler et al. (1986) note that "nowhere in the literature does one observe such a clear disparity between findings of analogue and clinical investigations as is true with regard to therapist self-disclosure" (p. 289). While analogue studies report positive effects on "clients" (actually college students) in brief, usually single-interview sessions, clinical studies find little effect. Orlinsky and Howard (1986) report on five outcome studies; results are mixed. They conclude that "the net impression is that therapist self-disclosure may occasionally be helpful, but is generally not a powerful mode of therapeutic intervention" (p. 330).

Beutler and colleagues (1994), in reviewing the research on therapist self-disclosure, lament that "research on clinical populations and/or outcome effects is still virtually nonexistent" (p. 256). They conclude that in the absence of a critical mass of studies concerning outcome, very little can be stated with certainty about therapist self-disclosure as a variable in psychotherapy.

Immediacy

There has been little research on immediacy. Referring to a study (Mitchell 1971) that found that clients of therapists who were significantly higher in immediacy than in empathy, warmth, and genuineness showed significant deterioration in therapy, Mitchell and co-authors (1977) note that it is possible that

> immediacy is related strongly to *positive* outcome only within the context of high levels of the interpersonal skills. It may be that high levels of immediacy so enhance the potential of the here-and-now therapist–client relationship for *therapeutic benefit or harm* that such therapist demands to intensify the alliance must be accompanied by high levels of empathy, warmth and genuineness. On the other hand, clinical wisdom suggests to us that a therapist who demands an intense relationship in the context of nonfacilitative levels of the interpersonal skills moves his client toward an intimacy with a person who is unable (or unwilling) to understand him, who remains unconcerned about him and lacking in respect, and who deals with him in a caricature of the professional relationship in a distant, stereotyped, and phony relationship. [p. 490]

Concreteness

Essentially no research has been done on concreteness or specificity in therapy.

These five conditions — confrontation, therapist self-disclosure, immediacy, and concreteness — differ from the three basic conditions. The basic conditions are attitudes; the others are essentially techniques. It appears that they are not necessary but may contribute to the efficiency of the therapy process in some instances in which they are appropriate and not inconsistent or in contradiction with the basic attitudes. Concreteness or specificity, particularly, would appear to be important in facilitating the process of self-exploration in clients.

7

The Client

Therapy . . . is figuring out what my being is.

Client

Introduction

The therapist's immediate goal is to initiate, and continue, a process leading to the ultimate goal. The client is a partner in this process. Therapy is a relationship of two people. A therapy relationship cannot exist without the client's participation. The client must voluntarily enter and actively engage in the process. Psychotherapy is not like medical treatment, where the physician can administer drugs, inject antibiotics, perform surgery, with little or no cooperation or participation by the client.

The client's contribution to a successful outcome is more important than that of the therapist. Frank (1974), following twenty-five years of research, concludes that "the most important determinants of long term improvement lie in the patient" (p. 339). Norcross (1986b) writes, "Experts estimate that about one-third of treatment outcome is due to the therapist and two-thirds to the client. Less than 10 percent of outcome variance is generally added for techniques" (p. 15). These experts presumably include Strupp (1972), who states, "In my judgment, by far the greatest proportion of the variance in therapeutic outcomes is accounted for by patient variables" (p. 411), and Bergin and Lambert (1978), who write:

We believe . . . that the largest variation in therapy outcome is accounted for by preexisting client factors such as motivation for change, and the like. Therapist personal factors account for the second largest proportion of change, with techniques coming in a distant third. [p. 80]

Bergin still held this belief in 1986 when he and his associates wrote, "It is becoming increasingly clear that the attributes of the patient as well as the therapist, play an important part in creating the quality of the therapeutic relationship and in the outcome of psychotherapy" (Lambert et al. 1986, p. 171). It is not clear what variables (other than motivation) these writers had in mind, however, since they are not specified.

There are two kinds of contributions of the client for successful therapy. First, conditions must be present in the client as he or she presents him- or herself for therapy. Those preexisting variables have two classes: demographic variables and client personal characteristics. Second, certain client conditions or activities must be present in the therapy process.

Preexisting Client Variables

Client Demographic Variables

Client age, gender, socioeconomic status, and education have been studied in relation to continuation in therapy and therapy outcome. Social class and education appear to have some influence on continuation in therapy. Neither age, gender, nor social class appears to be related to outcome. No data appear to be available on education in relation to outcome. Thus demographic variables are not useful in selecting clients for psychotherapy.

Client Personal Characteristics

Surprisingly, intelligence shows no clear relationship to either continuation in or outcome of psychotherapy. Performance on the Rorschach or the Minnesota Multiphasic Personality Inventory bears no clear relationship to continuation or outcome. Client expectations likewise show mixed findings. Garfield (1986) notes, "It appears that the degree of importance client expectations have as predictors of outcome in psychotherapy is still to be determined" (p. 243). The research on motivation is equivocal. While diagnosis might be expected to be related to continuation and outcome, no significant findings have been reported. The same is true for degree of disturbance.

It is certainly disappointing that Garfield's exhaustive review and analysis provide no support for predicting continuance or outcome from client variables. Not that such relationships may not exist. Experience and reason would seem to indicate that client expectations and motivation are important. Garfield notes the deficiencies in measurement and research in this area. Glencavage and Norcross (1990), in their review of fifty publications, found that 26 percent of the publications listed client positive expectations, hope, or faith as a common element.

In his classic article, Rogers (1957a) lists two client conditions as being necessary and sufficient for positive therapy outcome. The first must be present before, or when, therapy begins.

Client Vulnerability

Only two of fifty articles on commonalities list distress or incongruence in the client, and the same number list the clients' active seeking of help (Glencavage and Norcross 1990). This is surprising in view of the Rogers article (Rogers's article was not one of the fifty reviewed). However, only fifteen of the articles apparently consider client

128   *Successful Psychotherapy*

characteristics, so the percentage is actually thirteen of those including client characteristics.

Rogers's (1957a) condition states that "the client is in a state of incongruence, being vulnerable or anxious" (p. 200). Incongruence

> refers to a discrepancy between the actual experiences of the organism and the self picture of the individual insofar as it represents that experience. . . . [T]here is a fundamental discrepancy between the experienced meaning of the situation as it registers in his organism and the symbolic representation of that experience in awareness in such a way that it does not conflict with the picture he has of himself. . . . When the individual has no awareness of such incongruence in himself, then he is merely vulnerable to the possibility of anxiety and disorganization. . . . If the individual dimly perceives such incongruence in himself, then a tension state occurs which is known as anxiety. [pp. 96–97]

Simply put, the individual is in conflict and anxious; she or he hurts and is unhappy, discouraged, depressed, or dissatisfied. There are feelings of inadequacy, failure, unfulfilled desires or aspirations. Life lacks meaning, goals, a sense of direction. There is a discrepancy between the self-concept and the self-ideal: the individual is not what he or she wants to be or can be and is aware of this discrepancy. The following passage is a client statement of why she sought counseling:

> When I decided to see a counselor I was totally . . . "crazy" isn't the right word, because crazy is what I thought you had to be to go see a counselor. I don't think I'm crazy. I just think I have a lot of messed-up thoughts. What made me make the decision to come in was that my mind was so . . . I didn't have control over it. It seemed like everything in life was not working right and all I could do was cry.

Though the client may not, and usually does not, express it in these terms, she or he is not a self-actualizing person or is less self-actualizing than her or his potential. The drive for self-actualization is frustrated or not satisfied, which motivates a desire or drive to change. This state would appear to be the *prima facie* evidence of motivation for help. That the client presents her- or himself for therapy and continues in therapy is objective evidence of this motivation.

While it may appear that Rogers deals with internal conflicts, with intrapersonal problems, this is not actually the case. The conflicts originate in interpersonal experiences and are internalized by the client.

This condition of incongruence requires that a client is aware of the existence of a problem or problems, at least to the extent that she or he feels the need of help. In other words, the client voluntarily presents her- or himself for therapy. However, it is possible to offer therapy when this condition is not present, that is, with so-called involuntary clients (see Patterson 1990). In some cases the person will become aware of problems and recognize the need for psychotherapy.

Client Perception of the Therapist Conditions

Rogers's (1957a) second client condition states that "the communication to the client of the therapist's empathic understanding and unconditional positive regard is to a minimal degree achieved" (p. 96). He continues:

> Unless some communication of these attitudes has been achieved, then such attitudes do not exist in the relationship as far as the client is concerned, and the therapeutic process could not . . . be initiated. Since attitudes cannot be directly perceived, it might be somewhat more accurate to state that the therapist behaviors and words are perceived by the client as meaning that to some degree the therapist accepts and understands him. [p. 99]

The research evidence indicates that, in relating therapist qualities to outcome, "the proportion of positive findings is highest across all outcome categories when therapist warmth and acceptance are observed from the patients' process perspective. Here, again, the most decisive aspect of therapeutic process seems to be the patients' experience of it" (Orlinsky and Howard 1986, p. 348). This client statement exemplifies the felt condition of acceptance:

> . . . And it's like the major thing that I feel is there is a lot of the abandon feeling that I feel . . . because I'm afraid that I might say or do something to make someone leave. I guess that's why when I come here [to therapy] . . . that I don't worry about that because I don't. . . . It's like, you're not going to leave. . . . You're going to be there. . . . I can say anything I feel. I can look anyway I want to look. I can sit anywhere I want to sit and it doesn't matter. . . . Any other time it's like I can't be or do these things.

That external observations or ratings of the conditions also have been found to be related to outcomes suggests that observers are able to recognize if or when the client perceives the conditions in the therapist (see Watson 1984). The inability — or refusal — of the client to perceive the conditions is one of the reasons therapy is so difficult or even impossible with clients who are out of touch with reality (psychotic) or because of personality disorders (sociopathy) refuse to enter a relationship.

Thus, clients present themselves to the counselor or psychotherapist as persons who are motivated to change, at least to the extent that they are ready to commit time and, often, money to achieve this change. Clients have faith and confidence in the therapist and his or her methods, so that they trust themselves to the relationship. And they are able to perceive, at least to a minimal degree, the therapist's respect, interest, concern, and understanding. These are the conditions in the client that make possible the beginning of therapy.

While it would appear that some motivation to seek help is a necessary condition for psychotherapy, belief in the therapist and her or his methods, while desirable, may not be necessary. That this is so is suggested by the fact that some people get help and improve where no strong belief or faith is present (so-called "spontaneous remission"). Some clients may begin therapy out of a motive to relieve their pain, with little trust or even a manifested suspicion of the therapist. It is necessary, however, for the client to perceive the conditions and to begin to trust the therapist to progress in therapy.

Structuring the Client's Work

Clients present themselves to the therapist with some uncertainty, doubts, hesitations, anxiety, and even fear connected with the therapy situation and the therapist. They may not know what to expect or may have misconceptions about the process, what the therapist will do, and what they are expected to do. Some examples of client statements follow:

Client: I was real nervous because I didn't want to come over here and tell her. . . . First of all I didn't know what I was going to have to tell her. I didn't want to tell her my whole life because that was *my* whole life and it was *my* business. I didn't want to go telling anybody my whole life.

Client: Maybe I played out the fantasy where the prince [the therapist] comes for the princess—that I would want you to rescue me.

Client: When I first came in, I was wondering what you were going to do to make me better. After the session I wondered what that was all about. At first, I didn't feel any better. I didn't see anything to it. I'm not real sure why I kept coming back except that . . . I felt better after it was over. I guess I was letting a lot of stress out. I thought counseling was that I lay on the couch and you said things like, "You hated your mother" . . . you know, things like that. And where you ask me questions and I answer and everything is right, but it's not that way.

Although many clients do not need explanations about what they are expected to do, some clients are helped by having the therapist clarify the needed behavior through structuring. Part of the structuring consists of explaining to clients the nature of the client's work, which is essentially to talk about themselves, their feelings, attitudes, and experiences. Cultural norms may enter into the client's expectations and comfort level. Structuring clarifies the process so that the client has a choice to continue given the definition of therapy. Even when clients recognize and accept the task, it is often not easy for them to do it. They may begin in a perfunctory way or may only be able to give a general, superficial statement of their problems and then wait, depending on the therapist for help. This may be perceived by the therapist as a time to structure to ensure that the client knows what to do. A pause may be interpreted as the client asking the therapist to take the lead. However, a superficial summary statement and pause by the client may be a first attempt at evaluating the level of trust in the relationship. The prospect of revealing oneself openly to another is threatening. Before clients can speak honestly about their problems, they want to believe they are safe in doing so. The following is a client statement that exemplifies the point:

> I sort of told you a sweeping big picture of what happened because I wanted to see how you were going to react. If you thought I was horrible or were shocked, I sure wasn't going to tell you the rest of it.

If clients are to engage in their work, they need *at the very least* an absence of perceived threat to the self. The facilitative conditions provided by the therapist minimize threat. Love — real love — is challenging but not threatening. Learning, it is recognized, does not occur under conditions of severe threat. Behavior becomes restricted and narrowed rather than variable and exploratory, as is necessary for problem solving.

It is important that the therapist communicate these conditions and that the client perceive them. Only when the client feels accepted, respected, understood, safe, and secure with the therapist can she or he begin to make progress. With an anxious, fearful, threatened, and hesitant client, the therapist must be patient and persist in communicating the conditions to establish a nonthreatening atmosphere. There are no shortcuts or techniques to substitute for the core conditions. They stand as sufficient on their own. The only variable is the client's level of threat and how long that client needs to begin to trust the therapist. The therapist's role is to offer the conditions consistently.

The therapy relationship, like any other human relationship, takes time to develop. Prolonged silence on the part of the therapist can be highly threatening. On the other hand, profuse verbalization and reassurance can be inhibiting to the client. The process of therapy is an artful balance. It may be slow in beginning. There is and can be no such thing as instant intimacy.

Client Self-Exploration

When the therapist and client conditions are present, to at least a minimal degree, and the therapist conditions are perceived by the client, that client is enabled to engage in the necessary process of self-exploration. The therapist's attitudes, expressed through the core conditions, create an environment of nonjudgment and acceptance. When clients become aware of the acceptance, they become more accepting of themselves and their own range of feelings. A client statement elucidates the point:

> When you seem so laid-back, it's like I can be angry or afraid and you don't get angry back. Most people, I can't show how afraid I am because they get irritated. You don't. You just sit there and don't get upset. It feels like I can come here and get angry and complain all I want — get it all out just like it is — not pretending or holding back and because you just can take it and not get upset . . . you are patient. . . . It's OK to let it out. I'm not afraid to let it out with you.

Clients must be able, in some way and at least to some degree, to express or communicate their feelings, attitudes, thoughts, and experiences to the therapist. The most empathic therapist cannot understand clients or enter their frames of reference unless clients in some way communicate how they see themselves and the world. The most common and effective way is, of course, through verbalization. There are other ways of communicating in addition to verbalization, and the therapist must be sensitive to these; for example, sometimes the client's writing or such other expressive activities as art may communicate (see Pearson 1965). These, while helpful in addition to verbalization, are usually not adequate by themselves. They may be at least the bridge to a relationship.

There have been many discussions of the counseling process in terms of client involvement. But the basic activity of the client is to engage in a process of self-exploration or intrapersonal exploration. In every approach to psychotherapy, clients talk about themselves, about their beliefs, attitudes, feelings, experiences, thoughts, and actions. Considerable research supports the existence of a relationship between client self-exploration and successful therapy or favorable outcomes (Carkhuff 1969, Carkhuff and Berenson 1967, Truax and Carkhuff 1969). Much research also indicates that the level of client self-exploration is related to and influenced by the level of facilitative conditions provided by the therapist. However, there are differences among clients in their levels of self-exploration that are not related to therapist levels of the conditions (Truax and Carkhuff 1967, p. 192).

The process of self-exploration is a complex one, involving several aspects or (perhaps) stages. Self-disclosure is the first stage.

Self-Disclosure

Before clients can explore themselves, they must disclose or reveal themselves. In the beginning of counseling, this is most often the disclosure of negative aspects of themselves—problems, failures, inadequacies, and so on. Since these constitute the bases of the client's dissatisfaction and unhappiness, they are the reasons clients have sought counseling. But since they are negative—indicating a low or negative self-concept—they are difficult to express. Self-disclosure at this level represents self-exposure.

The question often arises among students about the desirability of accepting, or listening with acceptance to, extensive disclosures of negative feelings and emotions, self-negation and self-criticism, the expression of feelings of worthlessness, discouragement, depression, even suicide. Is this likely to reinforce these feelings and make the client worse? Should the counselor reassure clients that things are not as bad as they think they are, that clients are not as bad as they think they are? One client expressed her perception of reassurance:

> You know, when I told you how bleak it all looked to me, how I just thought I was crazy and would never make it out of this, you just stayed with me. You never told me not to feel the way I felt, or that I was stupid for feeling that way. My sister says, "Oh, don't say that. You don't really feel that way. Everything will be better tomorrow." I think then that she doesn't want to hear me. She can't stand it that I might feel bad. At that moment I do feel that way and sometimes I just want to say it. . . . I just want someone to hear it, to know.

The therapist must remember that clients come to therapy just because they have problems, negative feelings such as hate and fear, and to some extent a negative self-concept. Their low opinions of themselves are not (usually) simply a misperception or unrealistic — there is some basis in reality. They are failing to be their best selves, to be self-actualizing persons. To deny the client's feeling that this is the case is not to help clients but to prevent them from going on to recognize the positive aspects of themselves and their situations. The process of reaching the positive cannot be short-circuited. If clients are to reach a positive self-concept, they must be allowed to express negative feelings. The counselor must be willing and able to go with them to the depths and face the worst with them; the counselor must not allow his or her own anxiety, fears, and discomfort to prevent this descent. It is only when they have plumbed the depths and revealed themselves at their worst that clients can rise again and, accepting themselves, build a new positive self. This client expressed a need to experience feelings: "Don't try to alleviate suffering. I had to face it to get through it."

The assumption is that there is some good in every client, something positive in every situation, but that clients can only recognize this if they are allowed to express the worst:

Client: Things look pretty discouraging.
Therapist: It's pretty grim.
Client: It's worse than that—it's hopeless.
Therapist: There's just *no* hope.
Client: No—none at all. There's no way out.
Therapist: It's the end—a dead end—completely black, without a ray of light or hope.
Client: (pause) Well—maybe not completely. I'm not ready to give up completely yet.

Furthermore, such negative talk may be a real expression of the feeling the client has for self at that moment. To deny that feeling is to deny that the client knows her or his own feelings. Some clients suffer from not knowing how they feel, being out of touch with or not trusting their own feelings. By having others deny the client's feelings, there is the communication of two deeply destructive messages. One is that the *client* does not *know* how she or he feels. And the other is that *someone else knows* more about the client's feelings than does the *client*. Both messages alienate the client from his or her self. One of the goals of self-disclosure is self-awareness. This awareness is a sense of knowing how one feels and being able to say, "This is how I feel."

If a client can see no hope and does give up, possibly he or she is right—it is the end. And reassurance by or optimism on the part of the counselor is not likely to help.

The relationship between the therapist and client is an essential part of the initiation of change. When a client presents the worst to a therapist and that therapist can still accept the client as a human being worthy of respect, the client can begin to accept the self as worthy of respect. This is a starting point for positive changes.

Rogers (1961) developed an elaborate scale to cover the whole course of therapy. Clients who are able to disclose themselves are already at stage 4. Rogers gives this example of a client at stage 4: "I'm not living up to what I am. I really should be doing more than I am" (p. 139).

Rogers notes that successful cases begin at a higher level on the process scale than do unsuccessful cases. At stage 4, the client has perceived that the therapist understands him or her and is able to engage in self-disclosure. It is the difficulty of reaching this level with seriously disturbed clients that is responsible for many dropouts from therapy and thus the failures with the more severely disturbed. We should note that failure is not only cases of the client not being capable of communicating understanding to the therapist, but also of the therapist being unwilling to understand the worldview of the client, as the following client statement reveals:

Client: For years I didn't tell anyone what was going on because they always said, "Oh, you're crazy." My psychiatrist said, "You want someone to believe you!" as if what I was experiencing wasn't real. It was real for me, you can believe that. So I just didn't tell anyone. It wasn't until someone listened to me, really listened to what I was dealing with here, that I began to believe I could do something about it.

Rates of Self-Exploration

Once clients have disclosed themselves, put themselves out and on view to themselves and the therapist, and, importantly, *if* they have been accepted, they are able to look at themselves and to engage in the process of exploring what and who they are. It is a time to explore and try out new behaviors, thoughts and ideas, new ways of being. One client says of this practice, "This is my time to think things through without committing to it . . . to sort of try on various ideas." Clients can be themselves in a way they cannot in ordinary interpersonal relationships; they can be open, real, and honest with themselves as well as with the therapist. They are able to face themselves as they are. As the client expressed herself earlier in this chapter: "I can say anything I feel. I can look anyway I want to look. I can sit anywhere I want to sit and it doesn't matter. . . . Any other time it's like I can't be or do these things." The therapist's attitudes create an environment of acceptance where clients are free to express themselves without fear of being judged. When there is a low perceived threat to the self, the client can reveal even the most hidden thoughts and experiences.

The process of self-exploration does not proceed simultaneously and at equivalent levels in all areas of the client's life, with all problems, or in all aspects of his or her difficulties. Progress may occur to some extent in one area and then be blocked or slow down. The client shifts to another area only to reach a level beyond which he or she is not ready or able to go. This may repeat itself in still other areas. Eventually the client returns to the first area and each of the other areas, to progress further. Exploration in each area makes it possible to explore the other areas more deeply. It is not useful or possible to insist that the client stick to one area or problem until it is thoroughly explored before moving on to another. The total process is not a logical but rather a psychological one in which the areas or problems are interrelated and cannot be explored completely as independent problems. As in other areas of learning, in learning about oneself there are plateaus, places where the client may rest briefly, where there is an impediment to further progress in a particular area, perhaps because of some internal threat or discomfort. It may also represent an attempt to consolidate progress.

Client: I'm skipping around a lot.

Therapist: You're saying just what comes to mind. Right now it feels like you're going from one thing to another.

Client: Yeah. I feel like I'm repeating myself, too.

Therapist: Uh-huh, you've talked about the same thing before.

Client: But really it's different, something about it is different. Like I'm seeing it in a different light now. And it seems like all the pieces maybe fit into a puzzle, only now I'm just gathering up the pieces. They're important but I don't know the big picture yet. I wish I had your patience. You don't mind waiting for it to fall into place.

Therapist: You have a sense that all of the bits and pieces fit together in some way, but you really don't know how. You'd like to hurry it up.

> *Client*: Yeah, hurry it up . . . but also . . . I don't know what's there. It's sort of . . . scary, you know — I'm not sure what's there.
>
> *Therapist*: You seem to have two feelings at one time. Hurry it up and don't go so fast that you get too scared. You need to go at your own pace.
>
> *Client*: Yeah, keep a balance . . . not get too far ahead of myself.

Clients begin where they are able to begin and, usually, in areas where they are most conscious of a problem. They move to other relevant areas and problems when they are ready and able to do so in the nonthreatening relationship. To attempt to push clients or to direct them toward other areas the therapist considers important is to introduce threat and to risk retarding rather than facilitating the client's self-exploration. In cross-cultural counseling, it is even more apparent that therapists are less informed than clients on issues (especially cultural issues) relevant to the client's work. Assuming no two people have exactly the same experiences, then it is realistic to assert that any client has more personally relevant information with which to proceed than does the therapist (see Chapter 9).

Attempting to introduce action conditions (see Chapter 6), such as confronting in particular, as the client is beginning the exploration of new areas or problems, also can be inhibiting. These conditions can be threatening. The continuation of one of the client quotes from earlier in the chapter illuminates the importance of the client's sense of readiness:

> Maybe I play out the fantasy where the prince [the therapist] comes for the princess . . . that I would want you to rescue me, but then I realize that I may not want to be rescued . . . that maybe I'm a prisoner within myself . . . within my own right and only I have the key that unlocks my heart and soul when I'm ready. For you to attempt to do so may just push me further into seclusion since I may not be ready to come out of hiding.

This client and all clients decide what to say and when to say it. If that right to decide is violated or frustrated, clients have the option to resist. When the therapist trusts the client to lead the way, the client learns to trust her- or himself. The trusted self then can act as a knowledgeable guide — in therapy and in life.

In 1963, Truax (Truax and Carkhuff 1967) developed a nine-point Depth of Self-Exploration Scale. Carkhuff (1969, Vol. II) revised this into a five-level scale for measuring client self-exploration in interpersonal processes. These scales give descriptions and examples of levels of self-exploration.

Client Awareness and the Basic Self

The process of self-exploration leads to *self-discovery, self-understanding,* and *self-awareness,* among other things. This is more than what is commonly meant by insight, which is usually an intellectualized statement of a problem in terms of its origins or etiology. Self-understanding is not limited to intrapersonal processes but includes an understanding of the impact the client has on other people, or the nature of his or her functioning in interpersonal relationships. Clients begin to see themselves, at least to some extent, as others see them.

Self-exploration reveals inconsistencies and contradictions. Attitudes and feelings that have been experienced but denied to awareness are discovered. Experiences inconsistent with the self-concept or self-image, previously denied or distorted, become symbolized in awareness. Clients become more open to their experiences.

With increasing self-awareness, clients' self-concepts become clearer. And with clear self-concepts their vague dissatisfactions with themselves become more specific. They begin to see in what specific respects they are failing to measure up to their self-ideals. They begin to reorganize their self-concepts to assimilate all their experiences of themselves; the self-concept becomes more congruent with experiences and thus more realistic. In turn, clients' perceptions of their ideal selves become more realistic and more attainable, and their selves become more congruent with their ideal selves. With these changes in the self and self-concept, clients become more accepting of themselves and feel more confident and self-directing. They experience more acceptance from others, both because they perceive more realistically and accurately and because their changed selves elicit more positive reactions from others. They become fully functioning persons, more self-actualizing persons (Rogers 1959). Their feelings of adequacy and self-esteem increase.

In some cases clients have become so alienated from themselves that they must rediscover their own existence. These clients have been so discounted by criticism and harsh personal treatment that they barely have contact with their existence as a self. For them, part of the healing process is to become aware of the self—to listen to themselves, to trust themselves, to respect themselves again.

This change is initiated by the attitudes of the therapist through the core conditions. It is the therapist who first facilitates the client's awareness of her or his attitude toward the self. The therapist accomplishes this by listening to, trusting, and respecting the client. Thus the client becomes aware of the self as one who is worth listening to, can be trusted, and is worthy of respect. It is important for clients to be aware of others in their interpersonal environment, and it is equally important for clients to be aware of themselves as a part of their interpersonal world.

In the process of developing self-understanding and self-awareness, both positive and negative attitudes about the self arise. Not all that clients discover about themselves is negative or bad. Experiences that at first do not seem to belong to and cannot be integrated into the self become accepted as the self. Clients discover they can *be* themselves with all of their diverse and sometimes contradictory feelings and experiences. As the process continues, negative attitudes toward the self decrease and positive attitudes increase. For example, a client said, "I told you when we first started working that I felt I was evil. Now I don't think I'm evil, but I don't know if I'm good." Clients can then go beyond acceptance of self to actually *liking* themselves. The self that emerges—the deep, basic nature of the client—is not bad, antisocial, or destructive. The core of the self "is not bad, nor terribly wrong, but something positive. Underneath the layer of controlled surface behavior, underneath the bitterness, underneath the hurt, is a self that is positive, that is without hate" (Rogers 1961, p. 101).

In a very significant way, then, therapy does not necessarily require the changing of the basic self or its freeing so that the client can be his or her real, basic self. The conditions of therapy provide a nonthreatening environment in which the client does not have to respond negatively, aggressively, or defensively but can be the self that she or he really is or is capable of being. Therapy is, then, a situation in which clients can be themselves — their best selves, the potential selves that have been covered up or not allowed to develop by the absence of the conditions of good interpersonal relationships. In terms of the relation of the self-concept and the self-ideal, the discrepancy may be reduced by change in the self-ideal as much as, if not more than, by change in the self-concept. Or, perhaps more accurately, changes in the self-concept may occur without changes in the basic self.

It is important that the process of self-exploration not be confused with client talk *about* themselves. This is often a problem with students beginning supervised practice. By continued questioning, they get clients to make statements about themselves and mistake this for client self-exploration. But in such talk clients (as well as the therapist) are viewing themselves as objects and are not actually expressing or disclosing themselves. Their talk is externally oriented, abstract, generalized — an intellectual or rational discourse about themselves as objects.

Insight and Action

Insight, it frequently has been stated, is not enough. Self-understanding is not acceptable as a goal of counseling or psychotherapy. There must be action or changes in client behavior, or therapy cannot be considered successful. We have noted that Carkhuff and Berenson (1967) claim that traditional therapies stop at self-understanding and insight. They suggest that the core or facilitative conditions lead to insight but not to action and that new conditions, the action conditions, must be introduced in a second phase of psychotherapy to move the client beyond understanding to action.

In consideration of the counselor's implementation of the conditions, we have indicated that we prefer to think in terms of a single process rather than two processes, of a continuous process rather than two phases. Action conditions represent high levels of facilitative conditions within a mature therapeutic relationship. Although we agree that successful therapy includes changes in the client, the nature of these changes may vary from client to client. The client chooses the adaptations he or she will make. In fact, the client may choose not to change certain overt behavior at that time, while changing in awareness of the problem as it exists.

The choice of behavior change is up to the client and need not be evaluated by the therapist as a good or bad change. The manifestation of change is often a value judgment. The definition of what is an "action" is relative. No action, such as *not* leaving a poor relationship or *not* confronting a problem, is also an outcome of successful therapy. Perhaps a better word is *choice*. A self-aware client is capable of making an intentional choice concerning behavior. The best indication of change from the therapist's perspective is the development of this awareness in the client.

Action by the client or changes in behavior accompany or follow as a natural consequence of the development of self-awareness. In fact, as has been noted by many writers, action or changes in behavior may precede insight, or a clear verbalizable understanding, or self-awareness. Action and understanding are interacting or reciprocal processes. In healthy people understanding and action are often simultaneous. Carkhuff (1969, Vol. II) suggests that low-functioning persons, including the majority of clients, are unable to act on their self-understanding and must be pushed by the therapist. If, in the process of therapy, clients can develop self-understanding and begin to function in the therapy relationship at a higher level, why assume they cannot then act on their understanding? It is possible that the problem is one of time, with an impatient therapist being unable or reluctant to wait for the client to begin acting and changing behaviors.

Some might question, as Albert Ellis (1962) does, that when therapists know the problem, why "wait passively" for the client to come to an insight? The point goes deeper than an impatience or even a "time is money" issue. The focus should be on the consequences of how the client is being treated. For example, what message is given by doing something for those who can do it themselves? Whose needs are being fulfilled by jumping in and finishing off the task? The therapist who is so anxious might better respond to the client than to him- or herself.

It is apparent that the client's behavior does change in the therapy relationship itself. Clients disclose themselves and engage in productive self-exploration, which they were not able to do before. They develop and express self-awareness. They become more accepting of themselves. They become more accepting of others, including the therapist. They become more open, honest, and genuine. In other words, they become more like the therapist is in the relationship; they manifest the conditions of a good interpersonal relationship — empathic understanding, respect and warmth, genuineness, and concreteness. They become, within the therapy relationship, more self-actualizing persons. The following is a client quote explaining how she tries to take into her life what she has learned about relating in therapy:

> I try being myself in here and then I go out and I try being myself out there. Sometimes it works and sometimes it gets all confused with old stuff again. So I come here and kind of get back to who I am . . . then I try it again. I'm getting better at just being myself out there. I really am happier when I can do that.

The result of therapy, then, is that clients become more self-actualizing persons. The characteristics of the self-actualizing person include the facilitative conditions of a good human relationship. Clients, in becoming more like the therapist, manifest the conditions to which they are exposed. There is no question that the generalization of these changes outside the therapy relationship is a difficult and slow process. It does occur, and it is facilitated by the fact that, through the principle of reciprocal affect, the persons with whom the client relates become more accepting, understanding, and genuine.

Furthermore, in terms of more specific or more concrete changes in behavior, the client's basic drive toward self-actualization, freed from its frustration by a lack of facilitative interpersonal relationships, produces changes in the client. The motivation is there, the self-understanding is present, and, to the extent possible in his or her external environment, the client's behavior changes. In perceptual or phenomenological terms, the client's perceptions have changed, and her or his behavior changes accordingly. With a change in the self-concept, behavior then changes to become consistent with the self-concept, which is a basic determiner of behavior. Specific behavior changes occur as a by-product of self-actualization.

The Research Evidence

Research on client self-exploration is difficult to interpret. Orlinsky and Howard (1986), reviewing thirty-seven studies, write, "Somewhat surprisingly, the overwhelming majority of findings (26 out of 37) showed no significant process–outcome relationship, across all categories of outcome measurement" (p. 331), although over half of the studies of the relation of observer process ratings and therapist's outcome evaluations are positive. Orlinsky and Howard note that observers' ratings do not represent clients' experience of the process. They also note that only two of the nineteen studies using the Truax scale are positive, while five of thirteen using other measures are positive. In addition, they give as "another plausible reason for finding so low a proportion of significant effects . . . the likelihood that patient self-exploration is a very common occurrence in psychotherapy" and "would often be found in unsuccessful as well as successful cases" (p. 331).

Characteristics that would appear to be relevant to client participation in the process, if not in self-exploration, have been found to be related to success. Amount of patient speech is related positively to outcome (Orlinsky and Howard 1986). Patient expressiveness — such as feeling-oriented voice quality, variety of word usage, ease of communication of feelings, and use of polysyllables — also appears to be related to outcome. Patients' use of personal as opposed to nonpersonal language is also related to outcome (Orlinsky and Howard 1986). Orlinsky and Howard (1986) conclude that "patient expressiveness constitutes an especially significant influence on outcome" (p. 348). Also patient self-relatedness — openness to feelings — was found to be related to outcome in fourteen of sixteen studies (Orlinsky and Howard). Therapeutic realization ("all those signs *within the therapeutic process* that indicate that therapy is making a positive impact on the patient," such as insight) is also related to outcome (fourteen of eighteen studies) (Orlinsky and Howard 1986, pp. 360–361).

The Client in the Process

Rogers (1959) describes the client in the process:

The Process of Therapy
1. The client is increasingly free in expressing his feelings, through verbal and/or motor channels.
2. His expressed feelings increasingly have reference to the self, rather than nonself.
3. He increasingly differentiates and discriminates the objects of his feelings and perceptions . . . . [H]is experiences are more accurately symbolized.
4. His expressed feelings increasingly have reference to the incongruity between certain of his experiences and his concept of self.
5. He comes to experience in awareness the threat of such incongruence . . . because of the continued unconditional positive regard of the therapist. . . .
6. He experiences fully, in awareness, feelings which have in the past been denied to awareness, or distorted in awareness.

7. His concept of self becomes reorganized to assimilate and include these experiences which have previously been distorted or denied in awareness.

8. As reorganization of the self-structure continues, his concept of self becomes increasingly congruent with his experiences. . . . [D]efensiveness is decreased.

9. He becomes increasingly able to experience, without a feeling of threat, the therapist's unconditional positive regard.

10. He increasingly feels an unconditional positive self-regard.

11. He increasingly experiences himself as the locus of evaluation.

12. He reacts to experience less in terms of his conditions of worth and more in terms of an organismic valuing process. [p. 216]

The Client's Experience of the Therapist and the Therapy Situation

The experience of the client in the relationship is critical to the process of therapy. This is because change is initiated in response to the therapeutic relationship. A descriptive account of the client's experience is given by Rogers (1951) in his book, *Client-Centered Therapy: Its Practice, Implications, and Theory* (pp. 65–130; see also Rogers 1961, Chapters 5, 6, and 7). The client's perceptions are initially influenced by what the client expects of the therapist and the therapy situation. These expectations vary and include feelings ranging from fear to eager anticipation, but an ambivalent, fearful feeling seems most characteristic. Progress is facilitated when both the client and therapist perceive the relationship in the same way. It is important to note that verbal structuring of the relationship by the therapist, which was earlier considered desirable, does not necessarily lead to a common perception of the relationship.

Client perceptions of the relationship may vary initially but become more similar. When the therapist is perceived favorably as helpful, it is as someone who listens with warmth, interest, and understanding. At first, the client-centered therapist may frustrate the client who expects advice, but this way of being is later perceived as leading to self-exploration and understanding. Concerning her search for a therapist, a client said, "When I was hurting and wanted help, I think what I really want is for someone to listen to me, to acknowledge what I say, and accept me. I don't want to have to defend myself or my life. I'm not stupid or incompetent. I just need free time to work things through." The therapy hour becomes a stable, safe experience in an otherwise unstable life. The "free time" mentioned by the client is time unencumbered by the judgments of others. The client's experience is that the therapy session is a personally accepting environment in which to explore the self.

How Therapy Is Experienced by the Client

The experiencing of responsibility.   The client soon discovers that he or she is responsible for him- or herself in the relationship, which may lead to various feelings. Some clients experience a sense of being alone, annoyed, or angry and a growing sense and acceptance of responsibility. Many clients seek to maintain responsibility for themselves and recognize the therapist's effort to keep responsibility with the client as an act of respect. A client statement exemplifies this point: "I know what's going on with me, and therapists who try to tell me what's going on with me . . . are arrogant and usually off base. That's so disrespectful. It discounts me."

The experiencing of exploration.   As therapy develops, the client explores her or his attitudes and feelings. The client reacts with both fear and positive interest as inconsistencies and contradictions are discovered in the client's self. Honesty in facing this self develops in the nonthreatening therapeutic relationship. Verbal exploration takes place in the interview. Exploration continues, sometimes unverbalized, between interviews. The client may bring this exploration to the therapy session in the form of ideas, dreams, journals, poetry, and other art forms.

The discovery of denied attitudes. As a result of exploration, attitudes that have been experienced but denied to awareness are discovered. Both positive and negative attitudes arise. Experiences inconsistent with the self-concept, formerly denied or distorted, become symbolized in awareness.

The experiencing of reorganizing the self. The bringing of denied experiences into awareness necessitates the reorganization of the self. The client views him- or herself more positively, as a more adequate person; the client's acceptance of him- or herself increases. This changed perception of the self must begin before the client can become aware of and accept denied experiences. The permitting of more experiential data to enter awareness leads to a more realistic appraisal of the self, relationships, and the environment and to an acknowledgment of the basis of standards within her- or himself. The change in the self may be great or small, with more or less accompanying pain and confusion. More or less disorganization may precede the final organization, and the process may fluctuate up or down. The emotions that accompany the process, although fluctuating, appear to be mainly those of fearfulness, unhappiness, and depression; they are not consistent with actual progress, so that a deep insight may be followed by strong despair. The process of reorganizing the self, of becoming oneself or becoming a person, includes various aspects (see Rogers 1961, Chapter 6). One may be termed "getting behind the mask." In the atmosphere of freedom of the counseling relationship, the client begins to drop false fronts, roles, or masks and tries to discover something more truly him- or herself. The client is able to explore the self and its experience, facing the contradictions that are discovered and the facades behind which he or she has been hiding. The client may discover that he or she seems to have no individual self but exists only in relation to the values and demands of others. There is, however, a compelling need to search for and become oneself.

The part of being one's real self is the experiencing of feelings to their limits, so that the person *is* her or his fear, anger, love, and so on.

There is a

> free experiencing of the actual sensory and visceral reactions of
> the organism without too much of an attempt to relate these
> experiences to the self. This is usually accompanied by the
> conviction that this material does not belong to, and cannot be
> organized into, the self. The end point of the process is that the
> client discovers that he can *be* his experience with all of its variety
> and surface contradiction; that he can formulate himself out of
> his experience instead of trying to impose a formulation of self
> upon his experience, denying to awareness these elements which
> do not fit. [Rogers 1961, p. 80]

In experiencing these elements of the self, the client senses an
emerging unit, harmony, or pattern. All these experiences are part of
the potential self, which is being discovered.

The result of the reorganization of the self is not merely accepting
the self but also liking the self. It is not a bragging, self-assertive liking
but a "quiet joy in being one's self, together with the apologetic attitude
which, in our culture, one feels it is necessary to take toward such an
experience" (Rogers 1961, p. 87). It is a satisfying, enjoyable appreciation of oneself as a whole and functioning person.

The process of therapy is not the solving of problems; it is the
experiencing of feelings, leading to the being of oneself. It "is a process
whereby man becomes his organism — without self-deception, without
distortion" (Rogers 1961, p. 103). One becomes capable of perceiving
oneself as *acceptable* — without the need of pretending to be something
more. Thus, rather than acting in terms of the expectations of others,
a person acts in terms of her or his own experiences. It is the full
awareness of these experiences, achieved in therapy, that makes it
possible for the person to come to *be in awareness* what she or he *is in
experience* — a complete and fully functioning human organism.

The experiencing of progress.   Almost from the beginning, the
client feels that progress is being made. This progress is felt even when
confusion and depression are present. The facing and resolving of
some issues and the reconstructing of a segment of personality

represent progress and give the client confidence in continuing to explore him- or herself, even though the exploration continues to be upsetting.

The experiencing of ending. The client determines when to end the counseling. Sometimes the end is preceded by a period during which the time between interviews is lengthened. Often it is accompanied by feelings of fear, a sense of loss, or a reluctance to give up counseling, so that the ending may be postponed for an interview or two.

The Process of Conception of Psychotherapy

On the basis of listening to many therapy interviews, Rogers (1961, Chapter 7) made abstractions of the therapy process. A continuum emerges, not from fixity to flux but from stasis to process. Seven stages of the process are discriminated. At any one time, the client, taken as a whole, falls within a relatively narrow range on this continuum of personality change, although in given areas of personal meaning, the client may be at different stages. However, for any specific area, there is a regularity of progression through the stages, although there are some retreats along with the general advance.

First stage. In the first stage, there is "an unwillingness to communicate self. Communication is only about externals. Feelings and personal meanings are neither recognized nor owned. . . . Close and communicative relationships are construed as dangerous. No problems are recognized or perceived at this stage. There is no desire to change" (Rogers 1961, p. 132). Individuals at this stage do not come voluntarily for therapy.

Second stage. If the individual in the first stage can be reached through the providing of optimal conditions for facilitating change, then "expression begins to flow in regard of non-self topics" (Rogers 1961, p. 133). However, problems are seen as external, and the client accepts no personal responsibility. Feelings may be shown, but they are not recognized or owned. Experiencing is of the past. There is little differentiation of personal meanings and little recognition of contradictions. Clients may come for therapy voluntarily at this stage, but they often do not continue or make progress.

Third stage.   In the third stage, loosening continues, with freer expression about the self, about self-related experiences as objects, and "about the self as a reflected object existing primarily in others" (Rogers 1961, p. 135). Past feelings and personal meanings — usually negative — are expressed, with little acceptance of them. Differentiation of feelings is less global, and there is a recognition of contradictions in experience. Many clients begin therapy at this stage.

Fourth stage.   Acceptance, understanding, and empathy in the third stage enable the client to move to the fourth stage, in which feelings that are more intense, although not current, are expressed as well as some present feelings and experiences, but with some reluctance, fear, or distrust. Some acceptance of feeling is present. "There is a loosening of the way experience is construed. There are some discoveries of personal constructs; there is the definite recognition of these as constructs; and there is a beginning questioning of their validity" (Rogers 1961, p. 138). Differentiation of feelings is increased, and contradictions are of concern. Feelings of self-responsibility in problems occur. There is the beginning of a relationship with the therapist on a feeling basis. These characteristics are very common in much of psychotherapy, as are those of the next stage.

Fifth stage.   In the fifth stage, present feelings are freely expressed but with surprise and fright. They are close to being fully experienced, although with fear, distrust, exactness. Self-feelings are increasingly owned and accepted. Experiencing is loosened and current, and contradictions are clearly faced. Responsibility for problems is accepted. In this stage, the client is close to his or her organismic being, to the flow of his or her feelings. Experience is differentiated.

Sixth stage.   The sixth stage tends to be distinctive and dramatic. A feeling that has been "stuck" previously is experienced with immediacy, or a feeling is directly experienced with richness or flows to its full result. An experience and its accompanying feeling are accepted as something that *is*, not something to be feared, denied, or resisted. An experience is lived, not felt about. The self as an object disappears. Incongruence becomes congruence. "Differentiation of experiencing is sharp and basic. In this stage, there are no longer 'problems,' external or internal. The client is living, subjectively, a phase of his problem. It is not an object" (Rogers 1961, p. 150). Physiological concomitants of a loosening, relaxing nature are present — tears, sighs, muscular relaxations, and, it is hypothesized, improved circulation and conduction of nervous impulses. This stage is a highly crucial one and seems to be irreversible.

Seventh stage. In the seventh stage, the client seems to continue on her or his own momentum; this stage may occur outside the therapy hour and be reported in therapy. Clients experience new feelings with immediacy and richness and use feelings as referents for knowing who they (the clients) are, what they want, and what their attitudes are. Changing feelings are accepted and owned; there is a trust in the total organismic process. Experiencing is spontaneous, with an emerging process aspect, and "the self becomes increasingly simply the subjective and reflexive awareness of experiencing frequently something confidently felt in process" (Rogers 1961, p. 153). Since all the elements of experience are available to awareness, there is the experiencing of real and effective choice. This stage, which relatively few clients reach, is characterized by an openness to experience that leads to a quality of flow, motion, and change. Internal and external communication is free.

To summarize, the process involves the following stages:

1. a loosening of feeling,
2. a change in the manner of experiencing,
3. a shift from incongruence to congruence,
4. a change in the manner in which and the extent to which the individual is willing and able to communicate him- or herself in a receptive climate,
5. a loosening of the cognitive maps of experience,

6. a change in the individual's relationship to her or his problems, and
7. a change in the individual's manner of relating.

Conclusion

In psychotherapy, unlike in medical treatment, the client is not a passive recipient. Rather, the client is a partner—in fact, the more important partner, since the outcome depends more on the client than on the therapist. The client presents him- or herself to the therapist in a state of incongruence or conflict and suffering, with a desire to do something about it. The therapist is not an expert operating on the client but a facilitator of the client's work. The therapist conditions, when communicated to and perceived by the client, allow the client to begin the process of self-disclosure and self-exploration, which in turn lead to change and progress toward becoming a more self-actualizing person.

8

Multicultural Factors

Introduction

In this chapter, the rise of the multicultural movement in psychotherapy is considered. The nature of the movement has progressed from an emphasis on the differences among the various racial, cultural, and subcultural groups considered to an increasing recognition of their commonalities as members of the human race. With this recognition there has been a change of focus from specific techniques for different groups to consideration of the common or universal elements in effective psychotherapy. These are the elements or conditions developed in this book.

The multicultural movement in psychotherapy began some thirty years ago. An early statement was Wrenn's (1962) article "The Culturally Encapsulated Counselor." But the movement gained momentum from observations that "minority-group clients receive unequal and poor mental health services" (Sue 1977, p. 116). They were, it was claimed, underserved and poorly served. Sue cites as examples reports by Yamamoto and colleagues (1968) and others. He later (Sue 1988) refers to the President's Commission on Mental Health (1978), as had others before. It appears in Sue's study that minority clients were more likely to receive supportive treatment than white clients. Sue found, however, that African Americans and Native Americans "were heavily overrepresented" in the community mental health centers he studied in Seattle, while Chicanos and Asian-American clients were heavily underrepresented (Sue and McKinney 1975; Sue et al. 1974). The failure-to-return rate (after the first session) was over 50 percent for blacks, Native Americans, and Asian Americans; the Chicano rate was 42 percent; and the white rate was 30 percent. Blacks were the only group who received differential treatment, more often becoming inpatients and less often provided group and marital therapy (see also Wu and Windle 1980).

Mays and Albee (1992) summarize as follows:

Members of ethnic minority groups are neither users of traditional psychotherapy nor purveyors of psychotherapy in anything like their proportion in the population. . . . The pattern of usage should not be confused with levels of need or helpseeking for emotional problems. In general, ethnic minorities experience a higher proportion of poverty and social stressors typically regarded as antecedents of psychiatric and psychological disorders than Whites. . . . Yet, in spite of the preponderance of these events in their lives, ethnic minorities are often underserved by high quality mental health resources (Wu and Windle 1980). [pp. 552–553]

Early concern focused on minority groups in the United States (Sue 1978). Publications on these groups mushroomed. Sue's (1981a) book contains chapters on Asian Americans, African Americans (by Elsie Smith), Hispanics (by R. Ruiz), and American Indians (by E. H. Richardson). A special issue of the journal *Psychotherapy*, on psychotherapy with ethnic minorities (Dudley and Rawlins 1985), includes papers on these groups (see also Atkinson et al. 1993). Sue and Sue (1990) include chapters on American Indians, Asian Americans, African Americans, and Hispanic Americans.

But multiculturalism expanded to include other groups: various subcultures, racial groups, gender groups, age groups, and socioeconomic groups including the poor (see Goldstein 1973). Curiously, little has been written about psychotherapy in other cultures outside the United States. The book edited by Pedersen and colleagues (1976) does include some material on this topic.

The assumption was quickly made that a form of psychotherapy developed in the United States (and other Western countries) for upper-middle-class white clients was inappropriate for other groups, even within the same general culture. Pedersen (1976), in an early review, writes that "each cultural group requires a different set of skills, unique areas of emphasis, and specific insights for effective psychotherapy to occur" (p. 26).

Perspectives on Inadequacies of Mental Health Services for Minority Groups

Many reasons have been advanced for the inadequacies of mental health services for ethnic minority groups: a lack of bilingual therapists and therapists who are members of the minority groups; discrimination; prejudice in therapists from the majority group. Sue (1988) cites as one of the most frequent criticisms of therapy with minority clients "the lack of bilingual and bicultural therapists who can communicate and can understand the values, lifestyles, and backgrounds of these clients" (p. 302). Sue and Zane (1987) write that

the most important explanation for the problem in service delivery involves the inability of therapists to provide culturally responsive forms of treatment. The assumption, and a fairly good one, is that most therapists are not familiar with the cultural background and styles of the various ethnic-minority groups and have received training primarily developed for Anglo, or mainstream, Americans (Bernal and Padilla 1982, Chunn et al. 1983, Wyatt and Parham 1985). [p. 37]

In his early review, Pedersen (1976) writes, "There is increasing evidence that the trained counselor is not prepared to deal with individuals who come from different racial, ethnic, or socio-economic groups whose values, attitudes, and general life styles are different from and threatening to his own (Padilla et al. 1972)" (p. 35). And Mays and Albee (1992) refer to "the cultural insensitivity" of traditional psychotherapy and "a failure of the profession of psychology to develop and promote relevant and adequate mental health services for this population" (p. 554).

Since every client belongs to numerous groups, it does not take much imagination to recognize that the number of combinations and permutations of these groups is staggering. How different theories, methods, and techniques could be developed for each of these groups would be an insurmountable problem. Yet attempts have been made, limited to a few of the major ethnic-cultural groups.

Numerous authors attempt to remedy the lack of knowledge about ethnic, racial, and cultural groups. The literature is replete with the characteristics of these groups and how to treat or not treat them (e.g., Sue 1981a, Sue and Sue 1990, Vontress 1981).

Pedersen (1976) reports:

> Native American Indian culture presents its own unique requirements for effective counseling. When counseling Native American Indian youth, the counselor is likely to be confronted by passively nonverbal clients who listen and absorb knowledge selectively. A counselor who expects counselees to verbalize their feelings is not likely to have much success with Native American clients. The Native American is more likely to withdraw and using the advice he has received, work out the problems by himself. The Native American is very conscious of having to make his own decisions and is likely to resent being pushed in a particular direction by persons seeking to motivate him or her. [p. 30]

Ridley (1984) states that black clients distrust whites and do not self-disclose. "Thus both the clinical and research evidence converge in portraying a black client who, as a therapeutic participant, is generally reluctant to disclose intimately to a white therapist" (p. 1236). Ridley's statement on self-disclosure in African Americans applies to other groups as well, including Asian Americans. Yet not all blacks are non-self-disclosing, nor are all Asian Americans. Sue and Zane (1987) note that "many Asian American clients who were unacculturated seemed quite willing to talk about their emotions and to work with little structure" (p. 39). Trimble (1976) notes that "the Indian is not accustomed to self-analysis nor is there a familiarity with the process of discussing with a non-Indian one's emotional conflicts" (p. 79). Meadow (1982) recommends that counselors deemphasize the necessity for self-disclosure with Hispanic clients. Sue (1981a) writes that therapists who "value verbal, emotional and behavioral expressiveness as goals in counseling are transmitting their own values" (p. 38; cf. Sue and Sue 1990, p. 38). It appears that a lack of self-disclosure does not necessarily reflect an inability to do so but rather a reluctance to do so in certain situations with certain persons.

A second characteristic of many ethnic minority groups is the desire for a structured relationship in which the therapist is cast as an expert, giving advice and solutions to problems (e.g., Sue and Morishima 1982, Sue and Sue 1990, Szapocznik et al. 1982, Vontress 1976, 1981). Many clients from ethnic minority groups are dependent, desiring a therapist who is active, authoritative, directive, and concrete (Atkinson et al. 1978, Leong 1986, Sue 1981b, Sue and Zane 1987, Trimble 1976, 1981). It is usually stated that such clients *need* therapists who provide these conditions. However, it would be more accurate to say that they *want* or *prefer* such therapists. Virtually all of the research on the preferences of minority groups toward therapy includes subjects who are small, unrepresentative samples, not actual clients, involving statements of the kind of therapists the subjects would like if they were to go to a psychotherapist.

Yet, the almost universal recommendation is that therapists use techniques that "fit" the presumed characteristics of clients. Basic to this is "the assumption that different cultural and subcultural groups require different approaches" (Sue and Sue 1990, p. 161). Listing five publications (including Ridley 1984), the authors state:

All seem to endorse the *notion* that various racial groups may require approaches or techniques that differ from white Anglo-Saxon middle-class clients. Indeed, the *belief* held by many cross-cultural scholars is that minority clients tend to prefer and respond better to directive rather than nondirective approaches, that counseling approaches which are active rather than passive are more effective, that a structured, explicit approach may be more effective than an unstructured, ambiguous one, and that minority clients may desire a counselor who self-discloses his/her thoughts or feelings. [p. 160, italics added]

A plethora of publications have recommended that "culturally sensitive," "culturally relevant," and "culturally appropriate" techniques be developed (e.g., Sue 1991, Sue and Sue 1990, Chapter 8, "The Culturally Skilled Counselor," Sue et al. 1982). There are a number of problems with the attempt to provide information and knowledge about ethnic minority groups and to recommend specific methods or techniques to fit these characteristics.

Problems with a Technique Orientation to Multicultural Psychotherapy

Before discussing problems, it is important to distinguish psychotherapy from forms of mental health intervention, such as education and community advocacy. These interventions are active and forceful in taking responsibility for the client and assume the client is incapable or deficient in some way and needs an authoritative person to work on his or her behalf. Psychotherapy is defined here as a psychological relationship between a person or persons, designated as the client, whose progress in self-actualization has been blocked or impeded by the absence of good interpersonal relationships; and a person, designated as the therapist, who provides such a relationship. There is no assumption of personal deficit in the client and therefore no need to actively direct or take over responsibility from the client.

The first problem to recognize is that descriptions of the various groups are generalizations, describing the modal (abstract average) person. The result is the proliferation of stereotypes, a danger that a number of writers recognize. Sue (1983) cites Campbell (1963), who "warned that the finding of actual differences between groups often leads to exaggerated stereotyped images of these differences" (p. 585). Sue (1983) was one of the first to point out the existence of wide individual differences within each group. Statistically, when within-group variance is great compared to between-group variance, it becomes difficult, if not impossible, to assign individuals to groups or to differentiate among groups.

A note about the emphasis on value differences among cultures is relevant here. There are, to be sure, some value differences. Obviously, the more directive and active a therapist is with a client, the more opportunity there is to violate personal or culture-specific values of the client—knowingly or unknowingly. A therapeutic approach based on respect for the client, a belief in the inherent growth potential of the client, an acceptance of the client at an essential level of being, and an attempt to understand the client from her or his perspective provides an optimal environment for the client to determine her or his own values with reference to mental health.

But it needs to be pointed out that in some cases the word *values* is used too indiscriminately. Many so-called value differences among groups are actually customs, lifestyles, social norms or habits, and preferences. There are many values that are common to many different groups, and some universal values (Patterson 1989b). Brown (1991) writes that "universals exist, they are numerous. . . . [I]t will be irresponsible to continue shunting these questions to the side, fraud to deny that they exist" (see pp. 142–156).

Second, the assumptions regarding the characteristics of ethnic minority groups lead to the self-fulfillment prophecy. If clients from other cultural groups are believed to be non-self-disclosing, dependent, in need of structure, direction, advice, and so forth, then they will be treated as if these things are true, and they will respond to confirm the therapist's beliefs. It is thus assured that standard or traditional approaches will not be effective.

Third, the assumption that the therapist's knowledge of the culture of his or her client will lead to more appropriate and effective therapy has not been borne out. Sue and Zane (1987) state, "Recommendations that admonish therapists to be culturally sensitive and to know the culture of the client have not been very helpful" (p. 37). They continue:

> The major problem with approaches emphasizing either cultural knowledge or culture-specific techniques is that neither is linked to particular processes that result in effective psychotherapy. . . . [R]ecommendations for knowledge of culture are necessary but not sufficient for effective treatment. . . . [T]he knowledge must be transformed into concrete operations and strategies. [p. 39]

Fourth, perhaps the greatest difficulty with accepting assumptions about the characteristics and so-called needs of clients from differing cultures is that they will lead to failure, or a lack of success, in psychotherapy. The active, authoritative, directive, controlling therapist, providing answers and solutions to the client's problems, has not been considered competent or effective for many years. To provide this kind of treatment (it would not be called psychotherapy) to clients from other cultures would be providing poor or second-class treatment.

Fifth, Sue (1981a, p. 38) and Sue and Sue (1990, p. 40) refer to "the belief in the desirability of self-disclosure." But client self-disclosure is more than desirable—it is necessary for client progress. Sue and Sue (1990) appear to recognize its importance, referring to self-disclosure as an "essential" condition, "particularly crucial to the process and goals of counseling, because it is the most direct means by which an individual makes himself/herself known to another (Greene 1985, Mays 1985)" (p. 77). Vontress (1976) recognizes it as "basic to the counseling process" (p. 53). Ridley (1984) writes that "nondisclosure means that a client forfeits an opportunity to engage in therapeutic self-exploration. . . . [T]he result will most surely be nontherapeutic" (p. 1237).

Modifying or adapting psychotherapy to the presumed needs or desires of ethnic minority clients cannot lead to abandoning those things that are essential for therapeutic progress. Ho (1985) recognizes this: "there is a limit on the degree to which the fundamental psychological-therapeutic orientation [the Western model] can be compromised" (p. 1214). To attempt to apply all the techniques that have been suggested in working with ethnic minority clients is to water down the therapy process until it is no longer effective in any meaningful sense of psychotherapy. While clients may be pleased or satisfied with such treatment and even receive some immediate, temporary help, therapy that includes goals such as client independence, responsibility, and ability to resolve his or her own problems is not achieved.

Culture-specific techniques for all the innumerable groups that may appear to a therapist for help have not been clearly specified, described, or matched with the groups to which they apply. More important, there is little if any research support for the effectiveness of the theorized differential techniques or methods.

Sue (1988) notes that

considerable controversy exists over the effectiveness of psychotherapy for ethnic minority groups. . . . Despite the strongly held opinions over the problems ethnic clients encounter in receiving effective services, empirical evidence has failed to consistently demonstrate differential outcomes for ethnic and White clients. . . . Most treatment studies have failed to show differential outcomes on the basis of race or ethnicity of clients, [once clients enter and continue in treatment]. [pp. 301–302]

Psychotherapy with Members of Minority Groups: The Solution

What, then, is the solution to the problem of providing effective psychotherapy to members of minority groups? It is certainly not that traditional psychotherapy — that is, treatment as competently practiced in our current society — be abandoned.

Early on, before the emphasis on specific techniques for different groups, a number of writers listed certain therapist characteristics or attitudes as being necessary. Wohl (1976, p. 187) notes that McNeill (1965, p. vii) emphasized that the healing function includes a caring and concern on the part of the healer. And discussing Pande (1968), Wohl (1976) writes that "therapy provides a special, close, love relationship" (p. 189). Stewart (1976) emphasizes the importance of warmth, genuineness, and especially empathy. Torrey (1970, 1972), according to Pedersen (1976), "identified the expectations of troubled contrast culture clients and the personal qualities of a counselor as being closely related to the healthy change, accurate empathy, and nonpossessive warmth and genuineness that are essential to effective mental health care" (p. 30).

Vontress (1976) emphasizes the importance of rapport as "the emotional bridge between the counselor and the counselee. . . . Simply defined, rapport constitutes a comfortable and unconstrained mutual trust and confidence between two persons" (p. 45). He appears to include empathy in rapport. Richardson (1981) lists the following among the ways of working with Native American clients: listen, be accepting, respect their culture, be natural, be honest, honor their presence, do not be condescending. Vontress (1976) also comments on therapist training that

> what is needed most are affective experiences designed to humanize counselors. . . . Few counselors ever ask what they can do to change themselves; few want to know how they can become better human beings in order to relate more effectually with other human beings who, through the accident of birth, are racially and ethnically different. [p. 62]

Unfortunately, the emphasis on techniques overshadowed attention to the nature of the relationship between the therapist and the client. It now appears that this preoccupation with techniques is fading and that it is being recognized that therapist competence inheres in the personal qualities of the therapist (Bergin and Garfield 1994). The competent therapist is one who provides an effective therapeutic relationship. The nature of this relationship has long been known and is the same regardless of the group to which the client belongs.

Three basic therapist qualities are essentials for all effective psychotherapy (Rogers 1957a). First is *respect of the client,* which includes trust in the client. It assumes that the client is capable of taking responsibility for him- or herself, including during the therapy process, of making choices and decisions, of resolving problems, and, moreover, that the client should be allowed to do so, as a right.

The next therapist quality is *genuineness.* Psychotherapy is a real relationship. The therapist does not assume a role as an all-knowing expert, operating on the client with a battery of techniques. The therapist is not an impersonal, cold, objective professional but a real person.

Finally, *empathic understanding* is also essential. Empathic understanding is more than a knowledge of the client based on knowledge of the groups to which he or she belongs. It requires that the therapist be able to utilize this knowledge as it applies or relates to the unique client, which involves entering into the client's world and seeing it as he or she does. "The ability to convey empathy in a culturally consistent and meaningful manner may be the crucial variable to engage the client" (Ibrahim 1991, p.18).

The only way in which the therapist can enter the world of the client is with the permission of the client, who communicates the nature of his or her world to the therapist through self-disclosure. Thus, client self-disclosure is the *sine qua non* for psychotherapy. Therapist respect and genuineness facilitate client self-disclosure.

The conditions of empathy, respect, and genuineness must be perceived, recognized, and felt by the client if they are to be effective. This becomes difficult with clients who differ from the therapist in culture, race, socioeconomic class, age, and gender. Understanding of cultural differences in verbal and nonverbal behaviors (D. Sue 1989, Sue and Sue 1990) can be very helpful here.

Sue and Sue (1990) concede that

Qualities such as respect and acceptance of the individual, unconditional positive regard, understanding the problem from the individual's perspective, allowing the client to explore his or her own values, and arriving at an individual solution are core qualities that may transcend culture. [p. 187]

These therapist qualities are not only essential for effective psychotherapy but are also the elements of all facilitative interpersonal relations. They are not time bound or culture bound.

Structuring is another element in all psychotherapy that is of particular importance in intercultural therapeutic relationships. It appears to have been recognized by few writers. Vontress (1976) is one who has, and his statement bears repeating:

On the whole, disadvantaged minority group members have had limited experiences with counselors and related therapeutic professionals. Their contacts have been mainly with people who tell them what they must and should do. . . . Relationships with professionals who place major responsibility upon the individual for solving his own problems are few. Therefore, the counselor working within such a context should structure and define his role to clients; that is he should indicate what, how, and why he intends to do what he will do. . . . Failure to structure early and adequately in counseling can result in unfortunate and unnecessary misunderstanding. [p. 47; see also Sue and Zane 1987, pp. 41–43]

And, we might add, failure of the client to continue. Structuring is necessary whenever a client does not know what is involved in the therapeutic relationship—how the therapist will function and what is expected of the client—or holds misconceptions about the process.

The beginning of a change has appeared in the literature on multicultural counseling that could portend a return to a recognition of the basic nature of psychotherapy as an interpersonal relationship.

Patterson (1978) earlier had proposed such a view of multicultural therapy. Recently, change was introduced by Pedersen's (1990) statement that "to some extent all mental health counseling is multicultural" (p. 94). This was followed by his comment that "we are moving toward a genuine theory of multiculturalism" (Pedersen 1991, p. 6). He continues: "The obvious differences in behavior across cultures are typically over-emphasized, whereas the more difficult to discover similarities of expectations are typically underemphasized" (p. 9). Vontress (1988) earlier had emphasized the common humanness of all clients. Ibrahim (1991) also accepts multicultural counseling as generic. Speight and colleagues (1991) state it clearly: "All counseling is cross-cultural or multicultural because all humans differ in terms of cultural background, values, or lifestyle. . . . [M]ulticultural counseling is redefined as basic to all forms of helping relationships. All counseling is multicultural in nature" (pp. 29, 31). Unfortunately, the Statement of Standards of the Association for Multicultural Counseling and Development (Sue et al. 1992) does not adequately recognize this core of therapist competence.

All clients, as previously noted, belong to multiple groups, all of which influence the client's perceptions, beliefs, feelings, thoughts, and behavior. The therapist must be aware of these influences and of their unique blending or fusion in the client if therapy is to be successful.

The current (over)emphasis on cultural diversity and culture-specific therapy leads to (1) a focus on specific techniques (or skills, as they are now called), with the therapist becoming a chameleon, changing styles, techniques, and methods to meet the presumed characteristics of clients from varying cultures and groups, and (2) an emphasis on differences among cultures and their contrasting worldviews. This approach ignores the fact that we are rapidly becoming one world, with rapid communication and increasing interrelations among persons from varying cultures, leading to increasing homogeneity and a worldview representing the common humanity that binds all human beings together as one species.

Vontress (1979) has proposed an existentialist philosophical view of cross-cultural therapy, a "philosophical orientation that transcends

頁

culture" (p. 117). Freeman (1993), citing Pedersen's (1991) proposal for a search for a framework that recognizes the complex diversity of a plural society while, at the same time, suggesting bridges of shared concern that bind culturally different persons to one another, develops such a framework that includes the universal and the specific in therapy. Though she does not make this point, the universal is the process, while the specific deals with the content in therapy.

If multicultural psychotherapy is generic, and if all therapy is multicultural, then it becomes possible to develop a universal system of psychotherapy (Patterson 1989a).

9

Issues and Problems

Introduction

In this chapter, we consider some of the issues and implications deriving from the relationship therapy (and client-centered) position. First, we clear up some of the continuing misconceptions about relationship therapy. Then we move to the problem of short-term or long-term (interminable) therapy; the specific or nonspecific nature of the therapist conditions, whether they are sufficient as well as necessary conditions; and the problem of resistance to the system presented here. We will also consider the nature of the placebo in psychotherapy and in relationship therapy in particular. Finally, we clarify the nature of resistance in psychotherapy.

Some Implications

One of the oldest misconceptions about client-centered or relationship therapy is that the therapist is a purely passive participant in the process. The use of the term *nondirective* with reference to the therapist may have encouraged this view. The term might better be replaced with the word *noncontrolling*. The intent of the word is to focus on keeping responsibility for content and process with the client rather than having the therapist be in the role of director.

The therapist is far from being a passive participant. His or her responsibility is to actively create an environment that minimizes threat so that the client is free to work without the restrictions that occur under conditions of personal threat. The therapist is a highly sensitive, empathic listener. The focus of the therapist's energy is to understand the client accurately from the client's frame of reference and to communicate this understanding to the client. By working in this manner, the therapist keeps the client's attention focused on her- or himself. The client, in effect, continually listens to her- or himself in a process of clarification and validation of meanings. Rather than taking a dominant role of initiating or leading, the therapist is active in responding to the client.

Some misconceptions arise from a cursory understanding of client-centered therapy. First, therapists respond in ways that mirror the client's own perceptions. But it is not a parroting of the words of the client. The therapist's response is more complex than simple repeating. Responses are created with conscious intention of responding to varying depths of meaning. A verbatim repetition is a relatively shallow response. It indicates, at best, that the therapist has heard the client's most literal communication. It may be noted that repetition is a better response than that from a therapist who changes the subject, thereby ignoring and disrespecting the client altogether.

In this example the therapist is directing the client away from the intended focus, essentially ignoring the client:

> *Client*: I'm really confused about my family stuff. You know, with my brother and father. It seems like there was always this pressure to be a certain way and, I don't know, maybe jealousy of my brother . . . (pause)
> *Therapist*: What about your mother? She's in your family. Why didn't you mention her?

In this response, the therapist follows the client:

> *Client*: I'm really confused about my family stuff. You know, with my brother and father. It seems like there was always this pressure to be a certain way and, I don't know, maybe jealousy of my brother . . . (pause)
>
> *Therapist*: Though it is not clear, you're wondering if your own feelings play a part in family behavior . . . especially with your brother. Jealousy . . . that's hard to talk about.

The therapist's response is a reflection of the client's meaning, with specificity ("family behavior" instead of "family stuff") and depth (acknowledging jealousy is taboo). The response was calibrated to the client's awareness level. It allows clients to hear their own ideas.

Another misconception is that relationship therapy is a matter of only one technique — that of paraphrasing. It has become clear in this book that responding to the client derives from the whole therapist as a person — her or his attitudes and philosophy as exemplified in the core conditions. No array of techniques, no matter how skillfully practiced, can lead to a true therapeutic relationship. A trusted relationship is a matter of attitudes, not merely behaviors.

Another misconception is that relationship therapy has sometimes been thought only to be useful for a limited group of clients and problems, such as college students and mild adjustment problems. Studies in the 1960s proved relationship therapy is effective in treating schizophrenics (Gendlin 1962) and psychotics (Rogers et al. 1967), as well as less severe adjustment disorders.

A final misconception about relationship therapy is that it is purely or essentially affective in nature, dealing only with feelings while ignoring cognitive or intellective aspects of clients and their problems. While it is true that client-centered therapy in its beginnings focused on affect, in contrast to the exclusive focus on cognitions of behavioral approaches, it is also true that the therapist responds to the whole person of the client. When the client is working on cognitive aspects of the problem at hand, a therapist would respond to the client's focus on cognitive perceptions. The following is an example:

Client: Sometimes I think I go in gunning for a fight. You know, I figure they're going to give me trouble so . . . I go in with that attitude.

Therapist: You may create some conflict just by how you think about it beforehand.

Client: Yeah, maybe if I went in saying what I need and then be patient . . . I believe the outcome would be different. There wouldn't be so much fighting that way. I need to get my head on straight before I walk into it.

Therapist: So you want to avoid setting up a fight. And getting your "head on straight" . . . I'm wondering exactly what that means.

Client: Well, what am I aiming at here? What is my purpose? To fight? No, not really. To get some communication going here, yeah, so we can talk without all the yelling. So, uh, getting my head on straight means knowing what my purpose is and planning my way of being with them so that I keep to my purpose, and not going off and doing things that totally mess things up.

This client is focusing on cognitions rather than feelings. The therapist is following that focus, since this client at this time is recognizing his own contribution to conflicts. Cognitive, information-processing, and language factors in the therapy process are clarified in a volume edited by Wexler and Rice (1974).

Short-Term and Long-Term Psychotherapy

Length of Therapy: Motive and Severity

It is clearly a misconception that relationship therapy is necessarily long-term therapy. It is a mistake to believe that a method that leaves the initiative to the client must surely prolong therapy, as if the client has a motive to stall or digress rather than to grow. This error may have its roots in the medical model, which generally ignores the patient's capability to heal him- or herself. The medical model assumes that the doctor is the healer and that the source of healing is external to the patient.

The relationship therapist assumes the client is the healer and the source of healing is the client's own energy or motivation toward self-actualization. The therapist is the facilitator of the process. The client will take as long (or as short) as she or he needs to become fully aware of and work through the problem. This is based on the assumption that human beings have a natural tendency to heal and grow and that this process will occur given the conditions that free the growth tendency.

Beyond the variable of client motivation is the variable of the severity of the problem. Our experience as therapists suggests that a client who has been struggling for decades with psychotic or neurotic behavior will not be a short-term client. On the other hand, problems that arise as a result of an immediate life crisis may be resolved by the client through therapy in one or two sessions.

Brief Therapy as a Short-Term Alternative

An answer to the need for a quick fix in mental health treatment is brief therapy. A common characteristic of the brief therapies is that they are active, directing, and controlling. Three comments are in order here. First, the objectives of brief therapy are different from those of psychotherapy. The accepted objective is to provide immediate, if temporary, relief for the client's distress and to resolve current, specific problems.

This objective has unintended outcomes. The client gives over responsibility of problem resolution to the counselor. The use of directive methods means to some extent the abandonment of the objective of client responsibility for making choices, for solving problems, even for directing his or her own life.

The other side of the coin from relinquishing responsibility for self is that dependency is fostered by directive counseling. Whenever the client encounters another problem or difficult situation, he or she must return for help. Dependency is further reinforced by the attitude inherent in directive counseling that the client must look externally for solutions. The client is thus taught to trust others and not to trust him- or herself to solve problems. This attitude is disrespectful of the client's ability to understand his or her life and create appropriate solutions. The focus is on the client's neediness rather than on the client's strength. Many clients present themselves as helpless and often believe that about themselves. It is the therapist's responsibility to look beyond the neediness and to respect the strengths.

A therapist who focuses on empathic understanding and respect for the client is creating a relationship that demonstrates to the client that he or she is worthy of understanding and respect. This approach gives clients the courage to seek solutions of their own from a position of strength.

One client statement is relevant here:

When you so patiently listened to me — to what I had to say, what I thought was happening — without question, then I started to listen to me and give myself credit for knowing what was going on. I started to trust myself, trust myself to see accurately. When I did that, I knew what I should be doing. I wasn't so confused anymore. I knew what was happening and I knew what to do about it. I just thought I was stupid. So I didn't listen to my own, uh, view of things and became confused.

This client moved from looking to the therapist for guidance, to self-evaluation of the situation and self-construction of solutions. She initially appeared to the therapist as incapable, weak, and in need of rescue from her confusion. She viewed herself as incapable and thus did not access her own strength. Instead of taking control and reinforcing incapacity, the therapist listened to and valued the client's perceptions. The client then turned to herself as a credible witness and problem solver.

Feelings of confusion and incompetence are not an invitation for therapist control. They signal an opportunity to create an environment of clarity and personal responsibility. The effort of empathic understanding creates clarity. An attitude of valuing and respect toward the client encourages personal responsibility. Such characteristics are countered by an attitude of taking over and getting it done efficiently for the sake of insurance payment. For a clearer vision of the process of psychotherapy, therapists might just ask themselves what is the purpose of their work.

A second point about the more behaviorally oriented brief therapies is that the source of some problems is deeper than can be addressed with a cursory behavior change. Changing the behavior does not necessarily address the source or motive that created the maladaptive behavior. The quick fix is inefficient because the client will have to return again and again to have the counselor "cure" the problem unless the source is confronted and resolved. Furthermore, the client may be pushed out too soon and need to seek help elsewhere, potentially beginning a series of inconsistent short-term therapies known as the revolving-door phenomenon.

The third comment is that brief therapy in some applications is not therapy at all. It is often education or training. The brief therapy counselor may be training clients in such skills as parenting, relaxation techniques, or time management under the rubric of therapy. This service is not therapy. It is education. The person providing the service is a teacher, not a therapist. Such training may be initiated and completed in a few sessions and has been called "brief therapy."

The basic principle of the approach represented in this book is that the best way to provide therapy to any client, whether only for an hour or many hours, is to offer the highest level of a therapeutic relationship of which the therapist is capable.

The Relationship: Specific or Nonspecific?

There is currently general agreement among theorists and therapists that the relationship factors of empathic understanding, respect or warmth, and therapeutic genuineness are present in all systems or methods of psychotherapy (Bergin and Garfield 1994, Garfield and Bergin 1986). Therapy, by almost any definition, involves a personal contact between the therapist and the client. Yet difficulties remain with the concept of "the relationship" in psychotherapy. First is the problem of scientific study, and second is the nature of the effect of the relationship.

This universal presence of a psychological relationship constitutes an obstacle to research attempting to study the influence or effect of other factors, such as specific techniques, apart from the relationship. The relationship cannot be eliminated and is difficult to control. Because of the inability to control the relationship scientifically in experiments, evidence is unclear concerning the impact of various techniques. Do the techniques work, or is the relationship alone the change agent despite the techniques?

The fact that there are relationship factors in all psychotherapy is seldom denied, but many of those who recognize the importance of the relationship view it as a nonspecific factor. It is not considered by some to be directly related to the client's problems or to their resolution. It is considered as the general environment in which, or the base from which, the therapist operates, using specific methods or techniques. The relationship may be viewed as rapport, or the method of inducing the client to develop trust in the therapist. This is essentially the view of behavior therapists.

There are two arguments in favor of the view that the relationship is the specific treatment element in psychotherapy. First, if it is assumed, as is done here (and there is evidence for this view, as noted earlier) that the source of much if not most of clients' problems involves interpersonal relationships, mainly the lack of or inadequacy of good human relationships, then a therapy that provides and models a good human relationship is a relevant and specific treatment method.

Second, evidence suggests that the relationship, without the addition of any techniques, is effective with many clients with a broad spectrum of problems. Further, "there is massive evidence that psychotherapeutic techniques do not have specific effects" (Bergin and Garfield 1994, p. 822). Thus, the basic relationship common to all psychotherapy is the specific treatment leading to outcome in therapy.

The Relationship: Necessary and Sufficient?

The Necessity

In addition to the recognition of the relationship as a common element in all psychotherapy, there is widespread acceptance of its importance and even necessity. Goldstein, as early as 1962, concluded after reviewing the literature on therapist–patient expectancies in psychotherapy, "There can no longer be any doubt as to the primary status which must be accorded the therapeutic transaction" (p. 105).

Even behaviorists, who are determined to show there is a minimal effect of the relationship on outcome, are forced to admit its relevance. Lazarus acknowledges this: "Both Wolpe and I have explicitly stated that relationship variables are often extremely important in behavior therapy" (Klein et al. 1969, p. 262). Krumboltz (Freeman and Krumboltz 1992), in commenting on the counseling relationship, says, "Clearly good relationships are essential."

Behaviorists, however, view the relationship between therapist and client as a technical skill. Krumboltz, in the aforementioned discussion, went on to say "relationship building" is a behavioral technique (Freeman and Krumboltz 1992). This remark assumes "relationship" is a set of behaviors. However, behavior is a reflection of underlying attitudes, conscious or unconscious. When the behavior is simply a technique, the underlying attitude lacks genuineness, and it can be perceived as a fraud and its purveyor mistrusted. The relationship is being used to gain access for external manipulation.

A relationship therapist creates a relationship as a reflection of the client's deeper understanding of her- or himself. Underlying that bond are attitudes of valuing, honoring, and respecting the person's potential. The client recognizes her or his own sense of valuing, honoring, and respect. This is the basis from which clients may begin change in their lives. The relationship is necessary for self-respect to be brought to awareness.

The Sufficiency

The question of the presence and importance of the relationship in psychotherapy is no longer an issue, nor, it would appear, is the question of its necessity (Bergin and Garfield 1994). But there remains the debate as to whether the relationship is not only necessary but also sufficient for change.

A major implications of the model presented in this book is that the relationship is necessary and sufficient for therapeutic personality change. Note the adjective *therapeutic*. No one would deny that there are other ways to change behavior—force or threat of force, drugs, psychosurgery, brainwashing, and, to some extent with human beings, conditioning. But for positive changes in voluntary clients, the conditions of a therapeutic relationship are sufficient for a wide variety of changes with a wide variety of problems. If there are limits, there has not been scientific proof of what these limits are. As the conditions are tested in more and more situations, without the addition of other specific methods or interventionist techniques such as interpretation or behavior modification, they demonstrate their effectiveness.

A therapeutic relationship, based on the core conditions, effectively facilitates behavior change with all kinds of problems and all kinds of people—the poor and disadvantaged as well as the rich and middle class. The potential challenge with certain kinds of clients is not the ineffectiveness of conditions but the implementing or communicating of them. The conditions themselves are not time or culture bound (see Chapter 8).

The question of sufficiency involves the question, Sufficient for what? Rogers (1957a), in his initial statement of the hypothesis of necessary and sufficient conditions, uses the term *therapeutic personality change*. This needs definition. In this book strong support has been presented that a relationship characterized by empathic understanding, respect, and therapeutic genuineness leads, in the client who perceives these conditions, to progress in self-actualization. It leads in part to the development in the client of the three characteristics themselves, which constitute elements of self-actualization.

But what about specific outcomes? People often come to therapists with problems involving lack of information or knowledge, lack of skills of various kinds—deficiencies of a cognitive or motor nature. Surely where these are lacking or inadequate, the providing of a relationship is not sufficient. We maintain here that dealing with such problems is *education*. This is teaching, not therapy. While it may be difficult to draw a line between therapy and (remedial) teaching, there is value in doing so.

One difference is that therapy is concerned with persons who are not lacking in knowledge or skills but are unable for some reason to use their knowledge or skills effectively. Their problem, in the distinction made by many learning theorists, is not one of learning but of performance. Therapy as a relationship is sufficient for enabling them to do those things that they are capable of doing. On the other hand, the relationship is not sufficient when the client lacks information or skills. For example, your client, who was the victim of child abuse, is a parent who is abusing her child. Providing the core conditions in therapy to deal with the psychological wounds of victimization is the therapeutic application of the relationship. It is necessary and sufficient to help the client confront her own experience — past and present, as the client chooses. Parenting effectiveness training is an appropriate educational treatment to deal with a lack of knowledge and skill in healthy parenting. The former is therapy; the latter is education. In education, the relationship may not be sufficient, since information is required. In therapy, the relationship is necessary and sufficient for therapeutic personality change.

In the light of research indicating that the conditions alone are sufficient for a wide variety of outcomes, it becomes difficult to determine when other methods or techniques or other kinds of help should be included. In addition, it should be asked if these added interventions ultimately do more harm than good. A client who lacks information may be able to get that information. There are choices concerning ways or processes to give information.

The question may be asked if counselors encourage dependency by acting for people who are capable of learning to act for themselves. Client responsibility is increased when clients are guided to where to obtain information or instruction and, in some cases, referred or assisted in making contacts. Taking control in the name of service may actually be harmful to the client's sense of self, by creating dependency and a sense of personal inadequacy. It can be argued that, due to discrimination, some clients may be "outside the system" and need an advocate. Although the therapist acting as advocate may improve conditions of a client's life, advocacy is not psychotherapy.

Since therapy is effective without specific methods or techniques beyond the relationship itself with a wide variety of clients with a wide variety of problems, a number of questions arise. When is the relationship not sufficient? Since results are obtained without the use of information giving, advice, suggestions, interpretations, persuasion, and so on, then it is clear that none of these is necessary. The question then is, When added to the relationship, do these other techniques help without adding undesirable side effects? When do they help? And a final question, which has not been investigated: If the relationship is not only necessary but sufficient for so many outcomes, is it efficient (see Ellis 1980)? Again, are there other methods or techniques that would increase the efficiency of therapy, when added to the relationship, in achieving the same outcomes without undesirable side effects?

Resistance to Acceptance of the Model

There is resistance to acceptance of a model that says that a good interpersonal relationship is not only necessary but sufficient for therapeutic personality change. Such a model poses a threat to many psychotherapists for several reasons.

The idea that the essence of psychotherapy is a relationship between the therapist and the client appears to be too simple. Can there be healing in offering someone a relationship that is honest, respectful, and nonjudging? Research proves there is. Is there not some manipulation needed to force the client to change? Research proves added manipulation is not necessary for therapeutic personality change. As for the apparent simplicity, it is only simple in theory to offer the core conditions consistently. In practice, it takes discipline and training to listen consistently in a focused and empathic manner. It takes discipline and philosophical commitment to assume consistently an attitude free of judgment. It takes discipline and courage to be consistently genuine and honest in a working relationship. The idea and model are basic, but not simple.

The concept that the relationship is the essence of psychotherapy is potentially threatening to some because it places specific and clear responsibility on the person of the therapist. The research on the therapy relationship identifies and specifies those personality characteristics that are therapeutic and provides evidence that high levels of these characteristics lead to therapeutic personality changes, while low levels do not. If therapy is ineffective, the therapist is confronted with the possibility that she or he has not been able to provide or communicate the conditions adequately.

Another threatening implication of the relationship as the core of psychotherapy is that some therapists are concerned that this means psychotherapy is not a "profession." The fear, reflected by Strupp (1977), is that if a good human relationship is the major contribution to therapeutic outcome, then there is nothing left for a professional to give as a service. Bergin and Garfield (1994) also mention this concern. They point out that there is resistance to the massive research evidence that shows no support for techniques as outcome variables. They surmise that this may be a rationalization to preserve the professional legitimacy of psychotherapy. This fearful attitude assumes psychotherapy is only a set of techniques. An effective therapist's skill manifests in being capable of consistently offering an environment that promotes therapeutic personality change. This environment is not offered by everyone at this time. Most people can be philosophically and behaviorally (in that order) trained to offer the conditions consistently. That ability to offer consistently the conditions, rather than a bag of incidental techniques, is the claim to professionalism.

Finally, the greatest threat to academically trained psychiatrists, psychologists, and counselors is that they need not be in a dominant, directive, and controlling position. Along with education comes the expectation that they must "do" something: have an answer, create a cure, relieve the suffering—in short, be in control. This controlling stance is encouraged by the attitude that the "cure" comes from the professional and not from the client. It is difficult to believe that after all those years of taking in information, one has only to trust the client as a change agent. In relationship therapy ultimate power consciously and explicitly resides in the client.

The Placebo Effect

The placebo effect is a universal element in every method or theory of psychotherapy, yet it is almost never recognized or considered in these theories. Indeed, most of the effects of psychotherapists are placebo effects. Placebo means "to please," and most therapists want to, or try to, please their clients.

In his early discussion of the placebo effect in medicine and psychotherapy, Shapiro (1971) stated that he was presenting an examination of psychotherapy as a placebo effect. He was suggesting that psychotherapy is nothing more than a placebo. Later, in his review with Morris (Shapiro and Morris 1978), this position appears to be tempered somewhat when they noted that "the placebo effect functions primarily through psychological mechanisms. . . . *The placebo effect is an important component and perhaps the entire basis for the existence, popularity, and effectiveness of numerous methods of psychotherapy*" (p. 369). Shapiro and Morris view the total psychotherapy *relationship* as a placebo. They refer to a review by Luborsky and colleagues (1975) (see also Smith and Glass 1977, and Smith et al. 1980) that found several types of psychotherapy to be about equally effective. They conclude that this equal effectiveness related to the common therapist–patient relationship and point to this relationship as a demonstration of the placebo effect.

Shapiro and Morris (1978) defined a placebo as

any therapy or component of therapy that is deliberately used for its nonspecific, psychological, or psychophysiological effect, or that is used for its presumed specific effect, but is without specific activity for the condition being evaluated. The "placebo effect" is

defined as the psychological or psychophysiological effect produced by placebos. [p. 371]

All the variables in the psychotherapy relationship are psychological and all are active, having some direct or specific effects on the
client or patient. The placebo as an inert substance does not exist in
psychotherapy. Thus, the placebo in psychotherapy means nonspecific
effects—that is, though the placebo may have some specific effects,
these effects are not the objectives the therapist is attempting to
achieve.

Patterson (1959a) has for over thirty years suggested a division of
the common elements in all psychotherapies into those that were
essentially specific treatment variables (i.e., empathic understanding,
respect or compassion, and therapeutic genuineness), and those that
were nonspecific, essentially placebo, variables.

Nonspecific or placebo variables are the social-influence variables
(Strong 1978)—perceived therapist expertness or credibility, trustworthiness, and therapist expectations. These variables are among those
listed by Shapiro and Morris (1978) as variables through which the
placebo operates. Indeed, they are the essence of what Fish (1973)
boldly calls *placebo therapy*.

Recognizing that "the social influence process has been considered the active ingredient in the placebo," Fish (1973) states that
placebo therapy "denotes a broad frame of reference for considering all
forms of human interaction, especially psychotherapy, in terms of
social influence process" (p. xi). The therapist does everything possible
to establish him- or herself as an expert and an authority in the eyes of
the client. The client's susceptibility to influence and persuasion is
assessed. The impression is created that "once I know what is wrong
with you I can cure you."

A treatment strategy is then formulated and communicated to the
client in a plausible manner, tailored to the client's belief system. The
major technique used is that of behavior modification, together with
suggestion and hypnosis. "Placebo therapy is a strategy for getting the
maximum impact from such techniques regardless of their validity"
(Fish 1973, p. vii). Placebo communications are used not because they

are true, but because of their effects. The validity of the techniques, or the therapeutic ritual, to use Fish's term, is important only as it enhances the patient's faith — that is, how believable, impressive, or persuasive the technique is to the patient. The therapist "says things for the effect they will have rather than for his belief that they are true. Instead of speaking empathically because he believes that empathy cures, he does so because he sees that such statements add to credibility in the patient's eyes" (Fish 1973, p. 32). Further, "lying to a patient is desirable if the lie furthers the therapeutic goals, is unlikely to be discovered (and hence backfire) and is likely to be more effective than any other strategy" (p. 39).

Pentony (1981) provides a critical evaluation of Fish's placebo therapy. He says that "it seems questionable whether a treatment based on suggestion [or persuasion] alone will be universally applicable," given the existence of strong resistance to change. He raises three other questions about placebo therapy: "1. Is it ethical to mislead the client in regard to the therapeutic strategy? 2. Will the therapist be convincing when he is not a true believer in the ritual he is carrying through? 3. If placebo therapy becomes general and clients become aware of its nature, will they lose faith in the healing rituals and hence render these ineffective?" (pp. 63–64). Fish's attempts to answer these questions are less than convincing. No attention is given to the problem of therapist genuineness and the client's detection of its absence.

There are other problems with placebo therapy. Fish, who claims that it works, urges that the reasons be researched. There is probably no question that placebo therapy works with some clients some of the time. It is the basis for the success of charlatans and charismatics, who produce satisfied clients and testimonials.

There are three problems with the placebo as therapy, however. First, it is uncertain, or unreliable. Not all subjects are placebo reactors, and it is not possible to identify those who will respond positively to placebos. Fish attempts to determine who among his clients will be positive reactors. Although he notes that many are called but few are chosen, he does not tell how many. He refers to the problem client who expects and desires a different relationship with the therapist.

Second, placebo effects are not lasting. In a case where they do exist, they usually are not durable but tend to be transitory. None of the research on the social-influence variables has included long-term, or even short-term, follow-up of results.

Third, the possible side effects of placebo therapy are undesirable, including the fostering of dependence. Also, clients who become aware that the therapist is lying or posturing for their benefit only, may become disillusioned with treatment altogether.

The social-influence variables and the specific-relationship variables probably are not completely independent. LaCrosse (1977) found significant correlations between the Counselor Rating Form, which measures client perceptions of counselor expertness, attractiveness, and trustworthiness, and the Barrett-Leonard Relationship Inventory, which measures client perceptions of counselor empathic understanding, congruence, level of regard, and unconditional positive regard. Observer ratings were also highly correlated, although ratings by the counselors themselves were not, which raises some question about the presence of an artifact, such as the halo effect, in the client and observer ratings.

The presence of correlations between these two sets of relationship variables poses the question of which is primary, or which causes or leads to the others. That the core conditions are primary is suggested by studies that have shown them to be related to various therapy outcomes, while this has not been shown for the social-influence variables. Krumboltz and colleagues (1979) have indicated the direction of the relationship when they suggest, after reviewing the research, that "counselors who want to be seen as attractive should be empathic, warm and active" (p. 100). It would also appear, from LaCrosse's research, that counselors who want to be regarded as experts also should be empathic, respectful, warm, and genuine. Similarly, it might be suggested that counselors who want to be perceived as trustworthy should demonstrate the same qualities.

It appears that the complex therapeutic relationship cannot be prevented from being "contaminated" by placebo elements. Clients perceive therapists, to some extent at least, as authoritative and expert, regardless of the therapists' behavior. Clients normally trust their therapists. Therapists' belief in their theory is inextricable from their methods. If they did not have confidence in them, they would use other methods in which they did have confidence.

If placebo elements cannot be entirely eliminated from psychotherapy, they can be either maximized or minimized. If they are maximized, the therapist is engaging in placebo therapy, with the possibility that results may be limited, superficial, or temporary. The research on the social-influence variables has attempted to maximize the placebo effect in various ways, including favorable introductions of counselors to clients, display of degrees, diplomas, and professional books and journals, wearing of a white coat by the counselor, luxurious office furnishings, and cultivation of a self-confident, charismatic manner by the counselor. In spite of this, the research does not demonstrate the effectiveness of the variables. If, on the contrary, placebo elements are minimized and specific-relationship variables are maximized, therapy is effective.

All the variables in the psychotherapy relationship are psychological and all are active, having some direct or specific effects on the client or patient. The placebo as an inert substance does not exist in psychotherapy. Thus, the placebo in psychotherapy means nonspecific effects — that is, though the placebo may have some specific effects, these effects are not the objectives the therapist is attempting to achieve. Placebo elements may promote such effects, but they presumably are not used deliberately to achieve them. Lambert and Bergin (1994) have emphatically stated that the elements common to therapy are neither trivial nor inert. Research strongly supports the active role of such factors as warmth and empathy in client improvement.

Resistance in Psychotherapy

Client resistance in psychotherapy has been the concern of therapists since the time of Freud. He identified several kinds of resistance, all of which resided in the patient. This is still the case, as most therapists bear little, if any, responsibility for client resistance. Or, if any responsibility is accepted by the therapist, resistance is considered to be the client's nontherapeutic response to the good therapist's necessary and desirable methods of therapy. Resistance is thus inevitable, a universal and unavoidable element in psychotherapy. It is something to be overcome, not something to be avoided.

The questions arise as to whether to be successful psychotherapy must create resistance or whether successful therapy can be practiced in such a manner that creates little or no resistance. Resistance is a defense; defense is a response to threat. Therapist interventions can be, and often are, threatening to the client. Interpretations are often threatening to the client. Attempts to persuade the client through reasoning and argumentation, as in cognitive therapy, can be threatening. Even less overt and obvious therapist behavior can be threatening to the client. Rogers (1961) cites research by Dittes that found that "whenever the therapist's attitudes changed even slightly in the direction of a lesser degree of acceptance, the number of abrupt GSR deviations significantly increased" (p. 44). And "the psychogalvanic reflex . . . takes a sharp dip when the therapist responds with some word which is just a little stronger than the client's feelings" (Rogers 1961, p. 54). There is thus physiological evidence that therapist judgmentalism, evaluation, and interpretation are threatening.

It is well known that threat is inimical to learning and (voluntary) behavior change. Under threat people resist, cling to what they have and are, and become more fixed in their ideas and feelings. Perception is narrowed, as in tunnel vision, so that there is failure to perceive all the elements in a person's experience and environment (Combs and Snygg 1959).

But can threat be eliminated from psychotherapy, or at least minimized? Rogers (1942) deals extensively with resistance and its source in therapist's statements. The hypothesis, he writes:

is that resistance to counseling and to the counselor is not an inevitable part of psychotherapy, nor a desirable part, but it grows primarily out of poor techniques of handling the client's

expression of his problems and feelings . . . out of unwise attempts on the part of the counselor to short-cut the therapeutic
process by bringing into discussion emotionalized attitudes which
the client is not yet ready to face. [p. 151]

"Insight," he writes, "is an experience which is achieved, not an
experience which can be imposed" (p. 196).

The only effective learning in psychotherapy is self-discovered
learning. Anything that is really helpful, that leads to real and lasting
learning, is not the result of imposition. After years of research,
Rogers (1961) concludes, "I have come to feel that the only learning
which significantly influences behavior is self-discovered, self-
appropriated learning" (p. 276). Trying to speed up therapy or client
progress by interpreting, bestowing on clients the therapist's insights,
does not facilitate therapy but retards it. Learning can occur only at
the rate the client is able to progress on his or her own.

There is discussion in the literature about the need for the client
to experience an "optimum" level of anxiety if he or she is to be
motivated to make progress. For example, Strupp and Binder (1984),
writing about the therapist as "someone who evokes anxiety" then
suggest that "the trick is to steer a course which on the one hand
maintains sufficient tension, thereby keeping the patient motivated,
and on the other, prevents the experience of too much anxiety" (pp.
191–192). What is "optimum," "sufficient," or "too much" is not
specified; Strupp and Binder do not tell us how to perform the trick.

Bergin and Garfield (1994) make an important point in their
summary of the *Handbook of Psychotherapy and Behavior Change.* They
propose that rather than argue over whether "therapy works," we could
address ourselves to the question of whether "the client works!" (p.
825). This points directly to the original cause in psychotherapy: the
client. All action takes place in the client. If the attitude and behavior
of the therapist induce resistance to the process, then the "cause" will
resist an "effect."

Focusing on the therapeutic relationship and the core conditions
that support its presence in psychotherapy provides a simple, clear,
and valid method for maintaining optimum anxiety in the client. The

core conditions as the basis of the therapeutic relationship create an environment that frees the client as completely as possible from external threat. The client, having been freed from the need to defend and resist, can then turn her or his energy to explore personal experience and to deal with internal feelings and conflicts (Rogers 1961).

Some sources of resistance in the client are not caused by threatening aspects of the therapist's behavior. There are resistances to change, and resistances to facing negative and painful aspects of the self and one's behaviors. Clients may have difficulty in trusting the therapist and in experiencing self-disclosure. There is resistance against giving up old habits or symptoms.

Such resistance cannot be avoided or eliminated. They are accepted and responded to as any other statements or behaviors of the client. Therapy is accompanied by a certain amount of client anxiety. Learning is to some extent accomplished by anxiety; in fact, low levels of anxiety may facilitate learning.

When psychotherapy is based on the core conditions, threat is consciously minimized. A threatening environment in therapy creates resistance because a client who is threatened must defend the self from the perceived threat. The therapist conditions of empathic understanding, respect and warmth, and therapeutic genuineness provide an atmosphere and relationship that is perceived as nonthreatening, thereby releasing the client from the need for defensive behavior. A relationship between the therapist and client characterized by these conditions provides the optimum conditions for meaningful voluntary learning and progress on the part of the client.

Conclusion

The essential understanding of relationship therapy is that the client is the originator of all growth, all action, all initiation. The therapist creates the environment as free of threat as possible for the client to act and become her or his most highly actualized self. Attempts to establish faster results have not produced significant improvement in outcomes. These brief kinds of therapies may in fact be harmful by creating dependencies and revolving-door clients.

The therapeutic relationship is a specific treatment element in psychotherapy responding to a specific relationship deficit or inadequacy experienced by the client. Research evidence consistently reveals a lack of difference in the outcomes of various psychotherapy techniques and support for common elements in all or most therapies. The relationship is necessary and sufficient for therapeutic personality change. Relying on the relationship as the "curative" factor in therapy encourages the client to act as a self-healer, avoiding the externalized dependency of directive approaches. The core conditions of warmth/ valuing, empathy, and therapeutic genuineness are far from inert factors in therapy. They are relevant to theory and practice and have been supported as significant to outcome as active factors in client improvement (Bergin and Garfield 1994). Reliance on the therapeutic relationship in psychotherapy reduces client perception of threat and thereby resistance to the therapy process. The therapy relationship based on the core conditions creates an environment that facilitates personal exploration and personality change.

10

Primary Prevention

If we could raise one generation of children with unconditional love, there would be no Hitlers.

Elizabeth Kübler-Ross

Introduction

In Chapter 4 we concluded that the essence of psychotherapy is love. If love is the cure for psychosocial emotional disorders, then it should follow that the primary prevention of such disorders would be the providing of unconditional love and compassion to all infants and children.

Love and Society

William James (1902) long ago wrote, "I saw that the foundations of the world, of all the worlds is what we call love" (p. 391). Maria Montessori (1917) a decade and a half later noted that "scientists have at last perceived, after much research, this most evident fact: that it is love which preserves the animal species, and not simply the struggle for existence" (p. 326). Eric Hoffer (1979) wrote that the survival of the species will depend on the capacity to foster a boundless capacity for compassion. And Erich Fromm (1956) similarly wrote that love "is the most fundamental passion, it is the force which keeps the human race together, the clan, the family, the society. The failure to achieve it means insanity or destruction — self-destruction or destruction of others. Without love humanity could not exist for a day" (p. 15). Without love or some degree of altruism, the human race could not have survived.

Psychology, however, according to Batson (1990), denies the existence of altruism: *"Altruism,* the view that we are capable of valuing and pursuing another person's welfare as an ultimate goal, is pure fantasy. We are *social egoists"* (p. 336). But Batson goes on to present evidence that "we are not simply social egoists; we have the capacity for altruism" (p. 338). Walsh (1991), a sociologist, goes further. In exploring the scientific basis of love, he considers data from biology, physiology, and neurology, as well as the behavioral and social sciences.

Love and Its Deprivation in Infancy

While love is important throughout life for the well-being of the individual, it is particularly important, indeed absolutely necessary, for the survival of the infant and for providing the basis for the normal psychological development of the individual. Proposition 4, in the preface, states a unitary theory for the prevention of social-psychological pathology: the presence of at least one caregiver providing unconditional love for every infant (and young child) will prevent the occurrence of most social-psychological pathology. Pathology deriving from neurological or biochemical sources would not be included. Burton (1972), while discouraging the search for a single overriding trauma causing emotional disturbance, nevertheless states that "the basic pathogen is, for me, a disordered maternal or caretaking environment rather than any specific trauma as such" (p. 14). Disruptive behaviors related to the influence of peer pressures would decrease and eventually disappear, since (1) peers would be less likely to be disturbed, and (2) their influence would be reduced or eliminated since the peers would be secure and not vulnerable to such pressure. Other than neurological and biochemical disorders (some of which might be genetically based), such disruptive behaviors as existed would derive from the deprivation of the biological needs for existence; frustration of such needs could lead to aggressive and antisocial behaviors. But in a society permeated by love, such needs would be met — where there is love there will be bread.

We define love as an attitude that is expressed through empathic understanding, respect and compassion, and therapeutic genuineness, or honesty and openness toward others. In more personal — as distinguished from therapy — relationships, love may be defined as "that which satisfies our need to receive and bestow affection and nurturance; to give and be given assurance of value, respect, acceptance, and appreciation; and to feel secure in our unity with, and belonging to a particular family, as well as the human family" (Walsh 1991, p. 9).

In this chapter we focus on the nature of the love that is necessary for the normal development of infants and children.

Early Recognition of the Importance of Infant and Early Childhood Influences

A hundred years ago Freud emphasized the importance of infancy and early childhood on later development and psychological disturbance. Early on he attributed neuroses to the early trauma of being sexually molested. But a few years later he changed his views, concluding that it was not actual sexual experiences of seduction but false memories and fantasies that were the cause (the oedipal complex). Attention to the importance of real experiences of the infant and child was thus deflected to unreal or imagined experiences.

The object relations school of psychotherapy emphasizes the

importance of the infant's and child's relationship with a primary care person: "whatever a baby's genetic endowment, the mother's ability or failure to 'relate' is the *sine qua non* of psychic help for the infant. To find a good parent at the start is the basis of psychic health" (Guntrip 1975, p. 156).

During the 1940s several psychoanalytic therapists published reports of the effects of real experiences on children. The term *maternal deprivation* was applied to these experiences. In 1937 Levy published a study of children separated from their mothers at an early age. Lauretta Bender and Stella Chess, working in the child psychiatric service at Bellevue Hospital in New York, reported on children who experienced emotional deprivation during their early years (Bender and Yarnell 1941, Karen 1994).

Children in hospitals, even for brief periods of separation from their mothers, and children in institutions were found to be psychologically disturbed (Bakwin 1942, Bowlby 1959, 1973). Rene Spitz (1945, 1946) reported on his experience with children in a foundling home, comparing them with children in the nursery of a penal institution. The physical conditions in the foundling home were better than those in the penal institution, but the illness and death rates were higher. Although developmentally the foundling home infants were superior, after a year of institutionalization they were inferior to those in the prison setting. Within two years, 37 percent of the foundling home children were dead; all the prison children were alive five years later. The difference between the two settings was that in the prison the children's mothers cared for them, while in the foundling home the children were cared for by professional nurses.

John Bowlby became interested in the influence of the early environment in children in the late 1930s, and he published his first paper in 1940. In 1944 he published a paper reporting on forty-four children, ages 6 to 16 who were young thieves. The mothers of these children were described by social workers as "immoral, violent and nagging," "extremely anxious, fussing, critical," "drunken and cruel," "did not want the child," "unstable and jealous," and so on. One common objective factor was prolonged early separations of the child and mother, separations during which the child had never developed a true attachment and after separation had no opportunity to develop a true attachment.

In a study conducted for the World Health Organization, Bowlby (1951) surveyed the field and earlier studies. This survey included the work of Dorothy Burlingham and Anna Freud (1944) with children evacuated from London during the war whose behavior deteriorated in the absence of their mothers. Bowlby's survey showed that the behaviors and psychological disturbances of children subject to maternal deprivation and separation were many and varied. In addition to thievery, these disturbances included indifference, incorrigibility, hostility, lack of any feeling or empathy for others—a state of being affectionless and detached (characteristic of a psychopathic personality).

The conditions leading to such behaviors, in addition to early, even brief and later, longer separation from the mother, include the lack of or early loss of mother love and the emotional quality of the home, even before the child's birth. Bowlby refers to the British style of parenting—cold, impatient, demanding. But such an atmosphere of child rearing was not limited to Britain. For much of the first half of this century, child rearing in the United States followed Watson's (1928) approach:

Treat them as though they were young adults. Dress them, bathe them with care and circumspection. Let your behavior always be objective and kindly firm. Never hug and kiss them, never let them sit on your lap. If you must, kiss them once on the forehead when they say goodnight. Shake hands with them in the morning. Give them a pat on the head if they have made an extraordinary good job of a difficult task. [pp. 81–82]

Of course, not all, or even most, mothers and fathers followed the British and Watson precepts—fortunately so, considering the effects of such a program. The need for love in the normal development of infants and children would appear to be obvious.

The human infant is helpless and obviously unable to meet its needs for food, clothing, and shelter. In addition to the meeting of these needs, the infant needs more. It needs a nurturing, caring, compassionate caretaker who provides love. For the infant, love is communicated primarily through touch — stroking, cuddling, massaging, kissing. Walsh (1991) notes that "even the behaviorist John Watson believed that love was an innate human emotional need that is fed by the tactile stimulation an infant receives as it snuggles in its mother's arms" (p. 12). This care is "neurologically critical during the sensitive period in which the neural pathways are being laid down" (Walsh 1991, p. 44). Somatosensory deprivation (lack of touch, movement, massage, etc.) appears to be a basic cause of many physical and psychological disturbances.

Barry Stevens (Rogers and Stevens 1967) writes about an incident when her husband was in charge of a pediatric ward in a New York hospital in the 1920s. "There was an infant whom none of the doctors could find anything wrong with, but all of them agreed the infant was dying. My husband spoke privately to a young nurse who loved babies. He swore her to secrecy before telling her what he wanted her to do. The secret was, 'Take care of this baby as if it were your own. Just *love* it.' At that time love was nonsense even to psychologists. . . . The baby took hold. All the doctors agreed on that" (p. 31).

Recently a number of hospitals have been conducting experiments with hospitalized infants. Walsh (1991) refers to an Associated Press (1988) news story that reports on a volunteer program at St. Luke's–Roosevelt Medical Center in New York that took abandoned, neglected infants and those born drug addicted or with AIDS. Although given good physical care, they received no touching or stimulation, lying listless, and in time not even reacting to sound. But, when volunteers held, stroked, and cuddled them, they became alert, smiling, cooing, and reacting to stimuli.

At the University of Miami Medical School, psychologist Tiffany Field conducted an extensive study of premature infants (Ackerman 1990). The infants were stroked and massaged by nurses and volunteers three times daily. The massaged infants gained weight faster, became more active and alert, were more responsive to stimuli, and were discharged from the hospital sooner than nonmassaged infants.

Follow-up found that the massaged infants were larger and had fewer physical problems. They also did better in tests of mental and motor ability. Touch is a powerful expression of caring. Deprivation of this caring results in retarded physical and psychological development.

Walsh (1991) writes that there is a growing momentum among anthropologists, endocrinologists, physiologists, psychiatrists, psychologists, neuropsychologists, and others to recognize the role of mothers in "the critical task of humanizing the species. . . . [M]odern neurophysiology is reaffirming Freud's belief in the centrality of the mother's role in making us human. . . . [L]ove is a biological and psychological necessity" (p. 37).

Baumrind (1980), evaluating the research, concludes that "caretakers play a determining role in the ways their children develop. . . . [C]aretakers can have a determining effect on children's intelligence, character, and competence" (p. 640).

Ainsworth (1979), who with Bowlsby has spent much of her life studying mother–infant attachment, notes that while "it is an essential part of the growth plan of the human species — as well as that of many other species — for an infant to become attached to a mother figure, this figure need not be the natural mother but can be anyone who plays the role of principal caregiver" (p. 932).

Baumrind (1980) states that "there is no evidence of a biological need for an exclusive primary bond, and certainly not a bond to a particular person because she happens to be the child's biological mother" (p. 145). But "a primary commitment cannot be shared, although the care itself can and should be. Someone must, when no one else will, provide the attention, stimulation, and continuous personal relationship without which a child is consigned to psychosis, psychopathy, or marasmus" (p. 145). And fathers, men, can be principal caregivers, especially if they are socialized to give appropriate nurturing behaviors.

Consequences of Love Deprivation

The effects of being deprived of love are harmful to adults and devastating to children. "Individuals deprived of love become emotionally barren as they plod through dark lives" (Walsh 1991, p. 8). "Without love there can be no healthy growth or development" (Montagu 1981, p. 93).

Walsh (1991) opens his discussion of the effects of absence of a loving infant and early childhood environment with a general statement: "The human infant can be molded and cultivated into a decent and caring adult, or its development can be distorted horribly in a way no nonhuman animal can have its nature altered by experiences that occur within its species" (p. 8). He then proceeds to document this statement. The innate potentials of the infant or child, the inherent drive toward the actualization of these potentials in a process of self-actualization, can be inhibited and distorted by the absence of a nurturing environment of unconditional love. Furthermore, these human potentials can be nearly or totally destroyed by *abuse* in the caretaking relationship.

The Neuroses

The various neuroses originate in some form of emotional deprivation, resulting in a lack of satisfaction of the basic human needs for affection, security, respect, and self-esteem. The child's need for love has been thwarted by parents who are emotionally cold, controlling, and unloving. The neurotic engages in attempts to meet his or her needs for love and respect in ways that often turn other people off. Neurotics are unable to offer the love and respect that would lead to reciprocation by others. Henderson (1982) studied the difficulty of neurotics in forming attachments. Though they desperately desire such attachments and engage in what Henderson calls "care-eliciting behavior," involving crying (in children), attempts to draw sympathy, and "please love me" appeals, this behavior is not successful. Walsh (1991) relates this to Maslow's deficit love, an abnormal craving for love.

Depression and Suicide

One of the symptoms of depression is thoughts of suicide. However, depression itself is an amorphous category of emotional disturbance.

What has been called marasmus in infants is probably similar to depression in older persons. While there appears to be an increasing awareness of biochemical and even genetic factors in depression, it is still the case that depression is usually precipitated by environmental events, particularly the loss of a loved one. And it is possible that biochemical abnormalities are the result of psychosocial experiences. Akiskal and McKinney (1975), for example, suggest that rejection, lovelessness, and lack of relatedness lead to reduced brain catecholines, resulting in the behavioral disturbances characteristic of depression. Certainly, there are depressions that are the result of psychosocial factors rather than biochemical or genetic factors, though a genetic predisposition may be present in some cases. The evidence, at this time, is not consistent or absolutely definitive.

Suicide appears to be clearly related to psychosocial factors. Durkheim (1951), a French sociologist, a century ago noted the relation between social anomie and suicide. Suicide is higher in urban areas, among the unmarried and divorced, and among those living isolated lives. Among children, those who attempt suicide are more likely to have experienced abuse and neglect (Rosenthal and Rosenthal 1984). Adolescents who attempt suicide are usually isolated from their friends and family. Walsh (1991, p. 128) reports a study in which he and a colleague found suicide attempts among juvenile delinquents related to love deprivation.

Schizophrenia

As in the case of depression, many of those diagnosed as schizophrenic show evidence of brain malfunctioning and genetic factors. But there are wide differences among those with this diagnosis. While the concept of schizophrenogenic mother is no longer accepted, psychosocial factors are present; it is difficult, however, to discern cause–effect relationships, even though PET and CAT scans show brain abnormalities. Drugs (chlorpromazine and recently clozapine) relieve or remove the symptoms in many schizophrenics.

Seymour Kety (see Walsh 1991, p. 121), a researcher on the genetics of schizophrenia, points out that we cannot dismiss environmental factors, which can precipitate, intensify, or ameliorate symptoms. Love deprivation is viewed by many as an environmental factor that may operate by affecting chemical factors in the brain. Walsh (1991) cites studies by Robert Heath on Harlow's love-deprived monkeys that found brain disturbances. He concludes that "schizophrenia may very well be the result of the effects of early childhood experiences in the mechanisms of neurotransmitter metabolism for individuals with a schizophrenic predisposition" (p. 124). Lack of care and parental love, experienced as coldness and rejection, lead to passivity, isolation, and suspicion (Buss 1966, p. 352). Studies of the onset of schizophrenia find this isolation and lack of responsiveness prior to the onset. Walsh (1991) points out that genetic factors in parents may influence parenting behavior. In addition, we note that some attention should be given to historic psychosocial factors in parental behavior. What quality of caretaking experience did the parents have themselves as children, and how did that experience influence the parents' ability to love their children? The interactions of genetics, brain chemistry, and environmental factors are complex, but in the trend toward biologizing schizophrenia, environmental factors cannot be ignored.

Sociopathy and Criminality

Statements reminding us of the importance of early love in antisocial behavior abound. A Public Broadcasting System radio program recently quoted a former Los Angeles gang member as saying, "Kids aren't born bad. Kids are bad because they can't find love." Ashley Montague (1970), an anthropologist, writes, "Show me a murderer, a hardened criminal, a juvenile delinquent, a psychopath, or a 'cold fish' and in almost every case I will show you a tragedy that has resulted from not being properly loved during childhood" (p. 46). Lance Morrow (1992), in an essay in *Time* magazine, writes, "It is usually the want of love that makes children vicious and sends them out of control" (p. 68).

Not all criminal behavior is the result of lack of love, of course. Walsh (1991) estimates that about 10 percent of habitual criminals are psychopaths or sociopaths. They come from loveless homes, characterized by neglect, rejection, and abuse. Not having experienced love for themselves, they cannot feel love for others. They have had to alienate themselves from their own hurt at being unloved, from their feelings of unworthiness and eventually self-rejection. To protect the self from those feelings, they have alienated themselves to some degree from all feelings. They are unable to feel sympathy or empathy for others and are thus able to engage in cruelty toward others. Their consciences are not developed, so they feel no guilt or remorse and are not affected by punishment.

Walsh (1991) again presents evidence that the deprivation of love affects the functioning of emotional centers of the brain, leading to disruptive behaviors. "In fact, the physiological line of thought reasons that socialization and the development of conscience (the internalized control of behavior) are largely a function of autonomic conditioning in childhood" (p. 147). That early experiences can affect brain structure as well as function is becoming clear. Weil (1985) notes "that experiences induce neurophysiological structuring is increasingly recognized" (p. 336; see also Rourke et al. 1983). Whatever the interrelationships and relative weights of genetic, neurological, and psychological factors, sociopathic criminals appear to share some abnormalities in all these areas; genetic factors contribute susceptibility to the influence of other factors.

Not all mothers are good mothers or, to use Winnicott's (1965) term, *good enough mothers.* Not all mothers can or will love their infants. But it is not possible to remove infants or children from such mothers, unless and until there is evidence of abuse. Early intervention, beginning before the birth of the child, can have positive effects with some of these mothers. Intervention later to repair the effects of neglect and abuse is not highly effective (Parens and Kramer 1993). Didactic, cognitively oriented parent education is not likely to be effective when the parent is emotionally disturbed.

What Can Be Done?

Ideally, every infant and young child should have at least one principal caretaker who can and will provide the unconditional love necessary for normal physical and psychological development. This is clearly a tremendous task, and society is probably not yet ready or able to provide such care. Yet while it may be impossible in our world society to assure a loving caregiver for every infant and child, the desirability — indeed, the necessity — of doing so must be recognized, and steps taken toward its achievement. Walsh (1991) notes that while agencies are charged with assuring a minimal level of food and shelter (though not successfully doing this for all citizens), "there are no similar institutions monitoring the nation's love needs, nor is there likely to be any time soon" (p. 52).

Steps that can and should be taken include the following. First, the United States should ratify the United Nations Convention on the Rights of the Child (United Nations General Assembly 1989). This convention was adopted by the 159 Member States of the UN General Assembly on November 20, 1989, and has been ratified by 54 nations, but not by the United States. This convention includes the right of the child to affection, love, and understanding in a family, unless it is in the best interests of the child to remove the child from the parents.

Second, prenatal care, including preventing malnutrition in mothers, and education in infant needs and care can be increased. Here, the United States is behind some other countries.

Third, hospital practices should be modified, and the programs to provide infant stimulation through massaging and other contacts by touch, by the mother and other hospital personnel, should be extended.

Fourth, maternal — and paternal — leave from employment should be provided on, and for a period following, a child's birth. Desirably this should be paid leave, so that those with low incomes can afford it. The United States has lagged behind other countries. Over 100 countries provided this benefit before the United States, even though the United States was a signatory to the United Nations Convention on the Elimination of All Forms of Discrimination against Women that includes an agreement "to introduce maternity leave with pay or comparable social benefits without loss of former employment" (Walsh 1991, p. 53). In 1993, the United States finally joined the other developed countries when the family leave legislation was passed by Congress and signed by the president.

Fifth, education should be given to parents and potential parents about effective parenting behavior and the provision of love.

Finally, the public should be educated concerning the devastation of abuse. Part of the problem of abuse is that the issue has been avoided. From the time when Sigmund Freud bowed to the pressure of professional shunning to our own times when abuse is still denied as fantasy, human abuse reminds us too poignantly of our own fears. In avoiding our own sorrow we have allowed children to live the terror of abuse and to pass their inheritance to the following generations.

Conclusion

This chapter presents just a sampling of the voluminous evidence that the level of love in infancy and early childhood is the source of much, if not most, psychosocial disturbance and disorder. Love is a powerful prophylactic. The solution of the problem is startlingly simple: the provision of a safe and loving caregiver for every infant and child. The actual implementation of this solution is admittedly difficult. Isolated efforts are being made, and thus there is some hope that with recognition of love's importance, more will be done.

11

The Therapeutic Relationship: Case Studies

Introduction

It is difficult to find transcripts that, in a microcosm, exemplify the therapeutic process. Clients often go deeply into important experiences and then lighten up, almost as a breather, before diving in again to deeply personal experiences. The issue may not surface again until a subsequent session or sessions. In a linear sense, this approach may seem disconnected. If the patterns of a client's life can be viewed as a tapestry, the client's statements are the threads. When the client has had the opportunity to present the threads, they are ultimately woven into an understandable pattern or tapestry of experience.

To carry the metaphor further, the threads may seem at times unrelated. One thread may come from one part of the client's experience and one from another part. The therapist respectfully accepts the threads without judgment about relevance because sooner or later the connection will be made with the bigger picture. Life tapestries are made one thread at a time.

In the transcripts presented here, the reader may judge that the client is being evasive or vague. The therapist simply accepts that the client is expressing the experience as clearly as he or she is capable of at that moment. Often in a spiraling way, the client clarifies at deeper, more personally significant levels that which she or he is experiencing or has experienced. In other instances, the client is currently only willing to present information in a rather veiled way to test the reaction, as this client states: "I sort of told you a sweeping big picture of what happened because I wanted to see how you were going to react. If you thought I was horrible or were shocked, I sure wasn't going to tell you the rest of it."

We have placed some brief therapy transcripts into the chapters of this book where relevant. Here we provide blocks of therapy transcripts to give a broader sense of the process. All of these transcripts have been altered to protect the names and experiences of the client and of the people mentioned. New students of therapy may discover that most sessions are characterized more by caring patience than by excitement. In that sense, an important part of therapy is patiently and with unconditional acceptance walking with another human being through that person's experience.

Different clients benefit from different lengths of therapy. Clients themselves decide when to terminate. One of the following transcripts is of a one-session therapy process. The client asked for one session with the intention of relieving stress and bottled-up emotion. That was the client's intent, and that was the outcome. However, a client with thirty years of psychological distress, including treatments with psychotropic medication, shock, and multiple hospitalizations, is not a candidate for one-session therapy with any measure of success.

It is important to point out here that the process for working with the one- or two-session client is the same process for working with the client with a long history of distress who is a candidate for long-term therapy. The theory and process are consistent in each case. They are human beings dealing with their individual life experiences, motivated by the same essential energy to actualize their potential.

Empathic Responsiveness

The following transcript exemplifies the therapist empathically following the client. The client goes as deeply as she can into an issue and then stops when she has said enough for the time being. By "enough" is meant that she is too fearful to go further. She will wait until another time when she is prepared to step further into her fear.

Client: I guess it is about not being . . . not letting anyone run over me.

Therapist: OK. Is this part of the adult expectation . . . when he took you into his confidence?

Client: Yes, he started doing that when I was in high school. A while back I talked to him about my grandma. My grandmother and grandfather . . . my grandmother was adopted and Mary was her adopted mother. They lived with Grandmother and Grandfather, and after Dad was born, they moved to the next town. Dad didn't want to go, so they left him with Mary. When we had this talk, he opened up to me and said that he couldn't understand why they didn't make him go. If they'd cared they wouldn't have left him. I think with him, . . . they, Mary and John, spoiled him rotten. He said they'd have given him the moon if she could have gotten it . . . to make up for Grandpa and Grandma not being there. Grandpa was a good-looking man. I guess what I got from Grandpa . . . it's like an unconditional love, you know? But I guess that considering that Mom's mother died when she was young and her father drank all the time . . . and she didn't want to take anyone home with her because she didn't know what he might do. And with Dad not having his parents there and the hostilities they had, they . . . the two of them combined made for a really strange way of rearing us.

Therapist: Um-hum. You see the connection there to you . . .

Client: Yes, and it's like the major thing that I feel is there a lot of the abandon feeling that I feel. That's a lot of times that I don't say or do what I feel because I'm afraid that I might say or do something to make someone *leave*. And I guess that's why when I come here and that I don't worry about that because I don't . . . it's like you're not going to leave . . . and I guess it's because (fifteen-second pause) I don't know how to say this to make it sound like I want to make it sound, but it's like . . . you aren't part of my family; you aren't somebody that I go out and do things with. It's like you are the strong part, you know, or something that; you are going to be there, and I can say anything. . . . I can, I can say anything that I feel. I can look anywhere I look, that I want to look. I can sit anywhere I want to sit and it doesn't matter. And any other time it's like I can't be these things, and I guess with all the things that happened with Mom and Dad, they had expectations of me and they wanted me to be what they could never be. And they tried to make me be that way but they didn't know how because . . . they had always lived the way they'd lived.

Therapist: Hmm. And those expectations set conditions on you . . . seemed to you like you had to be something other than what you really are?

Client: Yeah. And I thought the other night, am I just doing that so I can get out of being what the hell I am? I thought, "Do you not like what you are? Is there something about you that you just don't like or what? I mean, you can't keep blaming them for what's going on with you here." And well . . . am I, am I, I don't know, if I'm being what I think they want me to be, and it goes back to the door again (client is referring to a dream). If I open the door, that's me. I know what is behind the door is me! (pause) And I don't know, I don't know if I am ready to be me . . . whatever me is, because I don't really know what me is.

Therapist: This would be giving up someone else's expectations . . .

Client: Right.

Therapist: . . . and not sure what's there, who is there.

Client: Right, and being what I've always been.

Therapist: Ah, you are aware of that part having always been . . .

Client: . . . Um-hum. And I know that there are parts of me that's already me . . . because I see them coming out of me. (laughs) This sounds like I have four or five different personalities, or something, like they are gushing out of me, or something, but I know . . . with my daughter most of the time I am me. But the other portion of the time I'm not, which is going to, which is going to make her end up like . . . I am . . .

Therapist: (quietly) Hm.

Client: Because I think that's what Mom and Dad did. They were themselves part of the time. And then, it's like, it's not like I am blaming them, and it's like I am like I am because I lived like I did. I know it's not their fault. They didn't intentionally *do* anything to *make* me think or feel or act or do anything that I have done.

Therapist: You can understand it, but still the effect is there.

Client: Right. It's kind of like if I open the door? . . . I'm going to lose them. (pause) If I am what I am, whatever it is, then . . .

Therapist: You may risk . . .

Client: . . . their affection . . . because I will be different, yes. And that's why with Bob (man with whom this client had a serious relationship) I couldn't be me. But the strange thing about it is . . . when I am me, that's when I get along better with everybody.

Therapist: Um-hum.

Client: That's like when I talked to Bob this morning, I was *me*.

Therapist: Yes, you felt more like your real self.

Client: And we could get along forever, when I'm me. Except . . . no that's not right. When I'm me and he's him, because he was him this morning.

Therapist: Um-hum. Both just being yourselves . . .

Client: So he's in sort of the same boat. When we got together everything was so good, because I was me and he was him. But we weren't "me and him" all the time, because of outside forces. But when I am me, I am happier . . . being me. But there's like, still, I can tell the difference; I can tell it's not as bad as it used to be. It used to be there wasn't a me. I mean, I couldn't . . . my me didn't start coming out until my daughter. And I guess if I open up the door that it will be different with Mom and different with Dad, especially with Dad. If I open up the door, there won't be anything left.

Therapist: That's what you're afraid of.

Client: Yeah.

Therapist: The worst-possible scenario, that there would be no . . . connection to Dad . . .

Client: And I don't know. I can't figure out why I have this feeling with him, because . . . it's like me being his favorite. It's almost like . . . I'm not sure if I am even his. (laughs)

Therapist: Not his?

Client: Mom had told me something about some guy she had really liked a lot. I'm not sure if I dreamed this; I'm not sure if she told me. I know she told me about this guy, but it's like for some reason it's real vivid in my mind as to she wasn't sure as to whether I was his or not, Daddy's. And . . . I don't know. That's one of my fears — is opening the door and realizing that I'm not . . . which I, even if I opened the door I wouldn't know that because the only person that knows that would be Mom.

Therapist: The door represents more than one kind of unknown to you, fears.

Client: Evidently. I didn't realize it did until just now. I didn't-. . . (pause)

Therapist: And some of those unknowns, when you look at them may not even . . .

Client: (interrupts) Have anything to do with anything. (Client looks puzzled and shakes her head no.)

Therapist: Or they don't make too much sense to you on a logical level right now.

Client: They don't and it's like the negative thoughts again. Thinking something like that seems so absurd. Or thinking it might be some kind of sexual harass . . . no, I've heard so much of that at work, it's all I can think of. Some kind of sexual abuse or physical abuse, and I don't think it's any of that and I can't figure out why. But the other night I was thinking about the blue room again, and I read my notes in my book and I wrote it's kind of like a ride at the fair that you can't stop, was what I wrote in that book. You know?

Therapist: A ride at the fair that you can't stop . . .

Client: And when I read it last night, and I had written it the other night. I looked at it and I thought, "That's strange." I had never thought of it as being like a ride at the fair that I couldn't stop. And it was always in that same . . . it was always in that blue room. I can't remember it happening in any other room. And I can't figure out why it was just that one room.

Therapist: Your bedroom when you were a girl . . .

Client: And I can't figure it out.

Therapist: Just bits and pieces come to you but not enough to understand . . .

Client: Not, no, enough to know why it's doing it. But it's like . . . (pause, then quietly) it's just like lost, (with a sigh) I don't know. (long pause) I'm tired.

Therapist: It is about time to quit for today.

Client: Yes, I need a break. Pull it all together and go back out for a while. I'll be back.

Trusting the Client

In the following transcript the client is of normal intelligence and quite capable of speaking for herself, but she is a fearful human being. The therapist chose to respond exactly at the same level of depth as the client presented so as not to threaten her. When the therapist responded at the same level, trusting the client to know her own way, this client would work toward the problem most effectively at her own pace.

Client: Some of this may sound really simple to some people, but, see, some of it I never got. Like I'm freer now than I have been . . . in my mind, inside, um, I didn't realize how much that all this stuff was inside. When it comes out . . . it freed up some things. I realized I'm afraid of being guilty. That's what pride is about . . . like being proud of being humble. Humble, though, is putting myself down. The more I put myself down, the more proud I was. The values were messed up, you know? Finally I feel like I know something that's true.

Therapist: You have been confused, really, and . . .

Client: Yeah, and I guess I've been angry that so much time has gone by that . . . but I'm also glad I'm realizing it now.

Therapist: At first you were angry that it's being going on so long and now you are feeling a shift. Like "What to do now?"

Client: (laughs) Wow!

Therapist: Now just a shift, more like "WOW!"

Client: (laughs and nods head yes)

(The client changed the subject and later returned to the subject from which she originally shifted.)

Client: It used to be "Why?" was the only question, but now there's more "What am I going to do?"

Therapist: Moving forward . . .

Client: (interrupts) Before that I was even afraid to ask why.

Therapist: So there is a progression from fear to ask, to asking why, to where to go from here.

Client: Yeah. And there's still some need to go back and deal with the why.

Therapist: Um-hum. You're not completely done with the why.

Client: Well, the anger of it.

Therapist: Um-hum. You want to go on but there is still some anger to be admitted.

Client: Yeah. This gets so deep. It's confusing.

(Another break here to another subject. Later returns.)

Client: When I made decisions then, when I was a child, and if they went wrong or I ended up with a guilt feeling because I was angry about having to do that in the first place—then that guilt kind of gave me security. That may sound kind of weird. But if I don't know what's going to happen, things are like really scary. And I would like to know what's going to happen before it happens, not like having surprises. If you're guilty at least you know who to blame. I don't have to stand around waiting for some uncertainty. Or waiting for what I know now is . . . I know I don't have that much control over the world. I kind of hang on to my guilt and I realize it served a purpose.

Therapist: It is the one thing you could control.

Client: Yeah, maybe so. (pause) This is what is happening to me when I'm not here. I'm remembering things like things that I would feel guilty about. I'm more free now because I understand that or something has happened because I don't feel a need for that guilt anymore. I'm realizing that. It's like a whole weight is lifted off of my shoulders. Part of this is like when I had that control and I was making those decisions, maybe I kind of enjoyed it. I can admit it now without like saying, "Oh, you enjoyed it. You must be a terrible person."

Therapist: You can just accept it.

Client: I can just accept it, yeah, and I'm glad it's not happening. I'm glad it's over with. That part of my life . . . that happened in that way.

Therapist: Um. You are looking back and . . .

Client: I have remembered so much, so much more than before. I have remembered that my brother was . . . I found out my cousin abused my brother. My brother was a strong enough person to admit what happened to him. And I believe him. I . . . felt responsible kind of in a way . . . that because somehow I made my cousin do it to my brother or something, I don't know. But now I am more free of that. That's an example of it. I also remember a time when something like that happened to me. And I don't know if you call it abuse or what, but a childhood game. I realize maybe that's why I felt inferior to other people. Looking back, I realize that inferiority has a lot to do with how I felt. That, uh, maybe that was why.

Therapist: This new freedom has helped you look back and remember experiences that weren't in your awareness and see them in a different light. Before you felt guilt, felt the blame . . . you feel differently now.

Client: Oh, yeah. And part of it is just realizing how I felt about those things in the first place . . . just being able to realize it how I felt inside.

Therapist: It is freeing . . . being able to know the feeling behind the guilt.

Client: Well, I guess it helps to tell it. I'm not sure. . . . Sometimes . . . how do you go about telling things about . . . like this situation . . . self-expression . . . but, uh . . . you don't ask me. You don't pry in. That's good in a way. But it's good when you ask me, too, because if I haven't told it, maybe I need to tell it.

Therapist: It sounds like you're saying it's good for you to tell these experiences, to bring them to the light, to be aware of them. There are more experiences you'd like to tell about, but you want me to ask about them. In a way you want me to ask you.

Client: In a way, but in a way not. (Client went on to change the subject.)

In the next session the client returned to the idea expressed previously about wanting the therapist to ask questions about her experience. Note that the client uses the same words (italicized) to pick up the issue where she left it off a week before.

Client: Sometimes I wish people would ask questions, to lead me.

Therapist: You want me to ask questions. Is that it?

Client: *In a way, but in a way not.* I guess in the short run, I want you to ask, but in the long run it's better to learn to assert myself.

Therapist: Assert yourself?

Client: Well, when I assert myself . . . part of it is to learn to say what I think. In the short run it's frustrating for me to have to get to . . . to tell you what I'm thinking. Other people can ask many questions and just tell you what you're thinking. That's what happened in my family.

Therapist: Your parents told you what to think.

Client: Yeah, sort of, but when other people speak for you it has an effect on your identity. It doesn't help me to grow. That's why I say in the long run it's better to learn to speak for myself.

Client Responsibility

This following transcript is a one-session therapy. It was agreed between the client and therapist before the session that this would be one session. The client's intent was to release emotion in a safe and protected environment. A portion of this transcript was edited out at the client's request because of its identifying nature.

Client: Well, I'm not sure what to talk about.

Therapist: We have this time set aside for you to use in whatever way is most meaningful for you. What do you want to talk . . . what would be best for you?

Client: (sobbing)

Therapist: This feeling is powerful for you.

Client: Yeah. I don't know where to begin . . . so . . . (pause, sobbing)

Therapist: It seems overwhelming.

Client: (sighs and pauses) I've pretty much done all this to myself, you know? It is very clearly my own creation.

Therapist: You've done all this to yourself? I'm not clear on that.

Client: (sighs) In the misguided effort or attempt to communicate with this girl in Ohio. I. . . . Number one, I was the impetus for her to do what I didn't want her to do. I had alternatives and I chose this and, um, so it's my doing in that sense. Plus, the more effort I put into it, the more personal and real it was for me, so that, the whole thing I did was very, uh, for lack of better words drew a lot of my personal nature out for me to look at. I guess I became very vulnerable.

Therapist: Um-hum. Left you open to being hurt.

Client: Hmm. So that just, uh, that was completely my situation. I'm sure she is in Ohio or somewhere and probably has not had my name cross her path. So this is all my stuff.

Therapist: You think she doesn't care about you, but you're still hurt.

Client: So I say, I did it to myself. I guess the, part of the question is, how long do I keep doing this to myself.

Therapist: Yes. You're still involved with it . . . a lot.

Client: I go through periods where I think it's somewhat resolved better. Then there are weak points when I find myself saying maybe I should have done this or what would I do if she sent me a postcard.

Therapist: I'm not clear on what you are talking about. It sounds like you are in a stage of a relationship where you are blaming yourself for a breakup. And continuing to think about it. Kicking yourself . . .

Client: Yeah, uh, I can get to that where I kick myself. That's usually not my frame of mind. I will give you a quick synopsis. I was finishing an advanced degree in Ohio. I went to an outdoor club on Friday afternoons and we met. She was the bartender. We didn't have real meaningful conversations, but she came to recognize me. So the last week before I left, my friend and I were there . . . to make a long story short. I got her phone number, so that was a big deal to me. I was pretty old, you know, because of college, for not having met anyone with any potential. So I'm getting older and I'm thinking to myself I need a girl. She was a nice, pretty girl, younger than me. She had just graduated. Probably at the cusp of youth that I would dare go out with, you know, possible. She was apparently interested and wanted me to write her. And we did. And in a couple of months, I called her up and asked her out. You know, I was in Texas and she was in Ohio. I would fly there and spend a few days there. On one of the days we would go out. So she said she would let me know when. I got a letter a month later and she said, "I don't know about this going-out thing, but you can come and enjoy good intellectual conversation." She was clearly saying, "No, not a date." I wrote back and said I am a mature man and I can take a no. You know, I know what it is like to go on a "not really" date and be a pain in the ass, and so I don't want that to happen. So, uh, make her choice. Let's go out or we don't go out. I figured that was it. Then I got a Christmas card, which was a surprise to me. I happened to be in the Ohio area a couple of weeks later, and a friend and I contacted her and stopped by. Then we started writing again. We wrote each other for the next year back and forth. Some was friendly, some was funny, but never got to anything personal. Then she asked me to come visit. I thought this would be good. I thought with a year she felt more comfortable. She was working and had me during the day going places with her roommate who was having an affair and I was the cover, so I put a stop to that, and that got the girl I was visiting angry and she withdrew. That left the rest of the weekend just totally sucked. As a result of that I wrote her a book, a long letter that instead of attacking her blatantly, I wrote her a letter that was a conversation between me and a therapist. Talking back and forth about my assumptions before I went to see her and I was surprised and how I thought she was a nice girl, but I noticed this and that about her and so forth.

Therapist: Um-hum.

Client: But it wasn't an attacking letter; maybe it should have been, I don't know. I got no response from that. I didn't think I would. Around Christmas time I sent her an invitation to go skiing and that stuff. Didn't get a response from that. I didn't think I would. So I sent her a really nice Valentine's Day letter, box of stuff. And, um, she sent me a postcard and said she was visiting a school she was going to be going to. She told me where she was and said she'd write me a real letter soon. So at least two months passed and I didn't get a letter, so I decided to let her know everything that I know and what I was able to see about her and her behavior and do it in a very delicate, gentle, interesting, thoughtful way. So I did that and got a response real fast in about five days. She said, "I don't know where you came up with this stuff that there is something between us. There will never be, never ever ever ever" or something like that. I responded very briefly that I never thought there was anything between us. So, uh, . . .

Therapist: It sounds like you weren't very honest. You did hope there was something between you.

Client: Well, yeah, actually I wrote her in the book-letter and at the end I say, OK, I've been lying and I think we'd make a good couple and the whole thing. So I admitted very clearly where I was at.

Therapist: Um-hum.

Client: But when she wrote and said I don't know where you ever got this idea, I said that I never had any idea that there was anything.

I'm not an idiot. So in my interpretation she . . . that's one of the places she was coming from, plus if she could upset me and that stuff, she could change the subject to something she could handle. But, so that was June and I wrote a letter to apologize that I was being too personal. So, I find myself now, if I hear the right or the wrong song on the radio, depending on how you look at it. . . . (emotional pause) I find myself just hoping that some of the stuff I wrote her, she'd look at it a second time and it would sink in and create enough interest in her or curiosity in her to just send something so I would have an address, so I could know where she is. I don't know where she is right now.

Therapist: Uh-huh. You still have a lot of emotion around this.

Client: Yeah, there is a lot of emotion tied up in . . . uh (crying), tied up in . . . rejection . . . tied up in the, uh, . . . the idea that I couldn't do what, . . . I wanted to do, the failure of it, uh, and uh, I think one of the reasons to the exhaustion I was at, she, depending on how this illness I have goes, she may well be the last girl that I knew who knew me who didn't know me as someone who has cancer.

Therapist: She's the last potential partner who would know you without the disease. Just you.

Client: It's like meeting people, getting to know people is already hard enough to begin with, but, uh, to have to say, "Hi, how ya doing? I'm Joe. I have cancer." Which is pretty much on your mind when you're having difficulty just walking. They can notice something's wrong. I don't have to bother doing that with her because she already knows me. It's like last . . . last-ditch effort.

Therapist: There's grief in that. You see it as the last time you can be yourself with a girl without the disease. . . . It seems along with that you're saying you believe no one would want to be with someone who has cancer.

Client: Well, . . . I wouldn't go so far as to say no one. But it certainly does make things difficult when they were already difficult the way they were. So, certainly does screw things up pretty good.

Therapist: And having a relationship with a woman is extremely important to you.

Client: (crying, long pause)

Therapist: You have a whole bundle of feelings all wrapped up tightly.

Client: Yeah. (long pause) If you follow me, the connections, the next thing that I come up with is that . . . , is . . . (pause) . . . is wanting to be taken care of. (crying)

Therapist: You want someone to take care of you.

Client: Um. Just like uh, I'm hurt.

Therapist: Um-hum.

Client: A little kid when he's hurt . . . runs to Mom.

Therapist: Um-hum. Kind of a fear of what's going to happen.

Client: Yeah. So the idea . . . that you can cry from now until doomsday . . . and no one will take care of you. Because, you know, it's not that bad a situation. . . . It would be nice to have someone to, uh, support you.

Therapist: You are wondering, "Can I get through this by myself?"

Client: (sobbing)

Therapist: You face a frightening, uncertain future.

Client: Yep.

Therapist: You aren't confident you can make it by yourself. And you need someone else . . . it would be good to have someone else.

Client: Yeah. That's a good way to put it. (pause) It would be very good.

Therapist: Um-hum. Someone for support, someone you could count on.

Client: Yep. (long pause)

Therapist: And is the other part that you don't know if you can do it yourself?

Client: Um, yeah. I don't know if I can do it myself. I'm pretty damn stubborn and determined. If there is any way through it myself, I will be able to do it myself. I won't be able to do it myself, or I'm not sure. It would be easier to know that I didn't have to do it with the disease, because the illness pretty much puts the stops on being able to do it.

Therapist: "Do it" is a broad category. What does that mean to you?

Client: Um. Being able to be successful, be independent . . . all the things that are assumed about an American male. Have a family, have a house, have a good job, be highly regarded, and all that stuff.

Therapist: So you have set standards for what you want.

Client: Yeah, sure. And I have clearly entertained the notion that I may not be able to have those things or get them in the ways I wanted. At this time I have not given up the idea. I may have to give those things up.

Therapist: You have thought of that.

Client: Yeah, sure, and life pretty much would suck if that were true. I suppose I'll get through that too. (pause) I feel the tears and emotions well up most, and it seems at least initially I haven't spent hours trying to follow them, but it seems to me that they, they head toward being taken care of. And if a little kid is hurt, he wants to be taken care of. (crying)

Therapist: To be taken care of.

Client: Hurt.

Therapist: It overwhelms you. A lot of hurt.

Client: So it has to do with acceptance. It seems I'm being what I perceive of as being taken unfair advantage of on my job. At least on the outside I am defensive. I can't make them do what they should do.

Therapist: A sense of powerlessness.

Client: Yeah. It's frustrating. The job is frustrating. I can't really challenge the system. So when that hurts . . . my response is help me . . . help. (sighs)

Therapist: You're looking at your watch. Are you concerned about the time?

Client: I need a few minutes to . . . this is not going to resolve itself.

Therapist: You're not prepared to resolve this today.

Client: So I gotta get my eyes wiped, leave in one piece. It does feel good to let the, uh, energy out.

Therapist: You hold it in.

Client: Yes and no. Sometimes I turn on emotional music and weep for a while. But, um, but . . . I'm not a big religious person. Not an atheist. I haven't prayed for years, but . . . (pause) the last three days, I've prayed. Prayed for myself. I prayed for cure. I prayed that this girl somehow would send me a postcard, anything where I could get back in touch with her.

Therapist: Um-hum. You need something. Seems strange to you that you are not religious and you are praying.

Client: A last ditch . . . shot in the dark, really.

Therapist: Um-hum.

Client: And a part of the prayer goes, well, if I do get a postcard, then I will entertain the possibility that maybe there is a higher power.

Therapist: Make God prove . . .

Client: That's not the purpose. If I sat there and I was praying, uh, that would be a complete lack of integrity and bullshit. So I gotta put something in that.

Therapist: Sounds like you feel like a hypocrite on the one hand and yet . . .

Client: Well, yeah, you know, I mean, I don't believe . . . but if I got a postcard, I would certainly consider. . . . But I'm so data oriented I need facts. I need data. And all my data tells me that if there is a God, He is probably asleep. Or doesn't have an impact on what goes on here.

Therapist: For you.

Client: For me and for anybody.

Therapist: You have to see the proof.

Client: None of the spiritual stuff pans out in reality. One can always get in touch with one's emotions to feel better. And I don't know if there is an afterlife or some kind of God or anything like that, I suppose I'll find out. I'm not going to sit around and worry about it now. I'm going to have fun tonight.

Therapist: You have plans?

Client: A little, but just the idea that I have . . . released some of this stuff will leave me in a rebound in the opposite direction.

Therapist: The sadness, the emotion drags you down.

Client: It takes work, so it drags me down, I guess. I put a lot of energy into keeping things going. I have to stay on a special diet and medication with side effects. And I have to deal with the illness, and I have to deal with not getting those things in life that others already have. If I had the house and family, I'd only be dealing with the illness. But I have to deal with all the rest of that stuff, too.

Therapist: The disappointment *and* the illness . . . it's a lot to deal with.

Client: Having put it off and waiting and thinking life would be better. I'm the kind of person who persists, perseveres, thinks of different ways to do things, works hard, like with this girl. I tried, and I shared a good deal of myself and my knowledge, and I just got total rejection.

Therapist: You work hard and really put yourself personally into something—like your life plan, the job, and this girl—and then it doesn't work out the way you want it. Totally rejected.

Client: Yeah, I never had much luck fighting things with their own will . . . like my boss. (pause) So the question becomes how much did I create . . . how much of the things with the two people, you know, how much did I make her do what I didn't want her to do. How much did I create that the people on the job, their attitude? To what extent did I create that, stuff like that, and how could I have done it differently? And the feeling that I could have done it better and that kind of stuff. So, uh, that doesn't help either.

Therapist: Looking at it that way isn't productive for you. You don't see anything coming out of that for you.

Client: I mean, you know, I think about it, not a lot, but some. I generally have some confidence in what I have done given the options that were available. Things could have worked out differently given this and given that, and how there are still chances today to do what I want. I took my chance and . . . blew it. Used it.

Therapist: It seems you're approaching those situations in ways that are not working for you. And yet you seem to be repeating the same situation over. You feel a great deal of frustration and anger and confusion . . . it's not working for you.

Client: (sigh) It's not working . . . not much I can do . . . very seldom do I get angry. Unless the anger is turning back inside and I'm not aware of it.

Therapist: You don't feel angry, or not aware of it if you are.

Client: Uh . . . no. Anger for me is like an external thing, like, you know, like a blame. It's a way of not taking responsibility, so sadness to me is, it's my fault. I had a choice and I blew it. I didn't make it. I failed. And, um, I usually don't go around being angry because I usually feel that I can impact them. I can do something to impact them. I'd get angry if someone took away my options, you know, completely stood in my way, I'd be angry. I wouldn't lay down and cry. I would fight.

Therapist: Um-hum. . . . It looks like we are running out of time.

Client: So what is my conclusion? It . . . it is as long as everything is screwed up and, uh, there's a lot of emotion in there and, uh, I should talk it out with somebody as much as I can, and I don't know if there is anything I can do to resolve any of that stuff.

Therapist: Talking may not end the problems but can help release the emotions you build up.

Client: I just have to accept the truth about things. Like with this girl. If you can deal with something that hurts and face the pain of that, eventually the pain of that goes away. Then you can move on to other things. If you don't, you get stuck with it. I'm willing to go through the pain, but I'm not, uh, if what I need to do is go through a bunch of emotional stuff to be comfortable with becoming a vegetable, I'm not interested in doing that right now.

Therapist: You can take it step by step.

Summary and Discussion

The system of psychotherapy in this book is based on what is known in medicine as the principle of minimal intervention. Berne (1966) provides a clear statement of this principle:

1. *Primum non nocere*: Above all, the therapist should do no harm. Intervention should be made only when necessary and only to the extent necessary.
2. *Vis medicatrix naturae*: The organism has a built-in drive toward health, which applies to the psychological as well as to the physical realm. The therapist's function is to remove the blocks to natural healing and growth.
3. *Je le pensay, Dieu le guarit*: The therapist treats the patient, but it is God who cures the patient; or, the therapist provides the best treatment possible, avoiding hurting or injuring the patient, and nature does the healing. [pp. 62–63]

Medicine has been moving toward the development and use of less invasive procedures, while paradoxically it appears that psychotherapy has been moving toward more invasive procedures or interventions. The movement in medicine recognizes that every intervention is accompanied by a risk of harm. Psychological interventions also include risks.

The system developed in this book is the least interventionist of current approaches to psychotherapy. It draws on the psychological growth principle that every organism works toward actualizing or developing its potentials, in the process of self-actualization. The therapist facilitates this process, allowing the client to take responsibility for and be in control of the process itself. That clients can and do take this responsibility when allowed to do so is demonstrated by the examples in this chapter and throughout the text. The client initiates; the therapist follows and responds. The client talks; the therapist listens. In the relationship with a therapist who provides empathic understanding, respect, and therapeutic genuineness, the client engages in the self-disclosure, self-exploration, self-awareness, and self-understanding that lead to therapeutic behavior changes, choices, and decisions.

This therapy process operates in ways consistent with known principles of learning and behavior change:

1. The therapist conditions create a nonthreatening environment, in which the client can feel safe in self-disclosing and

self-exploring. A high level of threat is inimical to learning or changing.

2. In conditioning terms, the therapist conditions are the most effective reinforcers of the client behavior of self-exploration.

3. The open, accepting atmosphere provided by the therapist contributes to desensitizing the client's anxieties and fears in human relating. Relating to the therapist is also reinforced.

4. The therapy process is not a simple straight-line progression. The client evidences the approach–avoidance conflict, progressing up to the point when internal threat or anxiety is too great, then retreating or pausing until anxiety subsides or is reduced by the therapist's acceptance.

5. Therapy is not a problem-solving process in which separate problems are worked on until each is resolved. If the therapist insists on a client focusing on a particular problem, threat is created, and resistance and blocking by the client follow. All problems interrelate, and the client moves from one to another problem, then another, and another, returning to each in a spiraling process.

6. The therapist conditions provide an environment for self-discovery learning. While discovery learning is not always possible or desirable in other areas, it is the most relevant and most effective method for learning about oneself. All of the information needed by the client is present but not fully available. The conditions create an environment in which clients are able to bring up the relevant information needed for their own psychological healing and behavior change.

7. The therapist conditions reflect attitudes characteristic of self-actualizing persons. These conditions are also the conditions of all good human relationships. The therapist becomes a model for the client. It follows that the therapist, to be an effective model, must represent a higher level of the conditions than the client. The client, in becoming more like the therapist, becomes a more self-actualizing person.

8. The conditions, when offered at a high level by the therapist, involve the expectation by the therapist of change in the client. Expectations have a powerful effect on the behavior of others.

The therapist conditions in this system of psychotherapy represent the essential conditions for the healthy, continuing existence of a society or culture. The enduring values of interpersonal relationships are necessary for human beings to live together and to survive as a society. They are neither time bound nor culture bound. They are thus universal in nature, and a psychotherapy based on these conditions is thus a universal system.

References

Ackerman D. (1990). *A Natural History of the Senses*. New York: Random House.

Ainsworth, M. D. (1979). Infant–mother attachment. *American Psychologist* 34:932–937.

Akiskal, H., and McKinney, W. (1975). Overview of recent research in depression. *Archives of General Psychiatry* 32:285–305.

Alexander, F., and French, T. M. (1946). *Psychoanalytic Therapy*. New York: Ronald.

Alland, A., Jr. (1972). *The Human Imperative*. New York: Columbia University Press.

American Psychiatric Association (1952). *Diagnostic and Statistical Manual of Mental Disorders*. Washington, DC: APA.

_____ (1980). *Diagnostic and Statistical Manual of Mental Disorders*, 3rd. ed. Washington, DC: APA.

_____ (1987). *Diagnostic and Statistical Manual of Mental Disorders*, 3rd ed. rev. Washington, DC: APA.

_____ (1994). *Diagnostic and Statistical Manual of Mental Disorders*, 4th ed. Washington, DC: APA.

American Psychological Association. (1992). Ethical principles of psychologists and code of conduct. *American Psychologist* 47:1599–1611.

Angyal, A. (1941). *Foundations for a Science of Personality.* New York: Commonwealth Fund.

———— (1952). A theoretical model for personality studies. In *Theoretical Models and Personality Theory,* ed. D. Krech and G. S. Klein. Durham, NC: Duke University Press.

Ansbacher, H. L., and Ansbacher, R. R., eds. (1956). *The Individual Psychology of Alfred Adler.* New York: Basic Books.

Arkowitz, H. (1992). Integrative theories of therapy. In *History of Psychotherapy: A Century of Change,* ed. D. K. Freedheim, pp. 261–303. Washington, DC: American Psychological Association.

Arnkoff, H., and Glass, C. R. (1992). Cognitive therapy and psychotherapy integration. In *History of Psychotherapy: A Century of Change,* ed. D. K. Freedheim, pp. 657–694. Washington, DC: American Psychological Association.

Associated Press News Service (1988). Wanted: someone to love babies, if only for an hour. *Idaho Press–Tribune,* September 18, p. D1.

Atkinson, D. R., Maruyama, M., and Matsui, S. (1978). Effects of counselor race and counseling approach on Asian Americans' perceptions of counselor credibility and utility. *Journal of Counseling Psychology* 25:76–83.

Atkinson, D. R., Morten, G., and Sue, D. W. (1993). *Counseling American Minorities: A Cross-Cultural Perspective,* 4th ed. Dubuque, IA: Brown.

Bakwin, H. (1942). Loneliness in infants. *American Journal of Diseases of Children* 63:30–40.

Batson, C. D. (1990). How social an animal? The human capacity for caring. *American Psychologist* 45:336–346.

Baumrind, D. (1980). New directions in socialization research. *American Psychologist* 35:639–652.

Bender, L., and Yarnell, H. (1941). An observation nursery: a study of 250 children in the psychiatric division of Bellevue Hospital. *American Journal of Psychiatry* 97:1158–1174.

Bergin, A. E., and Garfield, S. L. (1994). *Handbook of Psychotherapy and Behavior Change,* 4th ed. New York: Wiley.

Bergin, A. E., and Lambert, M. J. (1978). The evaluation of therapeutic outcomes. In *Handbook of Psychotherapy and Behavior Change,* 2nd ed., ed.

S. L. Garfield and A. E. Bergin, pp. 139–189. New York: Wiley.

Bergin, A. E., and Strupp, H. H. (1972). *Changing Frontiers in the Science of Psychotherapy*. Chicago: Aldine.

Bergin, A. E., and Suinn, R. M. (1975). Individual psychotherapy and behavior therapy. *Annual Review of Psychology* 26:509–556.

Bernal, M. E., and Padilla, A. M. (1982). Status of minority curricula and training in clinical psychology. *American Psychologist* 37:780–787.

Berne, E. (1961). *Transactional Analysis in Psychotherapy*. New York: Grove.

———— (1966). *Principles of Group Treatment*. New York: Oxford University Press.

Beutler, L. E. (1978). Psychotherapy and persuasion. In *Special Problems in Child and Adolescent Behavior*, ed. L. E. Beutler and R. Greene, pp. 119–159. Westport, CT: Tecnomic.

———— (1983). *Eclectic Psychotherapy: A Systematic Approach*. Elmsford, NY: Pergamon.

———— (1986). Systematic eclectic psychotherapy. In *Handbook of Eclectic Psychotherapy*, ed. J. C. Norcross, pp. 94–131. New York: Brunner/Mazel.

Beutler, L. E., and Clarkin, J. F. (1990). *Systematic Treatment Selection: Toward Targeted Therapeutic Interventions*. New York: Brunner/Mazel.

Beutler, L. E., Crago, M., and Arizmendi, T. G. (1986). Therapist variables in psychotherapy process and outcome. In *Handbook of Psychotherapy and Behavior Change: An Empirical Analysis*, 3rd. ed., ed. S. L. Garfield and A. E. Bergin, pp. 257–310. New York: Wiley.

Beutler, L. E., Machado, P. P. P., and Neufeldt, S. A. (1994). Therapist variables. In *Handbook of Psychotherapy and Behavior Change*, 4th ed., ed. A. E. Bergin and S. L. Garfield, pp. 229–269. New York: Wiley.

Bibring, E. (1958). The development and problems of the theory of instincts. In *Understanding Human Motivation*, ed. C. Stacy and M. F. DeMartino, pp. 474–498. Cleveland, OH: Howard Allen.

Black, J. D. (1952). Common factors of the patient–therapist relationship in diverse psychotherapies. *Journal of Clinical Psychology* 8:302–306.

Bonner, H. (1965). *On Being Mindful of Man*. Boston: Houghton Mifflin.

Bowlby, J. (1940). The influence of early environment in the development of neuroses and neurotic character. *International Journal of Psycho-Analysis* 1:154–178.

———— (1944). Forty-four juvenile thieves: their characters and homelife.

International Journal of Psycho-Analysis 25:19–52.

———— (1951). Maternal care and mental health. Geneva: World Health Monograph Series 2.

———— (1959). Separation anxiety. *International Journal of Psycho-Analysis* 41:89–113.

———— (1973). *Attachment and Loss. Vol. 2: Separation.* New York: Basic Books.

Brown, D. E. (1991). *Human Universals.* Philadelphia: Temple University Press.

Buhler, C. (1961). *Values in Psychotherapy.* New York: Free Press.

Burlingham, D., and Freud, A. (1944). *Infants without Families.* London: Allen & Unwin.

Burton, A. (1967). *Modern Humanistic Psychotherapy.* San Francisco: Jossey-Bass.

———— (1972). *Interpersonal Psychotherapy.* Englewood Cliffs, NJ: Prentice Hall.

————, ed. (1976). *What Makes Behavior Change Possible?* New York: Brunner/Mazel.

Buss, A. (1966). *Psychopathology.* New York: Wiley.

Campbell, D. T. (1967). Stereotypes and the perception of group differences. *American Psychologist* 22:817–829.

Carkhuff, R. R. (1969). *Helping and Human Relations.* Vol. I: *Selection and Training.* Vol. II: *Practice and Research.* New York: Holt, Rinehart & Winston.

Carkhuff, R. R., & Berenson, B. G. (1967). *Beyond Counseling and Therapy.* New York: Holt, Rinehart & Winston.

Carson, R. C. (1990). Needed: a new beginning. [Review of diagnosis and classification in psychiatry: a critical appraisal of *DSM-III*]. *Contemporary Psychology* 35:11–12.

Cartwright, D. S., and Cartwright, R. D. (1958). Faith and improvement in psychotherapy. *Journal of Counseling Psychology* 5:174–177.

Casement, J. P. (1991). *Learning from the Patient.* New York: Guilford.

Chunn, J. F., Dunston, P. J., and Ross-Sheriff, F., eds. (1983). *Mental Health and People of Color: Curriculum Development and Change.* Washington, DC: Howard University Press.

Colby, K. M. (1964). Psychotherapeutic processes. *Annual Review of Psychology*

15:347–370.

Collier, R. M. (1950). A basis for integration rather than fragmentation in psychotherapy. *Journal of Consulting Psychology* 14:199–205.

Combs, A. W., and Snygg, D. (1959). *Individual Behavior: A Perceptual Approach to Behavior*. New York: Harper & Row.

Corrigan, J. D., Dell, D. M., Lewis, K. N., and Schmidt, L. D. (1980). Counseling as a social influence process. *Journal of Counseling Psychology Monograph* 27:395–441.

Crussan, B. R. (1991). The unfolding of behavioral science. Review of *The Life of the Mind: Selected Papers,* by J. W. Brown. *Contemporary Psychology* 35:137–138.

Cudney, M. R. (1968). The use of immediacy in counseling. In *Counseling for the Liberal Arts Campus,* ed. J. C. Heston and W. B. Frick. Yellow Springs, OH: Antioch Press.

Cushman, P. (1992). Psychotherapy to 1992: a historically situated interpretation. In *History of Psychotherapy: A Century of Change,* ed. D. K. Freedheim, pp. 21–64. Washington, DC: American Psychological Association.

Dauphinais, R., Dauphinais, L., and Rowe, W. (1981). Effects of race and communication style on Indian perceptions of counselor effectiveness. *Counselor Education and Supervision* 21:72–80.

Day, W. F. (1972). Beyond bondage and regimentation. Review of B. F. Skinner, *Beyond Freedom and Dignity. Contemporary Psychology* 17:465–469.

De Grazia, S. (1952). *Errors in Psychotherapy.* Garden City, NY: Doubleday.

Derlega, V. J., Lovell, R., and Chasken, A. L. (1976). Effects of therapist self-disclosure and its perceived appropriateness on client self-disclosure. *Journal of Consulting and Clinical Psychology* 44:866.

Dickenson, W. A. (1969). Therapist self-disclosure as a variable in psychotherapeutic process and outcome. *Dissertation Abstracts International* 30:2434B.

Dimond, A. E., Havens, R. A., and Jones, A. C. (1978). A conceptual framework for the practice of prescriptive eclecticism in psychotherapy. *American Psychologist* 33:239–248.

Dollard, J., Doob, L. W., Miller, N. E., et al. (1939). *Frustration and Aggression.* New Haven, CT: Yale University Press.

Dormaar, M., Kijkman, S. I. M., and de Vries, M. W. (1989). Consensus in patient–therapist interactions: a measure of the therapeutic relationship related to outcome. *Psychotherapy Psychosomatica* 51:69–76.

Dudley, G. R., and Rawlins, M. L., eds. (1985). Psychotherapy with ethnic minorities. *Psychotherapy* 22:308–477.

Durkheim, E. (1951). *Suicide.* Glencoe, IL: Free Press.

Ellis, A. (1962). *Reason and Emotion in Psychotherapy.* Secaucus, NJ: Citadel.

———— (1980). The value of efficiency in psychotherapy. *Psychotherapy: Theory, Research and Practice* 17:414–419.

Emmelkamp, P. M. G. (1986). Behavior therapy with adults. In *Handbook of Psychotherapy and Behavior Change,* ed. S. L. Garfield and A. E. Bergin, 3rd ed., pp. 385–442. New York: Wiley.

English, H. B., and English, A. C. (1958). *A Comprehensive Dictionary of Psychological and Psychoanalytic Terms.* New York: McKay.

Fee, A. H., Elkins, G. R., and Boyd, L. (1982). Testing and counseling psychologists: current practices and implications for training. *Journal of Personality Assessment* 46:116–118.

Fiedler, F. (1950a). The concept of an ideal therapeutic relationship. *Journal of Consulting Psychology* 14:235–245.

———— (1950b). A comparison of therapeutic relationships in psychoanalytic, nondirective and Adlerian therapeutic relationships. *Journal of Consulting Psychology* 14:436–445.

———— (1951). Factor analyses of psychoanalytic, nondirective and Adlerian therapeutic relationships. *Journal of Consulting Psychology* 15:32–38.

Fish, J. M. (1973). *Placebo Therapy.* San Francisco: Jossey-Bass.

Flexner, A. (1960). *Medical education in the United States and Canada: a report of the Carnegie Fund for the advancement of teaching.* Originally published in 1910. New York: Carnegie Foundation.

Foote, N. N., and Cottrell, L. S., Jr. (1955). *Identity and Interpersonal Competence.* Chicago: University of Chicago Press.

Ford, D. H. (1971). Some historical and conceptual perspectives on psychotherapy and behavior change. In *Handbook of Psychotherapy and Behavior Change: An Empirical Analysis,* ed. A. E. Bergin and S. L. Garfield. New York: Wiley.

Ford, D. H., and Urban, H. B. (1963). *Systems of Psychotherapy.* New York: Wiley.

———— (1967). Psychotherapy. *Annual Review of Psychology.* Palo Alto, CA:

Annual Reviews.

Frank, J. D. (1959). The dynamics of the psychotherapeutic relationship. *Psychiatry* 22:17–39.

———— (1961). *Persuasion and Healing.* Baltimore: Johns Hopkins University Press.

———— (1973). *Persuasion and Healing,* 2nd ed. Baltimore: Johns Hopkins University Press.

———— (1974). Therapeutic components of psychotherapy. A 25-year progress report of research. *Journal of Nervous and Mental Disease* 159:325–342.

———— (1982). Therapeutic components shared by all psychotherapists. In *Psychotherapy Research and Behavior Change,* ed. J. H. Harvey and M. M. Parks, pp. 9–37. Washington, DC: American Psychological Association.

Frank, J. D., and Frank, J. (1991). *Persuasion and Healing,* 3rd ed. Baltimore: Johns Hopkins University Press.

Frankl, V. E. (1965). *The Doctor and the Soul,* 2nd ed. New York: Knopf.

Franks, C. M. (1984). On conceptual and technical integrity in psychoanalysis and behavior therapy: two fundamentally incompatible systems. In *Psychoanalytic Therapy and Behavior Therapy: Is Integration Possible?* ed. H. Arkowitz and S. B. Messer. New York: Plenum.

Freedheim, D. K., ed. (1992). *History of Psychotherapy: A Century of Change.* Washington, DC: American Psychological Association.

Freeman, S. (1993). Client-centered therapy and diverse populations. *Journal of Multicultural Counseling and Development* 21:248–254.

Freeman, S. C., and Krumboltz, J. D. (1992). *Client-Centered Therapy vs. Behaviorism: A Debate* (video). Lynchburg, VA: Lynchburg College.

Fromm, E. (1956). *The Art of Loving.* New York: Bantam.

Garfield, S. L. (1973). Basic ingredients or common factors in psychotherapy. *Journal of Consulting and Clinical Psychology* 41:9–12.

———— (1980). *Psychotherapy: An Eclectic Approach.* New York: Wiley.

———— (1982). Eclecticism and integration in psychotherapy. *Behavior Therapy* 13:610–623.

———— (1986). Research on client variables in psychotherapy. In *Handbook of Psychotherapy and Behavior Change,* 3rd ed., ed. S. L. Garfield and A. E. Bergin, pp. 213–256. New York: Wiley.

Garfield, S. L., & Bergin, A. E., eds. (1971). *Handbook of Psychotherapy and Behavior Change,* 2nd ed. New York: Wiley.

———— (1994). *Handbook of Psychotherapy and Behavior Change,* 4th ed. New York: Wiley.

Garfield, S. L., and Kurtz, R. M. (1974). A survey of clinical psychologists: characteristics, activities and orientation. *The Clinical Psychologist* 28(1):7–10.

———— (1976). Clinical psychologists in the 1970s. *American Psychologist* 31:1–9.

Gelso, C. J., and Carter, J. A. (1985). The relationship in counseling and psychotherapy: components, consequences, and theoretical antecedents. *The Counseling Psychologist* 13:155–243.

Gendlin, E. T. (1962). Client-centered developments in work with schizophrenics. *Journal of Consulting Psychology* 9:205–212.

Gill, M. M. (1976). Three on a match but no light. Review of *Three Psychotherapies: A Clinical Comparison,* ed. C. H. Loew, H. Grayson, and G. H. Loew. *Contemporary Psychology* 21:291–292.

Glencavage, L. M., and Norcross, J. C. (1990). Where are the commonalities among the therapeutic factors? *Professional Psychology: Research and Practice* 21:372–378.

Goldfried, M. R. (1980). Toward a delineation of therapeutic change principles. *American Psychologist* 35:991–999.

———— (1982). On the history of therapeutic integration. *Behavior Therapy* 13:572–593.

Goldfried, M. R., and Castonguay, L. G. (1992). The future of psychotherapy integration. *Psychotherapy* 29:4–10.

Goldfried, M. R., and Davison, C. (1970). *Clinical Behavior Therapy.* New York: Holt, Rinehart & Winston.

Goldfried, M. R., and Newman, R. (1986). Psychotherapy integration: an historical perspective. In *Handbook of Eclectic Psychotherapy,* ed. J. C. Norcross. New York: Brunner/Mazel.

Goldfried, M. R., and Safran, J. D. (1986). Future directions in psychotherapy integration. In *Handbook of Eclectic Psychotherapy,* ed. J. C. Norcross. New York: Brunner/Mazel.

Golding, W. (1955). *Lord of the Flies.* New York: Coward McCann.

Goldstein, A. P. (1962). *Therapist–Patient Expectancies in Psychotherapy.* New

York: Macmillan.

———— (1966). Psychotherapy research and extrapolation from social psychology. *Journal of Counseling Psychology* 13:38–45.

———— (1973). *Structured Learning Therapy: Toward a Psychotherapy for the Poor.* New York: Academic.

Goldstein, A. P., Heller, K., and Secrest, L. B. (1966). *Psychotherapy and the Psychology of Behavior Change.* New York: Wiley.

Goldstein, K. (1939). *The Organism.* New York: World Book.

Goodstein, L. D. (1977). Dialect in psychotherapy. Review of *What Makes Behavior Change Possible?*, ed. A. Burton. *Contemporary Psychology* 22:578–579.

Greene, B. A. (1985). Considerations in the treatment of black patients by white therapists. *Psychotherapy* 22:389–393.

Guntrip, H. (1975). My experience of analysis with Fairbairn and Winnicott. *International Review of Psycho-Analysis* 2:145–156.

Gurman, A. S. (1977). The patient's perception of the therapeutic relationship. In *Effective Psychotherapy: A Handbook of Research,* ed. A. S. Gurman and A. M. Razin, pp. 503–543. New York: Pergamon.

Hahn, M. E., and MacLean, M. S. (1955). *Counseling Psychology,* 2nd ed. New York: McGraw-Hill.

Hall, B., ed. (1959). *A Psychiatrist's World: The Selected Papers of Karl Menninger.* New York: Viking.

Halleck, S. L. (1971). *The Politics of Therapy.* New York: Science House.

Hart, J. T. (1983). *Modern Eclectic Therapy.* New York: Plenum.

———— (1986). Functional eclectic therapy. In *Handbook of Eclectic Psychotherapy,* ed. J. C. Norcross, pp. 201–224. New York: Brunner/Mazel.

Hathaway, S. R. (1948). Some considerations relative to nondirective counseling as therapy. *Journal of Clinical Psychology* 4:226–235.

Hawking, S. (1993). *Black Holes and Baby Universes and Other Essays.* New York: Bantam.

Hayward, R. H. (1974). Process and outcome consequences of therapist self-disclosure. *Dissertation Abstracts International* 34:6210B–6211B.

Hebrink, R. (1950). *The Psychotherapy Handbook.* New York: New American Library.

Held, B. S. (1984). Toward a strategic eclecticism: a proposal. *Psychotherapy* 21:232–241.

Henderson, S. (1982). The significance of social relationships in the etiology of neuroses. In *The Place of Attachment in Human Behavior,* ed. C. Parkes and J. Stevenson-Hinkle. New York: Basic Books.

Hilgard, E. R. (1949). Human motives and the concept of the self. *American Psychologist* 4:374–382.

———— (1962). *Introduction to Psychology,* 3rd ed. New York: Harcourt, Brace & World.

Ho, D. Y. F. (1985). Cultural values and professional issues in clinical psychology: the Hong Kong experience. *American Psychologist* 40:1212–1218.

Hoffer, E. (November 24, 1979). *Saturday Review.*

Hovland, C. L., Janis, I. L., and Kelley, H. H. (1953). *Communication and Persuasion: Psychological Studies of Opinion Change.* New Haven, CT: Yale University Press.

Ibrahim, F. A. (1991). Contribution of cultural worldview to generic counseling and development. *Journal of Counseling and Development* 70:13–19.

Jahoda, M. (1950). Toward a social psychology of mental health. In *Symposium on the Healthy Personality.* Supplement II. *Problems of Infancy and Childhood,* ed. M. J. E. Senn, pp. 211–231. New York: Josiah Macy Foundation.

———— (1958). *Current Concepts of Positive Mental Health.* New York: Basic Books.

James, W. (1902). *Varieties of Religious Experience.* New York: Modern Library.

Jones, M. R., ed. (1962). *Nebraska Symposium on Motivation.* Lincoln: University of Nebraska Press.

Jourard, S. (1964). *The Transparent Self.* Princeton, NJ: Van Nostrand Reinhold.

Kanfer, F. H., and Phillips, J. A. (1969). A survey of current behavior therapies and a proposal for classification. In *Behavior Therapy: Appraisal and Status,* ed. C. M. Franks, pp. 445–475. New York: McGraw-Hill.

Karasu, J. B. (1986). The specificity versus nonspecificity dilemma: toward identifying therapeutic change agents. *American Journal of Psychiatry* 143:687–695.

Karen R. (1994). *Becoming Attached.* New York: Warner.

Kell, B. L., and Mueller, W. J. (1966). *Impact and Change: A Study of Counseling*

Relationships. New York: Appleton-Century-Crofts.

Kelley, E. C. (1962). The fully functioning self. In *Perceiving, Behaving, Becoming,* ed. A. W. Combs, pp. 9-20. Washington, DC: National Education Association.

Kelly, E. L. (1961). Clinical psychology—1960. *Newsletter, Division of Clinical Psychology of the American Psychological Association* 14:1-11.

Kelly, G. A. (1958). Man's construction of his alternatives. In *Assessment of Human Motives,* ed. G. Lindzey. New York: Rinehart.

———— (1962). Europe's matrix of decision. In *Nebraska Symposium on Motivation,* ed. M. R. Jones, pp. 83-123. Lincoln: University of Nebraska Press.

Kisch, J., and Kroll, J. (1980). Meaningfulness versus effectiveness: paradoxical implications of the evaluation of psychotherapy. *Psychotherapy: Theory, Research and Practice* 17:401-413.

Kitchner, K. S. (1984). Intuition, critical evaluation and ethical principles: the foundation for ethical decisions in counseling psychology. *The Counseling Psychologist* 12:43-55.

Klein, M., Dittman, A. J., Parloff, M. B., and Gill, M. M. (1969). Behavior therapy: observations and reflections. *Journal of Consulting and Clinical Psychology* 33:259-266.

Krumboltz, J. D. (1966). Promoting adaptive behaviors: new answers to familiar questions. In *Revolution in Counseling.* Boston: Houghton Mifflin.

Krumboltz, J. D., Becker-Haven, J. F., and Burnett, K. F. (1979). Counseling psychology. *Annual Review of Psychology* 30:555-602.

LaCrosse, M. B. (1977). Comparative perceptions of counselor behavior: a replication and extension. *Journal of Counseling Psychology* 24:464-471.

———— (1980). Perceived counselor social influence and counseling outcome: validity of the Counselor Rating Form. *Journal of Counseling Psychology* 27:320-327.

LaCrosse, M. B., and Barak, A. (1976). Differential perceptions of counselor behavior. *Journal of Counseling Psychology* 23:170-172.

Lambert, M. J., and Bergin, A. E. (1983). Therapist characteristics and their contributions to psychotherapy outcome. In *The Handbook of Clinical Psychology,* vol. 1, ed. C. E. Walker, pp. 205-241. Homewood, IL: Dow Jones Irwin.

_____ (1994). The effectiveness of psychotherapy. In *Handbook of Psychotherapy and Behavior Change,* ed. A. E. Bergin and S. L. Garfield, 4th ed., pp. 143–189. New York: Wiley.

Lambert, M. J., DeJulio, S. S., and Stein, D. (1978). Therapist interpersonal skills. *Psychological Bulletin* 85:467–489.

Lambert, M. J., Shapiro, D. A., and Bergin, A. E. (1986). The effectiveness of psychotherapy. In *Handbook of Psychotherapy and Behavior Change,* 3rd ed., ed. S. L. Garfield and A. E. Bergin, pp. 157–211. New York: Wiley.

Lang, P. J., Melamed, B. G., and Hart, J. T. (1970). A psychophysical analysis of fear modification using an automated desensitization procedure. *Journal of Abnormal Psychology* 76:220–234.

Larson, D. (1980). Therapeutic schools, styles, and schoolism: a national survey. *Journal of Humanistic Psychology* 20(3):1–20.

Lasch, C. (1979). *The Culture of Narcissism: American Life in an Age of Diminishing Expectations.* New York: Norton.

Lazarus, A. A. (1967). In support of technical eclecticism. *Psychological Reports* 21:415–416.

_____ (1981). *Multimodal Therapy.* New York: McGraw-Hill.

_____ (1988). Eclecticism in behavior therapy. In *Advances in Theory and Practice in Behavior Therapy,* ed. P. M. G. Emmelkamp, W. T. A. N. Everald, F. Kraaimast, and J. J. M. vanSon, pp. 63–70. Amsterdam: Swets & Zeitlinger.

Lazarus, A. A., and Beutler, L. E. (1993). On technical eclecticism. *Journal of Counseling and Development* 71:381–386.

Lazarus, A. A., Beutler, L. E., and Norcross, J. C. (1992). The future of technical eclecticism. *Psychotherapy* 29:11–20.

Lecky, P. (1945). *Self-consistency: A Theory of Personality.* New York: Island.

Lederman, L., and Teresi, D. (1993). *The God Particle: If the Universe Is the Answer, What Is the Question?* New York: Houghton Mifflin.

Lee, H. (1960). *To Kill a Mockingbird.* Philadelphia: Lippincott.

Leo, J. (1985). A therapist in every corner. *Time,* December 23, p. 59.

Leong, F. T. (1986). Counseling and psychotherapy with Asian-Americans. *Journal of Counseling Psychology* 33:196–206.

Levy, D. (1937). Primary affect hunger. *American Journal of Psychiatry* 94:643–652.

Littman, R. A. (1958). Motives, history and causes. In *Nebraska Symposium on Motivation*, ed. M. R. Jones, pp. 114–168. Lincoln: University of Nebraska Press.

Luborsky, L., McLellan, A. T., Woody, G. E., et al. (1985). Therapist success and its determinants. *Archives of General Psychiatry* 42:602–611.

Luborsky, L., Singer, B., and Luborsky, L. (1975). Comparative studies of psychotherapy. *Archives of General Psychiatry* 32:995–1008.

Lynch, J. J. (1977). *The Broken Heart: The Medical Consequences of Loneliness.* New York: Basic Books.

Maddi, S. (1973a). Ethics and psychotherapy: remarks stimulated by White's paper. *The Counseling Psychologist* 4(2):26–29.

———— (1973b). Creativity is strenuous. *The University of Chicago Magazine.* September–October, pp. 18–23.

Mahalik, J. R. (1990). Systematic eclectic models. *The Counseling Psychologist* 18(4):665–679.

Mahoney, M. J., Norcross, J. C., Prochaska, J. O., and Missar, C. D. (n.d.). *Human psychological development and psychotherapy: convergence among American clinical psychologists.* Unpublished manuscript.

Mahrer, A. H., ed. (1967). *The Goals of Psychotherapy.* New York: Appleton-Century-Crofts.

Maslow, A. H. (1943). A theory of human motivation. *Psychological Review* 50:370–396.

———— (1949). Our maligned human nature. *Journal of Psychology* 28:273–278.

———— (1954). *Motivation and Personality.* New York: Harper & Row.

———— (1955). Deficiency motivation and growth motivation. In *Nebraska Symposium on Motivation*, ed. M. R. Jones, pp. 1–30. Lincoln: University of Nebraska Press.

———— (1956). Self-actualizing people: a study of psychological health. In *The Self: Explorations in Personal Growth*, ed. C. E. Moustakas, pp. 160–174. New York: Harper & Row.

———— (1962). *Toward a Psychology of Being.* Princeton, NJ: Van Nostrand Reinhold.

———— (1970). *Motivation and Personality,* 2nd ed. New York: Harper & Row.

May, R. (1954). A psychologist looks at mental health in today's world. *Mental Hygiene* 38(1):1–11.

———— (1967). *Psychology and the Human Dilemma.* Princeton, NJ: D. Van Nostrand.

Mays, V. M. (1985). The Black American and psychotherapy: the dilemma. *Psychotherapy* 22:379–388.

Mays, V. M., and Albee, G. W. (1992). Psychotherapy and ethnic minorities. In *History of Psychotherapy,* ed. D. K. Freedheim, pp. 552–570. Washington, DC: American Psychological Association.

McNeill, J. T. (1965). *A History of Souls.* New York: Harper & Row.

Meadow, A. (1982). Psychopathology, psychotherapy, and the Mexican-American patient. In *Minority Mental Health,* ed. E. E. Jones and S. J. Korchin, pp. 331–361. New York: Praeger.

Menninger, K., Ellenberger, H., Pruyser, P., and Mayman, M. (1958). The unitary concept of mental illness. *Bulletin of the Menninger Clinic* 22:4–12.

Menninger, K., and Holzman, P. S. (1973). *Theory of Psychoanalytic Techniques,* 2nd ed. New York: Basic Books.

Menninger, K., Mayman, M., and Pruyser, P. (1963). *The Vital Balance.* New York: Viking.

Messer, S. B. (1986). Eclecticism in psychotherapy: underlying assumptions, problems, and tradeoffs. In *Handbook of Eclectic Psychotherapy,* ed. J. C. Norcross, pp. 379–397. New York: Brunner/Mazel.

Mitchell, K. M. (1971). Relationship between therapist response to therapist-relevant client expressions and therapy process and client outcome. *Dissertation Abstracts International* 32:1853B.

Mitchell, K. M., Bozarth, J. D., and Krauft, C. C. (1977). A reappraisal of the therapeutic effectiveness of accurate empathy, non-possessive warmth, and genuineness. In *Effective Psychotherapy,* ed. A. S. Gurman and A. M. Razin, pp. 482–502. New York: Pergamon.

Montagu, A. (1962). *The Humanization of Man.* Cleveland: World Publishing.

———— (1970). A scientist looks at love. *Phi Beta Kappan* 51:463–467.

———— (1981). *Growing Young.* New York: McGraw-Hill.

Montessori, M. (1917). *Spontaneous Activity in Education.* New York: Stokes.

Mook, D. G. (1988). The selfish paradigm. (Review of *The Battle for Human Nature: Science, Morality and Modern Life*). *Contemporary Psychology* 33:5–7.

Moore, T. (1992). *Care of the Soul: A Guide for Cultivating Depth and Sacredness in Everyday Life.* New York: HarperCollins.

Morrow, L. (1992). Video warriors in Los Angeles. *Time,* May 11, p. 68.

Muehlberg, N., Pierce, R., and Drasgow, J. (1969). A factor analysis of therapeutically facilitative conditions. *Journal of Clinical Psychology* 25:93–95.

Murray, E. J. (1986). Possibilities and promise of eclecticism. In *Handbook of Eclectic Psychotherapy*, ed. J. C. Norcross, pp. 398–415. New York: Brunner/Mazel.

Nietzel, M. T., Russell, R. L., Hemmings, K. A., and Gretter, M. L. (1987). Clinical significance of psychotherapy for unipolar depression: a metanalytic approach to social comparison. *Journal of Consulting and Clinical Psychology* 55:155–161.

Norcross, J. C. (1986a). *Handbook of Eclectic Psychotherapy*. New York: Brunner/Mazel.

_____ (1986b). Eclectic psychotherapy: an introduction and review. In *Handbook of Eclectic Psychotherapy*, ed. J. C. Norcross, pp. 3–24. New York: Brunner/Mazel.

_____ (1990). Commentary: eclecticism misrepresented and integration misunderstood. *Psychotherapy* 27:297–298.

_____ , ed. (1992). The future of psychotherapy. Special issue of *Psychotherapy* 29:1–150.

Norcross, J. C., and Prochaska, J. O. (1982). A national survey of clinical psychologists: affiliations and orientations. *The Clinical Psychologist* 35(3):1–6.

Oberndorf, C. P. (1946). Constant elements in psychotherapy. *Psychoanalytic Quarterly* 15:435–449.

Orlinsky, D. E., and Howard, K. I. (1978). The relation of process to outcome in psychotherapy. In *Handbook of Psychotherapy and Behavior Change: An Empirical Analysis,* 3rd ed., ed. S. L. Garfield and A. E. Bergin, pp. 283–330. New York: Wiley.

_____ (1986). Process and outcome in psychotherapy. In *Handbook of Psychotherapy and Behavior Change: An Empirical Analysis,* 3rd ed., ed. S. L. Garfield and A. E. Bergin, pp. 311–381. New York: Wiley.

Orne, M. E. (1962). On the social psychology of the psychological experiment: with particular reference to demand characteristics and their implications. *American Psychologist* 17:776–783.

Orwell, G. (1949). *1984.* New York: Harcourt Brace Jovanovich.

Padilla, E., Boxley, A., and Wagner, N. (1972). *The desegregation of clinical psychology training.* Mimeographed.

Palmer, S. (1979). *A Primer of Eclectic Psychotherapy.* Monterey, CA: Brooks/ Cole.

Pande, S. (1968). The mystique of Western psychotherapy: an Eastern interpretation. *Journal of Nervous and Mental Disease* 146:425–432.

Parens, H., and Kramer, S., eds. (1993). *Prevention in Mental Health.* New York: Jason Aronson.

Parloff, M. B. (1967). Goals in psychotherapy: mediating and ultimate. In *Goals of Psychotherapy,* ed. A. R. Mahrer, pp. 5–19. New York: Appleton-Century-Crofts.

———— (1976). Shopping for the right therapy. *Saturday Review,* February 21.

———— (1982). Psychotherapy evidence and reimbursement decisions: Bambi meets Godzilla. *American Journal of Psychiatry* 139:718–729.

Parloff, M. B., Waskow, I. E., and Wolfe, B. E. (1978). Research on therapist variables in relation to process and outcome. In *Handbook of Psychotherapy and Behavior Change: An Empirical Analysis,* 2nd ed., ed. S. L. Garfield and A. E. Bergin, pp. 233–282. New York: Wiley.

Patterson, C. H. (1948). Is psychotherapy dependent upon diagnosis? *American Psychologist* 3:155–159.

———— (1949). Diagnosis and rational psychotherapy. *Journal of Nervous and Mental Disorders* 109:440–450.

———— (1959a). *Counseling and Psychotherapy: Theory and Practice.* New York: Harper & Row.

———— (1959b). Counseling as a relationship. *Journal of Rehabilitation* 25:13–15.

———— (1962). *Counseling and Guidance in Schools: A First Course.* New York: Harper & Row.

———— (1974). *Relationship Counseling and Psychotherapy.* New York: Harper & Row.

———— (1978). Cross-cultural or intercultural counseling or psychotherapy. *International Journal for the Advancement of Counseling* 1:231–247.

———— (1980). Williamson and the Minnesota point of view. In *Theories of Counseling and Psychotherapy,* 3rd ed., pp. 19–64. New York: Harper & Row.

———— (1984). Empathy, warmth, and genuineness in psychotherapy: a review of reviews. *Psychotherapy* 21:431–438.

_____ (1985a). *The Therapeutic Relationship: Foundations for an Eclectic Psychotherapy.* Monterey, CA: Brooks/Cole.

_____ (1985b). What is the placebo in psychotherapy? *Psychotherapy* 22:163–169.

_____ (1986). *Theories of Counseling and Psychotherapy,* 4th ed. New York: Harper & Row.

_____ (1989a). *A universal system of psychotherapy.* Keynote speech, Southeast Asian Symposium on Counseling and Guidance in the 21st Century, Taipei, Taiwan, December.

_____ (1989b). Values in counseling and psychotherapy. *Counseling and Values* 33:164–176.

_____ (1989c). Eclecticism in psychotherapy: Is integration possible? *Psychotherapy* 26:157–161.

_____ (1990). Involuntary clients: a person-centered view. *Person-Centered Review* 5:316–330.

Patterson, C. H., and Watkins, C. E., Jr. (1996). *Theories of Psychotherapy.* New York: HarperCollins.

Paul, G. L. (1967). Outcome research in psychotherapy. *Journal of Consulting Psychology* 31:109–118.

Pearson, L., ed. (1965). *The Use of Written Productions in Counseling and Psychotherapy.* Springfield, IL: Charles C Thomas.

Pedersen, P. B. (1976). The field of intercultural counseling. In *Counseling across Cultures,* ed. P. B. Pedersen, W. J. Lonner, and J. G. Draguns, pp. 17–41. Honolulu: University Press of Hawaii.

_____ (1990). The multicultural perspective as a fourth force in counseling. *Journal of Mental Health Counseling* 12:93–95.

_____ (1991). Multiculturalism as a generic approach to counseling. *Journal of Counseling and Development* 70:6–12.

Pedersen, P. B., Lonner, W., and Draguns, J. G., eds. (1976). *Counseling across Cultures.* Honolulu: University Press of Hawaii.

Pentony, P. (1981). *Models of Influence in Psychotherapy.* New York: Free Press.

Perls, F. S. (1969a). *Ego, Hunger and Aggression.* New York: Random House.

_____ (1969b). *Gestalt Therapy Verbatim.* Moab, UT: Real People Press.

Persons, J. B. (1991). Psychotherapy outcome studies do not accurately represent current models of psychotherapy: a proposed remedy. *Amer-*

ican Psychologist 46:99–106.

Phillips, C. (1991). To be whole again. *Parade,* August 11, pp. 10–12.

Piper, W. E., Azim, H. F., Joyce, A. S., and McCallum, M. (1991). Transference interpretations, therapeutic alliance, and outcome in short-term individual psychotherapy. *Archives of General Psychiatry* 48:946–953.

Postman, L. (1956). Is the concept of motivation necessary? Review of *Nebraska Symposium on Motivation,* ed. M. R. Jones, 1955. *Contemporary Psychology* 1:229–230.

President's Commission on Mental Health (1978). *Report to the President.* Washington, DC: United States Government Printing Office.

Prochaska, J. O. (1988). The devaluation of psychotherapy. Review of *The Evaluation of Psychotherapy. Contemporary Psychology* 33:305–306.

Prochaska, J. O., and DiClementi, C. C. (1984). *The Transtheoretical Approach: Crossing Traditional Trends of Therapy.* Chicago: Dorsey.

Prochaska, J. O., and Norcross, J. C. (1983). Contemporary psychotherapists: a national survey of characteristics, practices, orientations and attitudes. *Psychotherapy: Theory, Research, and Practice* 20:161–173.

Raimy, V., ed. (1950). *Training in Clinical Psychology.* Englewood Cliffs, NJ: Prentice Hall.

Reik, T. (1948). *Listening with the Third Ear.* New York: Farrar, Straus.

Richardson, E. H. (1981). Cultural and historical perspectives in counseling American Indians. In *Counseling the Culturally Different: Theory and Practice,* ed. D. W. Sue, pp. 216–255. New York: Wiley.

Ridley, C. R. (1984). Clinical treatment of the non-disclosing black client. *American Psychologist* 39:1234–1244.

Rioch, D. (1951). Theories of psychotherapy. In *Current Trends in Psychological Theory,* ed. W. Dennis. Pittsburgh: University of Pittsburgh Press.

Robertson, M. (1979). Some observations from an eclectic therapist. *Psychotherapy: Theory, Research and Practice* 16:18–24.

Rogers, C. R. (1942). *Counseling and Psychotherapy: Newer Concepts and Practice.* Boston: Houghton-Mifflin.

———— (1951). *Client-centered Therapy.* Boston: Houghton-Mifflin.

———— (1956). Client-centered therapy: a current view. In *Progress in Psychotherapy: 1956,* ed. F. Fromm-Reichmann and J. L. Moreno. New York: Grune & Stratton.

_____ (1957a). The necessary and sufficient conditions of therapeutic personality change. *Journal of Consulting Psychology* 21:95–103.

_____ (1957b). A note on "The Nature of Man." *Journal of Counseling Psychology* 4:199–203.

_____ (1959). A theory of therapy, personality, and interpersonal relationships as developed in the client-centered framework. In *Psychology: A Study of a Science,* vol. 3, ed. S. Koch, pp. 184–256. New York: McGraw-Hill.

_____ (1961). *On Becoming a Person.* Boston: Houghton-Mifflin.

_____ (1963a). Psychotherapy today or where do we go from here? *American Journal of Psychotherapy* 17:516.

_____ (1963b). The concept of the fully functioning person. *Psychotherapy: Theory, Research and Practice* 1:17–26.

_____ (1969). *Freedom to Learn.* Columbus, OH: Merrill.

_____ (1975). Empathic: an unappreciated way of being. *The Counseling Psychologist* 5(2):2–10.

_____ (1980). *A Way of Being.* New York: Houghton-Mifflin.

_____ (1986). A client-centered/person-centered approach to therapy. In *Psychotherapist's Casebook,* ed. I. Kutash and A. Wolf, pp. 197–208. New York: Jossey-Bass.

Rogers, C. R., and Dymond, R. F., eds. (1954). *Psychotherapy and Personality Change.* Chicago: University of Chicago Press.

Rogers, C. R., Gendlin, E. T., Kiesler, D. J., and Truax, C. B., eds. (1967). *The Therapeutic Relationship and Its Impact: A Study of Psychotherapy with Schizophrenics.* Madison, WI: University of Wisconsin Press.

Rogers, C. R., and Stevens, B. (1967). *Person to Person: The Problem of Being Human.* Lafayette, CA: Real People Press.

Rosenthal, R. (1966). *Experimenter Effects in Behavioral Research.* Englewood Cliffs, NJ: Prentice Hall.

Rosenthal, R., and Rosenthal, S. (1984). Suicidal behavior in preschool children. *American Journal of Psychiatry* 141:520–524.

Rosenzweig, S. (1936). Some implicit common factors in diverse methods of psychotherapy. *American Journal of Orthopsychiatry* 6:412–415.

Rounsaville, B. J., Chevron, E. S., Prusoff, B. A., et al. (1987). The relation between specific and general dimensions of the psychotherapy process in interpersonal psychotherapy of depression. *Journal of Consulting and*

Clinical Psychology 55:379–384.

Rourke, B. P., Bakker, J. D., Fisk, J. L., & Strang, J. D. (1983). *Child Neuropsychology.* New York: Guilford.

Rudolf, L. (1991). *Die therapeutische Arbeitsbezeihung.* Berlin: Springer.

Safran, J. D., and Wallner, L. K. (1991). The relative predictive validity of two therapeutic alliance measures in cognitive therapy. *Psychological Assessment* 3:188–195.

Sapolsky, A. (1960). Effect of interpersonal relationships upon verbal conditioning. *Journal of Abnormal and Social Psychology* 60:241–246.

Schofield, W. (1964). *Psychotherapy: The Purchase of Friendship.* Englewood Cliffs, NJ: Prentice Hall.

Schwitzgebel, R. K., and Traugott, M. (1968). Initial note on the placebo effect of machines. *Behavioral Science* 13:267–272.

Seligman, L. (1990). *Selecting Effective Treatments: A Comprehensive, Systematic Guide to Treating Adult Mental Disorders.* San Francisco, CA: Jossey-Bass.

Shapiro, A. K. (1971). Placebo effects in medicine, psychotherapy, and psychoanalysis. In *Handbook of Psychotherapy and Behavior Change: An Empirical Analysis,* ed. S. L. Garfield and A. E. Bergin. New York: Wiley.

Shapiro, A. K., and Morris, L. A. (1978). The placebo effect in medical and psychological therapies. In *Handbook of Psychotherapy and Behavior Change: An Empirical Analysis,* ed. S. L. Garfield and A. E. Bergin, 2nd ed., pp. 369–410. New York: Wiley.

Singer, J. (1974). *Imagery and Daydream Methods in Psychotherapy and Behavior Modification.* New York: Academic Press.

Skinner, B. F. (1948). *Walden Two.* New York: Macmillan.

———— (1958). Reinforcement today. *American Psychologist* 14:94–99.

Smith, D. (1982). Trends in counseling and psychotherapy. *American Psychologist* 37:802–809.

Smith, M. B. (1950). Optima of mental health: a general frame of reference. *Psychiatry* 13:503–510.

———— (1973). Comment on White's paper. *The Counseling Psychologist* 4(2):48–50.

Smith, M. B., and Glass, G. V. (1977). Meta-analysis of psychotherapy outcome studies. *American Psychologist* 40:1285–1295.

Smith, M. B., Glass, G. V., and Miller, J. (1980). *The Benefits of Psychotherapy.*

Baltimore: Johns Hopkins University Press.

Snyder, M. (1992). The meaning of empathy: comments on Hans Strupp's case of Helen R. *Psychotherapy* 29:318–322.

Snygg, D., and Combs, A. W. (1949). *Individual Behavior: A New Frame of Reference for Psychology.* New York: Harper.

Speight, S. L., Myers, L. J., Cox, C. I., and Highlen, P. S. (1991). A redefinition of multicultural counseling. *Journal of Counseling and Development* 70:29–36.

Spence, J. T. (1985). Achievement American style: the rewards and costs of individualism. *American Psychologist* 40:1285–1295.

Spitz, R. (1945). Hospitalism. *Psychoanalytic Study of the Child* 1:53–74. New York: International Universities Press.

———— (1946). Anaclytic depression. In *Psychoanalytic Study of the Child* 2:313–342. New York: International Universities Press.

Stainbrook, E. (1953). Some historical determinants of contemporary diagnostic and etiological thinking in psychiatry. In *Current Problems in Psychiatric Diagnosis,* ed. P. H. Hock and J. Zubin. New York: Grune & Stratton.

Standal, S. (1954). The need for positive regard: a contribution to client-centered theory. Unpublished Ph.D. dissertation, University of Chicago.

Stanton, A. H. (1956). Theoretical contribution to the concept of milieu therapy. In *Theory and Treatment of the Psychoses: Some Newer Aspects.* St. Louis: Washington University Press.

Stewart, E. C. (1976). Cultural sensitivities in counseling. In *Counseling across Cultures,* ed. P. Pedersen, W. J. Lonner, and J. Draguns, pp. 98–122. Honolulu: University of Hawaii Press.

Stiles, W. B., Shapiro, D. A., and Elliott, R. (1986). Are all psychotherapies equal? *American Psychologist* 41:165–180.

Strecker, E. A. (1957). General principles of psychiatry and psychotherapy. In *The Handicapped and Their Rehabilitation,* ed. H. A. Pattison. Springfield, IL: Charles C Thomas.

Strong, S. R. (1968). Counseling: an interpersonal process. *Journal of Counseling Psychology* 15:215–224.

———— (1978). Social psychological approach to psychotherapy research. In *Handbook of Psychotherapy and Behavior Change,* 2nd ed., ed. S. L. Garfield and A. E. Bergin, pp. 101–135. New York: Wiley.

Strong, S. R., and Claiborn, C. D. (1982). *Change through Interaction: Social Psychological Processes of Counseling and Psychotherapy.* New York: Wiley.

Strong, S. R., and Matross, R. (1973). Change processes in psychotherapy. *Journal of Counseling Psychology* 20:25–37.

Strupp, H. H. (1972). *Changing Frontiers in the Science of Psychotherapy.* Chicago: Aldine.

———— (1977). A reformulation of the dynamics of the therapist's contribution. In *Effective Psychotherapy,* ed. A. S. Gurman and A. M. Rozrin, pp. 3–21. New York: Pergamon.

———— (1990). The case of Helen R: A therapeutic failure? *Psychotherapy* 4:644–656.

Strupp, H. H., and Bergin, A. E. (1969). Some empirical and conceptual bases for coordinated research in psychotherapy. *International Journal of Psychiatry* 7:18–90.

Strupp, H. H., and Binder, J. L. (1984). *Psychotherapy in a New Key: A Guide to Time-limited Dynamic Psychotherapy.* New York: Basic Books.

Sue, D. W. (1978). Eliminating cultural oppression in counseling: toward a general theory. *Journal of Counseling Psychology* 25:419–428.

———— (1981a). *Counseling the Culturally Different: Theory and Practice.* New York: Wiley.

———— (1981b). Evaluating process variables in cross-cultural counseling and psychotherapy. In *Cross-cultural Counseling and Psychotherapy,* ed. A. J. Marshall and P. Pedersen. New York: Pergamon.

———— (1989). *Cultural specific techniques in counseling: a counseling framework.* Paper presented at the Southeast Asia Symposium on Counseling and Guidance in the 21st Century. Taipei, Taiwan, December.

———— (1990). Culture specific techniques in counseling: a conceptual framework. *Professional Psychology: Research and Practice* 21:424–433.

———— (1991). A model for cultural diversity training. *Journal of Counseling and Development* 70:99–105.

Sue, D. W., Arredondo, P., and McDavis, R. J. (1992). Multicultural counseling competencies and standards: a call to the profession. *Journal of Counseling and Development* 70:477–488.

Sue, D. W., Bernier, J. E., Durran, A., et al. (1982). Position paper: cross-cultural counseling competencies. *The Counseling Psychologist*

10(2):45-52.

Sue, D. W., and Sue, S. (1990). *Counseling the Culturally Different,* 2nd ed. New York: Wiley.

Sue, S. (1977). Community mental health services to minority groups: some optimism, some pessimism. *American Psychologist* 32:616-624.

———— (1983). Ethnic minorities in psychology: a reexamination. *American Psychologist* 38:583-592.

———— (1988). Psychotherapeutic services for minorities: two decades of research findings. *American Psychologist* 43:301-308.

Sue, S., and McKinney, H. (1975). Asian Americans in the community mental health system. *American Journal of Orthopsychiatry* 45:111-118.

Sue, S., McKinney, H., Allen, D., and Hale, J. (1974). Delivery of community mental health services to black and white clients. *Journal of Consulting and Clinical Psychology* 42:794-801.

Sue, S., and Morishima, J. K. (1982). *The Mental Health of Asian Americans.* San Francisco: Jossey-Bass.

Sue, S., and Zane, N. (1987). The role of culture and cultural techniques in psychotherapy. *American Psychologist* 42:37-45.

Sullivan, H. S. (1947). *Conceptions of Modern Psychiatry.* Washington, DC: William Alanson White Psychiatric Foundation.

Swan, G. E., and MacDonald, M. L. (1978). Behavior therapists in practice: a national survey of behavior therapists. *Behavior Therapy* 9:799-807.

Szapocznik, J., Santisteban, D., Kurtines, W. M., et al. (1982). Life enhancement counseling: a psychosocial model of services for Cuban elders. In *Minority Mental Health,* ed. E. E. Jones and S. J. Korchin. New York: Praeger.

Taft, J. (1933). *The Dynamics of Therapy in a Controlled Relationship.* New York: Macmillan.

Thorne, F. C. (1961). *Personality: A Clinical Eclectic Viewpoint.* Brandon, UT: Clinical Psychology.

———— (1967). Personal communication, June 2.

Torrey, E. F. (1970). *The irrelevancy of traditional mental health services for urban Mexican-Americans.* Paper presented to the American Orthopsychiatric Association, San Francisco, CA, March.

———— (1972). *The Mind Game: Witch Doctors and Psychiatrists.* New York: Emerson Hall.

Trimble, J. E. (1976). Value differences among American Indians: concerns for the concerned counselor. In *Counseling across Cultures,* ed. P. Pedersen, W. J. Lonner, and J. Draguns, pp. 65–81. Honolulu: University Press of Hawaii.

———— (1981). Value differences and their importance in counseling American Indians. In *Counseling across Cultures,* ed. P. Pedersen, W. J. Lonner, and J. Draguns, pp. 203–226, 2nd ed. Honolulu: University Press of Hawaii.

Truax, C. B., and Carkhuff, R. R. (1967). *Toward Effective Counseling and Psychotherapy.* Chicago: Aldine.

Truax, C. B., and Mitchell, K. M. (1971). Research on certain therapist interpersonal skills in relation to process and outcome. In *Handbook of Psychotherapy and Behavior Change,* ed. S. L. Garfield and A. E. Bergin, pp. 299–344. New York: Wiley.

Ullmann, L. P., and Krasner, L., eds. (1965). *Case Studies in Behavior Modification.* New York: Holt, Rinehart & Winston.

Ungersma, A. J. (1961). *The Search for Meaning.* Philadelphia: Westminster.

United Nations General Assembly (1989). *Adoption of a convention on the rights of the child.* New York: Author.

Urban, H. B., and Ford, D. H. (1971). Some historical and conceptual perspectives on psychotherapy and behavior change. In *Handbook of Psychotherapy and Behavior Change: An Empirical Analysis,* ed. S. L. Garfield and A. E. Bergin, pp. 3–35. New York: Wiley.

Vontress, C. E. (1976). Racial and ethnic barriers in counseling. In *Counseling across Cultures,* ed. P. Pedersen, W. J. Lonner, & J. Draguns, pp. 42–64. Honolulu: University of Hawaii Press.

———— (1979). Cross-cultural counseling: an existential approach. *Personnel and Guidance Journal* 58:117–122.

———— (1981). Racial and ethnic barriers in counseling. In *Counseling across Cultures,* ed. P. Pedersen et al., 2nd ed. Honolulu: University of Hawaii Press.

———— (1988). An existential approach to cross-cultural counseling. *Journal of Multicultural Counseling and Development* 16:73–83.

Wachtel, P. L. (1977). *Psychoanalysis and Behavior Therapy: Toward an Integration.* New York: Basic Books.

Walsh, A. (1991). *The Science of Love.* Buffalo, NY: Prometheus Books.

Watkins, C. E., Jr. (1990). The effects of counselor self-disclosure: a research review. *The Counseling Psychologist* 18:477–500.

Watkins, C. E., Jr., Lopez, F. G., Campbell, V. L., and Himmell, C. D. (1986). Contemporary counseling psychology: results of a national survey. *Journal of Counseling Psychology* 33:301–309.

Watson, J. B. (1928). *Psychological Care of Infant and Child.* New York: Norton.

Watson, N. (1984). The empirical status of Rogers's hypothesis of the necessary and sufficient conditions for effective psychotherapy. In *Client-centered Therapy and the Person-centered Approach: New Directions in Theory, Research, and Practice,* ed. R. F. Levant and J. M. Shlien, pp. 17–40. New York: Praeger.

Weaver, W. (1966). Confessions of a scientist-humanist. *Saturday Review,* May, 49:12–15.

Weil, A. P. (1985). Thoughts about early pathology. *Journal of the American Psychoanalytic Association* 33:335–352.

Weinberg, S. (1993). *Dreams of a Final Theory: The Search for the Fundamental Laws of Nature.* New York: Pantheon.

Wexler, D. A., and Rice, L. N., eds. (1974). *Innovations in Client-Centered Therapy.* New York: Wiley.

White, B. F. (1973). The concept of the healthy personality. *The Counseling Psychologist* 4(2):3–12, 67–69.

White, R. W. (1952). *Lives in Progress: A Study of the Natural Growth of Personality.* New York: Sloane.

——— (1959). Motivation reconsidered: the concept of competence. *Psychological Review* 66:297–333.

——— (1964). *The Abnormal Personality,* 3rd ed. New York: Ronald.

Whiteley, J. M. (Producer/Director). (1987). *Recollections: Celebrating the Life of Carl R. Rogers* [Film]. The Carl Rogers Memorial Fund.

Williams, K. E., and Chambless, D. L. (1990). The relationship between therapist characteristics and outcome of in vivo exposure treatment for agoraphobia. *Behavior Therapy* 21:111–116.

Williamson, E. G. (1950). A concept of counseling. *Occupations* 29:182–189.

——— (1958). Value orientation in counseling. *Personnel and Guidance Journal* 36:520–528.

——— (1963). The social responsibilities of counselors. *Illinois Guidance and Personnel Association Newsletter,* Winter, pp. 5–13.

_____ (1965). *Vocational Counseling.* New York: McGraw-Hill.

Winnicott, D. W. (1965). *The Maturational Processes and the Facilitating Environment.* New York: International Universities Press.

Wohl, J. (1976). Intercultural psychotherapy: issues, questions, and reflections. In *Counseling across Cultures,* ed. P. Pedersen, W. J. Lonner, and J. Draguns, pp. 184–207. Honolulu: University of Hawaii Press.

Wolfe, T. (1976). The "ME" decade. *New York Magazine,* August 23, pp. 26–30.

Wolpe, J. (1958). *Psychotherapy by Reciprocal Inhibition.* Stanford, CA: Stanford University Press.

_____ (1969). *The Practice of Behavior Therapy.* New York: Pergamon.

_____ (1987). The promotion of a scientific psychotherapy: a long voyage. In *The Evolution of Psychotherapy,* ed. J. K. Zeig, pp. 133–142. New York: Brunner/Mazel.

Woodworth, R. S. (1958). *Dynamics of Behavior.* New York: Holt.

Wrenn, C. G. (1962). The culturally-encapsulated counselor. *Harvard Educational Review* 32:444–449.

_____ (1985). Afterword: the culturally-encapsulated counselor revisited. In *Handbook of Cross-cultural Counseling and Therapy,* ed. P. B. Pedersen, pp. 323–329. Westport, CT: Greenwood.

Wu, I. H., and Windle, C. (1980). Ethnic specificity in the relative minority use and staffing of community mental health services. *Community Mental Health Journal* 16:156–168.

Wyatt, F. (1948). The empirical status of Rogers's hypotheses of the necessary and sufficient conditions for effective psychotherapy. In *Client-centered Therapy and the Person-centered Approach: New Directions,* ed. R. F. Leviant and J. M. Shlien, pp. 17–40. New York: Praeger.

Wyatt, G. E., and Parham, W. D. (1985). The inclusion of culturally sensitive issue materials in graduate school and training programs. *Psychotherapy* 22:461–468.

Yamamoto, J., James, T. C., and Palley, N. (1968). Clinical problems in psychiatric therapy. *Archives of General Psychiatry* 19:45–49.

Zeig, J. K., ed. (1987). *The Evolution of Psychotherapy.* New York: Brunner/Mazel.

Zilboorg, G. (1941). *A History of Medical Psychology.* New York: Norton.

Ziskind, E. (1949). How specific is psychotherapy? *American Journal of Psychiatry* 106:285–291.

Credits

The authors gratefully acknowledge permission to reprint material from the following sources:

Index

action conditions, 111–113
research evidence on, 123
Thorne, F. C., 7, 28
Torrey, E. F., 164
Traugott, M., 19
Treatment paradigms, described,
3–5
Trimble, J. E., 159
Truax, C. B., 70, 77, 81, 82, 83,
84, 86, 87, 93, 97, 98, 103,
119, 134, 140
Trust
case studies, 211–214
therapeutic relationship, 89–90

Ullmann, L. P., 19
Ungersma, A. J., ix
United Nations, 202
Universality, theory and, xii, 22
Urban, H. B., 4, 46, 50, 69

Values, goals as, 65–67
van Kaam, A., 55
Vontress, C. E., 158, 159, 162,
164, 166, 167
Vulnerability, of client, 127–129

Wachtel, P. L., 6
Wallner, L. K., 100

Walsh, A., 51, 192, 193, 196, 197,
198, 199, 200, 201, 202
Watkins, C. E., Jr., xii, 8, 54, 123
Watson, J. B., 195, 196
Watson, N., 130
Weaver, W., xii
Weil, A. P., 201
Weinberg, S., xii
Wexler, D. A., 172
White, B. F., 38
White, R. W., 28, 31, 36, 48, 56
Whitehorn, J. C., 55
Whiteley, J. M., 58, 61
Williams, K. E., 100
Williamson, E. G., 7, 35, 36
Windle, C., 156
Winnicott, D. W., 201
Wohl, J., 164
Wolfe, T., 36
Wolpe, J., 2, 18, 19, 20, 55, 177
Woodworth, R. S., 28
Wrenn, C. G., 66, 155
Wu, I. H., 156
Wyatt, F., 12
Wyatt, G. E., 157

Yamamoto, J., 155
Yarnell, H., 194

Zane, N., 157, 159, 162
Zeig, J. K., 2
Zilboorg, G., 43, 45
Ziskind, E., 12